KT-212-413

Freedom and Nature in Schelling's Philosophy of Art

Devin Zane Shaw

continuum

UNIVERSITY OF WINCHESTER
LIBRARY

Continuum International Publishing Group

The Tower Building	80 Maiden Lane
11 York Road	Suite 704
London SE1 7NX	New York NY 10038

www.continuumbooks.com

© Devin Zane Shaw, 2010

First published 2010
Paperback edition first published 2012

All rights reserved. No part of this publication may be reproduced or transmitted in any form or by any means, electronic or mechanical, including photocopying, recording, or any information storage or retrieval system, without prior permission in writing from the publishers.

British Library Cataloguing-in-Publication Data
A catalogue record for this book is available from the British Library.

ISBN: HB: 978-1-4411-5624-2
     PB: 978-1-4411-1732-8

Library of Congress Cataloging-in-Publication Data
Shaw, Devin Zane.
Freedom and nature in Schelling's philosophy of art / Devin Zane Shaw.
   p. cm.
Includes bibliographical references (p.   ).
ISBN: 978-1-4411-5624-2
1. Schelling, Friedrich Wilhelm Joseph von, 1775–1854. 2. Art–Philosophy. I. Title.

B2898.S53 2010
111'.85092–dc22   2010012593

UNIVERSITY OF WINCHESTER

Typeset by Newgen Imaging Systems Pvt Ltd, Chennai, India
Printed and bound in Great Britain

Freedom and Nature in Schelling's Philosophy of Art

KA 0388095 8

Continuum Studies in Philosophy
Series Editor: James Fieser, University of Tennessee at Martin, USA

Continuum Studies in Philosophy is a major monograph series from Continuum. The series features first-class scholarly research monographs across the whole field of philosophy. Each work makes a major contribution to the field of philosophical research.

Contents

Acknowledgments

My interest in the philosophy of Friedrich Schelling can be traced back to Jeffrey Reid's graduate seminar 'The Self and Its World in Fichte, Schelling and Early German Romanticism.' My work, as it has progressed from conference papers, through my dissertation, to this book, would not have been the same without his constant encouragement and constructive criticism. In the process of writing and refining, I have benefitted from the helpful comments and suggestions of Frederick C. Beiser, Denis Dumas, Iain Hamilton Grant, Douglas Moggach, and Sonia Sikka. I would also like to thank my editor, Tom Crick, at Continuum for his support and patience.

Thanks are also due to my family and friends, in academia and elsewhere, who listened, nodded, and gave support through the process of my writing and researching. Mark Raymond Brown, Dean Wm. Lauer, and Mark Young all had to listen to endless philosophical speculations as I worked through Schelling's philosophy of art, Sascha Maicher helped out when Schelling's German appeared to be opaque, and Jeff Renaud read and commented on the penultimate draft. Finally, my wife Caroline had patience during the time I was knee-deep in the absolute.

Note on Citations

Several abbreviations referring to the collected works of Schelling, Fichte, Kant, and Hölderlin appear in this text. I have indicated them below. Full information to all references is given in the bibliography. Some translations have been modified for textual consistency or other qualms, and have been designated with a 'tm.' I have also tried to utilize where possible the gender neutral term 'humanity' for my own discussions of Schelling's philosophy, where he uses the German *Mensch* and its cognates, which, while implying a neutral gender, too often meant, in his time, men.

Schelling

All references to Schelling cite the English translation, when available, and the volume (in Roman numerals) and page of K. F. A Schelling's edition of *Schellings sämmtliche Werke*. 14 volumes (Stuttgart: Cotta, 1856–1861), which is reproduced in *Schellings Werke. Nach der Original Ausgabe in neuer Anordnung*. 12 volumes. Ed. Manfred Schröter (Munich: Beck, 1927–1959). In addition, I have made reference to the *Historisch-kritische Ausgabe.* (Abbreviated as AA) Ed. H. M. Baumgartner, W. G. Jacobs, H. Krings (Stuttgart: Frommann-Holzboog, 1976–). It contains three divisions: I: Works, II: the Nachlass, III: Letters (Cited as AA, Division [in Roman numerals]/Volume/Page).

Fichte

All references to Fichte (except to his letters) cite the English translation followed by the volume and page of *Johann Gottlieb Fichtes sämmtliche Werke*. 8 vols. Ed. I. H. Fichte (Berlin: Veit, 1845–1846) as reproduced in *J. G. Fichte. Gesamtausgabe der Bayerischen Akademie der Wissenschaften* (Abbreviated as GA). Ed. Reinhard Lauth, Hans Jacobs, and Hans Gliwitsky (Stuttgart-Bad

Cannstatt: Fromann-Holzboog, 1964–). For Fichte's letters, I have cited the *Gesamtausgabe* by division (in Roman numerals)/volume/page.

Kant

All references to Kant are cited by the English translation followed by the volume (in Roman numerals) and pagination of *Gesammelte Werke* (Berlin: de Gruyter, 1900–), with the exception of the *Critique of Pure Reason*, which references the pagination of the 1781 (A) and 1787 (B) editions.

Hölderlin

I have used the *Sämtliche Werke*. Ed. Friedrich Beissner (Stuttgart: Verlag W. Kohlhammer, 1943–1985). I cite the English translation and then the HSA by volume (in Roman numerals) and page.

. . . is Achilles possible with powder and lead? Or the Iliad with the printing press, not to mention the printing machine? Do not the song and the saga and the muse necessarily come to an end with the printer's bar, hence do not the necessary conditions of epic poetry vanish?

But the difficulty lies not in understanding that the Greek arts and epic are bound up with certain forms of social development. The difficulty is that they still afford us artistic pleasure and that in a certain respect they count as a norm and as an unattainable model.

—*Karl Marx*, Grundrisse *(1973: 110–111)*

Introduction

The philosophy of Friedrich Schelling has a remarkable depth and breadth. It can move, often rapidly, from Plato to Spinoza, from physics to mythology, from art to astronomy, from medicine to theology. Once his philosophy is examined on its own merit, and not as the incomplete anticipation of some other figure in the history of philosophy, it becomes clear that Schelling made important and original contributions to philosophically thinking many of these fields. The present study is oriented around three of these original contributions as they are expressed in his work from 1795–1810: his idea of freedom, his philosophy of nature, and his philosophy of art. Schelling's idea of freedom is developed out of a critique of the formalism of Kant's and Fichte's practical philosophies, and his nature-philosophy is developed to show how subjectivity and objectivity emerge from a common source in nature. The philosophy of art plays a dual role in the system. First, Schelling argues that artistic activity produces through the artwork a sensible realization of the ideas of philosophy. Second, he argues that artistic production creates the possibility of a new mythology that can overcome the socio-political divisions that structure the relationships between individuals and society.

In the *Philosophy of Art*, which is comprised of lectures given in Jena in 1802–1803 and in Würzburg a year later, Schelling asks his audience not to

> confuse this science of art with anything previously presented under this or any other title as aesthetics or as a theory of the fine arts and sciences. There does not yet exist anywhere a scientific and philosophical doctrine of art. At most only fragments of such a doctrine exist, and even these are little understood and can be comprehended only within the context of the whole. (1989: 11/V, 361)

There have been, he says, theories of judgment and taste, technical training, art histories, and even virtual 'cookbooks in which the recipe for a tragedy reads approximately as follows: a great deal of fright, but not too much, as much sympathy as possible, and tears without end' (1989: 12/V, 362). There has, however been no philosophy of art that has sought to think the absolute *truth* of art, the *idea*, taken in the Platonic sense. A philosophy of art, according to Schelling's original account, requires one to think art within the totality of the system, with freedom, with nature-philosophy, and with a new mythology.

Schelling's contributions to a philosophy of freedom and a philosophy of nature have drawn a considerable amount of interest, especially because his work offers a contrast to, and critique of, his erstwhile friend Hegel.[1] By contrast, much of the attention paid to Schelling's philosophy of art has focused on its presentation in the *System of Transcendental Idealism* at the expense of the others: the lectures collected as the *Philosophy of Art*, the address *Über das Verhältnis der bildenden Künste zu der Natur* of 1807, and, even if Schelling's remarks about art are much more critical, the *Stuttgart Seminars*. Nor is much consideration paid to Schelling's discussions of art and mythology in the *Philosophical Letters on Dogmatism and Criticism* (1795–1796) and the *Allgemeine Übersicht der neuesten philosophischen Literatur* (1797–1798), and their relationship to the later texts of the philosophy of art. Although the reasons vary, the standard or accepted interpretation holds that the *System of Transcendental Idealism* is the only text in which artistic production is central to the system.[2] One of the main reasons offered for this interpretation is that the philosophy of art is necessary only for the subjective idealism of the *System of Transcendental Idealism* while it is not necessary for the absolute idealism of the *Darstellung meines Systems der Philosophie* (1801) and beyond.

In contrast to this standard interpretation of Schelling's philosophical development, I argue that the philosophy of art is central to his thought, not only in the *System of Transcendental Idealism* (1800), but through the entire period from 1800 to 1807. To return the philosophy of art to its proper place within the totality of Schelling's system requires a new interpretation of his philosophical development from 1801 to 1810 through the often overlooked or underappreciated *Philosophy of Art* (1802–1804), *Über das Verhältnis der bildenden Künste zu der Natur* (1807) and the *Stuttgart Seminars* (1810). These texts all show that Schelling is working toward a philosophy that can incorporate history, mythology, and revelation. I argue that one of the central problems that connects the *Philosophy of Art* to the *Philosophical Investigations into the Essence of Human Freedom* (1809) and the *Stuttgart Seminars* is Schelling's attempt to render a philosophy of history, nature, and revelation consistent. Once, in fact, Schelling turns to the investigation of the idea of a universal religion and the idea of freedom, he no longer pursues his philosophy of art.[3]

Let us begin with the first point. In order to establish a measure for evaluating the continuity of his philosophy of art, I focus on demonstrating the features that are consistent within the period from 1800 to 1807. I will show that these conditions for the philosophy of art are maintained even after Schelling abandons the subjective idealism of the *System of Transcendental Idealism* in the *Darstellung* (1801); in fact, they are found in the *Philosophy of Art* (written during the period of absolute idealism), and in his philosophy through 1807. Three *conditions* are necessary for Schelling's philosophy of art:

C1. What philosophy constructs in the ideal, art produces in the real. Thus artistic activity is the highest human vocation (*Bestimmung*) because practical philosophy can only approximate its object, which is the moral law.

C2. While both the natural organism and the artwork embody the same identity of real and ideal, of necessity and freedom, the work of art overcomes these oppositions through the identity of conscious and unconscious production, whereas the organism's activity is unconscious.

C3. Artistic production has a socio-political task: it aims to overcome the fragmentary condition of modernity through a new mythology and artistic renewal.

All these features are first established in the *System of Transcendental Idealism* and are maintained through 1807. Let us just look briefly at Schelling's turn from subjective or transcendental idealism to absolute idealism, which has been the focus of the standard interpretation. The *Darstellung* (1801), the turning point, concludes with the suggestion that a full system of absolute idealism would develop truth and beauty as 'highest expressions of indifference' (IV, 212), and the 'Further Presentations from the System of Philosophy,' state that the *System of Transcendental Idealism* sketches the 'general framework of construction, whose schematism must also be the foundation of the completed system' (2001a: 396/IV, 410).

The three conditions are part of this 'general framework.' As I argue, they should be understood in relation to Schelling's ideas of freedom and nature. The philosophy of art emerges as a solution to the problem of how to show that human activity – and this includes philosophy – can be objectified within the real world. For the philosophy of art, the objective result is the artwork. For Schelling, artistic production exhibits a power or *ethos* of free activity that is 'more free than freedom.' This idea of 'freedom' is an idea of absolute creativity, rather than conceived, as in Kant and Fichte, in conformity to the moral law. Though he thinks practical reason – like Kant and Fichte – as an infinite approximation to a regulative ideal, Schelling adds that the 'creative freedom' of artistic activity produces its own law, as beauty, in the harmony of form and content of the work, and in doing so, this creativity exhibits the identity of freedom and necessity, the self and nature, and the ideal and the real. Art presents and produces the absolute in the finite world.

To give a fuller picture of Schelling's philosophy of art, I begin with its 'pre-history' by tracing the development of the philosophical problems to which artistic activity is his solution. In the first chapter, I show how Schelling begins to outline the relationship between freedom, nature, and art in his *Philosophical Letters on Dogmatism and Criticism* of 1795–1796. He manages to mediate between several of the most important intellectual debates of his time, in ten short letters, written to a fictional Spinozist, who is more than likely based on his friend Friedrich Hölderlin. There, Schelling defends critical philosophy as a superior system of philosophy over Spinozist dogmatism, a judgment that is determined through the way in which each system interprets the relationship between the self and the world. The dogmatist relinquishes his or her autonomy to the idea of an ultimate power outside of the self (to necessity), while the critical philosopher asserts, through theory and practice, the primacy of the self's freedom.

I begin with the *Letters* because it contains an analysis of Greek tragedy in comparison to criticism and dogmatism. Schelling argues that tragedy exhibits the identity of freedom and necessity through the interplay of the protagonist acting freely and yet ultimately succumbing to the power of fate. Despite his praise for Greek tragedy, which Schelling calls the most sublime presentation of the human condition, he argues that it cannot provide a model for a system of freedom. Instead, any attempt to forfeit the power of human freedom to the external world acts against the truth of practical philosophy. While not yet presenting a philosophy of art, the *Letters* anticipate some of Schelling's later philosophical concerns, to which the philosophy of art comprises the answer.

In Chapter 2, I reconstruct Schelling's sketch of what he calls the 'history of self-consciousness' from the *Ideas for a Philosophy of Nature* of 1797 and the *Allgemeine Übersicht der neuesten philosophischen Literatur* (or *Survey*), which was published in installments from 1797–1798 in Immanuel Niethammer's and Fichte's, *Philosophisches Journal*. The 'history of self-consciousness' is

Schelling's attempt to develop a critical idealism that could demonstrate how self-consciousness arises within nature and within human history, that is, how self-consciousness progressively overcomes its previous limitations through its interaction with nature and history. Thus, on the one hand, Schelling develops this system *ideally* in the *Survey*, and on the other, he proposes a nature-philosophy in the *Ideas* that outlines a *real* 'natural history' (*Naturlehre*) of the mind (1988: 30/II, 39). The purpose of both is to show how a completed system of critical idealism could reconcile the differences that marked humanity's 'modern condition,' and the philosophical assumptions that separated humans from nature, and freedom from necessity. As this history of self-consciousness develops, I argue, it appears, in vague outline, that both parts of the system – idealism and nature-philosophy – require a third to resolve their contradictions. This third part of philosophy is a philosophy of art. The chapter closes with a reading of the 'Älteste Systemprogramm des deutschen Idealismus,' a dense fragment that argues that beauty, poesy, and a mythology of reason are the highest realizations of philosophy. These are all features that will reappear in Schelling's philosophy of art.

In Chapter 3, I outline Schelling's philosophy of art found in the *System of Transcendental Idealism*. I argue that the introduction of the philosophy of art should be read as a subversion of Fichte's emphasis on practical reason. So, where Fichte grounds his system in the self's free activity, Schelling now argues that the true realization of human activity is in the work of art, which is produced objectively. Whereas freedom – as conceived as an infinite approximation of the moral law – can only strive toward its object, artistic activity is grounded in the identity of freedom and necessity because it produces the inner harmony and beauty of a work of art. Thus artistic production, through genius, is an activity that is 'more free than freedom itself,' a kind of *ethos* that produces according to its own creative laws. In addition, I also show that all three conditions, listed above, are established in the *System of Transcendental Idealism*. While it is the first systematic presentation of Schelling's philosophy of art, it is not his last.

Therefore, in the first half of Chapter 4, I demonstrate that the three conditions obtain in Schelling's *Philosophy of Art*, which was written and delivered as lectures during the period of his system of absolute idealism or 'system of identity.' Even if the first principle of the system shifts from the self's activity to, according to Schelling, the standpoint of reason itself, the *Philosophy of Art* still maintains all three conditions. Furthermore, in outlining the task of the new mythology, we discover that Schelling's absolute idealism encounters a contradiction it cannot resolve, a contradiction between substance (the first principle of the system) and history (the mythological revelation of its content). This occurs because Schelling holds that the first principle of the system of identity is an eternal and infinite substance, an identity of form and content, while at the same time presenting a historical construction of art that presents a series of divine revelations within history. This series begins with Greek mythology and leads to Christian revelation, in which Christ is revealed as the closure of antiquity and the origin of the modern era. The *Philosophy of Art* results in the following dilemma: either retain the first principle, and reduce the historical revelation to mere appearances (contradicting the infinite quality of the gods, and the Christian God), or maintain the historical revelation of Greek and Christian mythology, and abandon the immutable and eternal Spinozist substance.

Schelling will attempt to grapple with the problem of history within the system of identity until 1807, in his address to the *Akademie der Wissenschaft* in Munich. In the *Über das Verhältnis der bildenden Künste zu der Natur*, Schelling departs from the system of absolute idealism and turns to a system of historical revelation that anticipates his later philosophy of freedom that begins in 1809. In Chapter 5, I argue that this neglected text deserves more attention because, at the turning point between the philosophy of art and the philosophy of freedom, Schelling proposes a singular account of an *ethos* that unifies the true, the good, and the beautiful through artistic production. Artistic activity reveals the true, because art reproduces the history of natural production itself, as it reveals the divine in humanity; it reveals the good, because artistic production presents an ethic of moderating the passions through the creation of beauty. Schelling invokes this *ethos* to call for a renewal of art within the public sphere, which would express the essence of the German people on the stage of history.

Yet if *Über das Verhältnis der bildenden Künste zu der Natur* presents such a singular *ethos*, it is important to search for the reasons why Schelling abandons his philosophy of art. Therefore the last chapter also traces the end of the philosophy of art to Schelling's shift toward a philosophy of freedom and his interest in the relationship between freedom, revelation, and theology. This shift leads to the *Stuttgart Seminars*, where I argue that Schelling's orientation turns from a hopeful future of humanity, to an account of the distant past of humanity's Fall. While Schelling develops the Fall and its consequences as real historical events, his focus turns to Christian revelation, the figure of Christ, and the idea of human freedom as positive capacity for good or evil. In this account, Schelling diminishes the role of art to the production of a work based either in the artist's individuality, or as a work of nostalgia for a lost connection to nature. Art is reduced to this role because Schelling now conceives of freedom, and virtue, as the highest activity of human being; but this idea of freedom is of an ecstatic nature. Schelling elevates human freedom to the pinnacle of the system when he finally surpasses the conception of freedom as an activity that approximates the moral law; in the *Philosophical Investigations into the Essence of Human Freedom* of 1809, and the *Stuttgart Seminars* a year later, freedom is rethought as a positive, ecstatic act of inner law-giving, which is realized as virtue.

After showing how Schelling returns to the primacy of freedom, through the criticism of Kant, Fichte, and his own previous work, I close Chapter 5 by evaluating the political implications of Schelling's call for a new mythology and renewal of art. Over the course of its development, the idea of the new mythology shifts from a revolutionary and utopian vision to a kind of apologetic statism, in which the realization of a new mythology will be the perfection of the ideal state and vice versa. The shifting implications of the philosophy of art and the new mythology should not pass uncriticized, although some Schelling scholars might find my criticism of his 'mythologization of politics' to be too harsh.[1] Nevertheless Schelling's insistence on the socio-political potential of artistic production remains one of his more influential and enduring contributions to philosophy. It is remarkable that, long after Schelling had given up on the political and social effects of art, both visions, one revolutionary and the other conservative, continued to resonate through the 19th and 20th centuries. The idea that a new mythology can, and should, express the essence of a people, nation, or community, had a long history, while the revolutionary and utopian conception of artistic production reemerges in the avant-gardes of the 20th century, and still inspires philosophical debate in the 21st. If my concluding critique of the conservative sequence is sharp or even polemical, it is only because I think the potential of the revolutionary sequence has yet to be exhausted.

Chapter 1

Dogmatism, Criticism, and Art

1.1. 'The Alpha and Omega of all Philosophy'

Although Schelling's *System of Transcendental Idealism* (1800) is the first systematic account of his philosophy of art, he first proposes art – more specifically, the content of Greek tragedy – as a solution to the problem of freedom in the *Philosophical Letters on Dogmatism and Criticism* (1795–1796). In ten densely written epistles, Schelling begins to develop his own system of philosophy through a discussion guided by the prominent philosophical debates at the end of the 18th century – the Pantheism Controversy and the ascendancy of the critical philosophy of Kant, Reinhold, and Fichte. With the inclusion of a discussion of Greek tragedy, Schelling also considers the relationship between philosophy and art that was of interest to his friend Friedrich Hölderlin.

In this chapter, I focus on the relationship between philosophy and art in the *Letters,* and more precisely on the relationship between practical reason, the world, and art. Schelling argues that the relationship between the three is determined by the distinction between critical and dogmatic philosophy, or, to attach a proper name to the two systems, the distinction between Fichte and Spinoza. These two systems are grounded in mutually opposed first principles. All post-Kantian philosophy, Schelling claims, must choose between the absolute I as first principle or the absolute object. The former leads to a critical system of freedom, the latter to a dogmatic system of necessity.

At this early juncture, Schelling chooses critical philosophy. As he states in a letter to Hegel, dated February 4, 1795, the 'Alpha and Omega of all philosophy is freedom' (AA, III/1: 22). If we cast the distinction between criticism and dogmatism as a rivalry within the domain of philosophy, Schelling dedicates the *Letters* to testing the ability of these rivals to explain freedom. By the ninth letter, Schelling has shown that, unlike the critical affirmation of freedom, dogmatism risks 'moral ruin' because it cannot account for freedom. Nevertheless, in the tenth letter he introduces one more rival: Greek tragedy. The content of tragedy presents what both criticism and dogmatism cannot attain: the identity of freedom and necessity. Yet, while tragedy presents this identity in the mortal's struggle against fate, Schelling ultimately rejects it as a model of practical action. This rejection rests on Schelling's commitment to the 'alpha and omega of all philosophy' that is freedom; he concludes the *Letters* by stating that recourse to fate, in the post-Kantian condition, can prevent the full realization of the idea of freedom. Instead of attributing the creative powers of the self's activity to an external source like the dogmatist, Schelling argues that it is in the 'interest of reason' to explain them at all times through freedom. It is this defense of freedom that prevents him from proposing tragedy as a system of action.

Before showing how this conflict between criticism and dogmatism unfolds in the *Letters* (in Sections 1.4 and 1.5), we will address how Schelling came to oppose Fichte to Spinoza. The controversies surrounding critical philosophy and the Pantheism Controversy had shaken the intellectual life of German Enlightenment, and their reverberations had traveled at least as far as the Tübingen *Stift*, which is the seminary where Hegel, Hölderlin, and Schelling pursued their studies. In Section 1.2, we will analyze Jacobi's *Concerning the Doctrine of Spinoza in Letters to Herr Moses Mendelssohn*, which is the book that initiated the Pantheism Controversy by claiming that all philosophical demonstration is atheistic and fatalistic, because at its basis, all philosophy is some form of Spinozism. In Section 1.3, we will outline how Fichte's philosophy attempted to overcome these claims with a system grounded in practical reason and freedom rather than theoretical reason.

Fichte visited the *Stift* twice in the early 1790s, and it is possible that he and Schelling met during the second visit in May 1794 (the first visit was in June 1793; see Tilliette, 1999b: 28–29). By this time, Fichte's work, along with that of Kant and Reinhold, had become a decisive influence on the young Schelling's thought. By his second visit to the *Stift*, Fichte had produced an outline of a systematic unification of theoretical and practical philosophy in his *Über den Begriff der Wissenschaftslehre*, which he subsequently developed in his *Grundlage der gesamten Wissenschaftslehre* (1794).[1] The system that Fichte calls the *Wissenschaftslehre* (the doctrine of science), seeks to unify theory and practice in the self-positing subject, the absolute I. This self-positing is the act whereby the subject recognizes him or herself through freedom, through the practical demand to act as if one's freedom were unconditional. Although he soon recasts Fichte's (and Kant's) work to different ends, the influence of the new professor at the University of Jena (called, incidentally, to take Reinhold's chair) is visible in Schelling's insistence on the practical primacy of a freely acting subject. Such excitement is discernable in Schelling's early 'critical' texts, *On the Possibility of a Form of All Philosophy* and *Of the I as Principle of Philosophy*.[2]

While the *Letters* defends the critical emphasis on freedom and practical action, Schelling's interest in Spinoza leads him to recast dogmatism as a practical system of philosophy opposed to criticism. Like many of his contemporaries, such as his former classmates Hegel and Hölderlin, and others such as Friedrich Schlegel and – above all – Goethe, Schelling was a serious reader of Spinoza. The resurgence of interest in Spinoza was the result of the Pantheism Controversy, which was ignited by the publication of Jacobi's *Concerning the Doctrine of Spinoza in Letters to Herr Moses Mendelssohn* in 1785. The book opens in a dramatic fashion by disclosing an avowal by G. E. Lessing – a prominent figure of the German Enlightenment – of Spinozism, which at the time referred to some combination of fatalism, atheism, and materialism. The *Doctrine of Spinoza* shook German intellectual life because it treated Lessing as a synecdoche for *Aufklärung* philosophy as a whole. Through the conversations he reports to have had with Lessing, Jacobi develops the charge that all philosophical demonstration, if consistent, leads to Spinozism. Any consistent philosophy, according to Jacobi, is atheistic because it can only provide proofs of an immanent God or nature (which produces a disguised materialism), and fatalistic because it precludes the possibility of freedom and morality. These consequences can only be avoided, according to Jacobi, by grounding knowledge and practice in revelation and faith in a personal God.

Despite all his efforts, Jacobi's polemic backfired, and it inspired an entire generation of German philosophers to read Spinoza, who, in Lessing's words, was once considered a 'dead dog' (Jacobi, 1994: 193). Though Kant claimed not to understand Spinoza (while nevertheless intending to refute his philosophy), and Fichte subordinated Spinozist dogmatism to a necessary step toward critical idealism, Schelling argues that consummate dogmatism (Spinoza's system) is a coordinate practical rival to criticism. Yet, after establishing this rivalry, and after arguing that dogmatism could be refuted neither theoretically nor practically, Schelling sets out to refute it in both domains. Criticism ultimately demonstrates its practical superiority in its use of the principle of intellectual intuition, which Schelling introduces to answer Jacobi's demand for an immediate intuition into the supersensuous world, to account for Spinoza's third kind of knowledge, and to name the foundational activity of Fichte's absolute I. Criticism proves itself superior to its rival by interpreting this intuition as a regulative ideal for practical action, which prevents this intuition from being hypostatized as a thing in itself, as it is by dogmatism. This opposition between criticism and dogmatism ultimately allows for the confirmation of freedom through the choice of two systems. As we will see, when Schelling claims that these two systems are coordinate rivals, he departs from the letter of Fichte's and Kant's works.

The *Letters* parts ways with Fichte when Schelling argues that the absolute is beyond either the subject or object, which implies a higher standpoint than Fichte's first principle. However, at this point Schelling still argues for the primacy of criticism because it recognizes the regulative status of the absolute for the practical subject. The ambiguity over the absolute in the *Letters* allowed for different readings of the text. Hölderlin found an important departure from Schelling's previous convictions, while Fichte saw no reason to publicly break with his younger ally. This ambiguity also underlies Schelling's later claim that the *Letters* contains the first hints of absolute idealism (see Chapter 4), and then, decades later, his claim that the *Letters* provides the first statement regarding the necessity of a system to *complement* criticism, much as positive philosophy was the complement of negative philosophy (2007a: 146/XIII, 82).

It is from this perspective that we can understand Schelling's reference to Greek Tragedy in the tenth epistle of the *Letters*. While Schelling recognizes the aesthetic power of tragedy for thought, he tempers this power by demonstrating that a true practical philosophy must always promote and defend the idea of freedom. Hence while he recognizes that the drama of Greek tragedy presents the absolute identity of freedom and necessity in the free struggle of the mortal hero against fate, Schelling prohibits its use as a model for a system of ethics because the struggle presented in tragedy always results in the hero's defeat through fate. It is, he says, in the interest of practical reason to expose any attempt to place the creative powers of the self, which *should be* realized in freedom, in the objective world. Although Greek tragedy presents the highest standard of art, Schelling argues that critical philosophy demonstrates the standard for practical action through freedom.

1.2. The Pantheism Controversy

Before turning to Fichte's *Wissenschaftslehre*, we will begin with the Pantheism Controversy, which went public after the publication of Jacobi's *Concerning the Doctrine of Spinoza in Letters to Herr Moses Mendelssohn* in 1785 and rapidly transformed the philosophical landscape of Enlightenment Germany.[3]

Of course, the first edition of Kant's *Critique of Pure Reason* preceded the *Doctrine of Spinoza* by four years and had a longer lasting impact on philosophy, but at the time critical appraisal of Kant's philosophy would primarily take place in the rhetorical framework of the Pantheism Controversy. Both Kant and Jacobi attacked the dogmatism of Leibnizian-Wolffian philosophy, and this, perhaps, is where their similarities end. While Kant utilized refined philosophical criticism to question the domain and application of synthetic a priori judgments, Jacobi very bluntly accused all theoretical philosophy of atheism, fatalism, and materialism. While Kant separated the noumenal and phenomenal worlds, demolishing the speculative proofs for the soul, freedom, and God in order to open the possibility of their application for practical action, Jacobi opposed faith and revelation to all theoretical demonstration.

Common to Kant and Jacobi is the critique of dogmatic philosophy, which is what they also have in common with Fichte and Schelling. In their own respective ways, each prioritizes practical action over theoretical reason. In retrospect, the crucial differences concerning the role of theoretical reason between Jacobi and these critical philosophers are more than obvious, especially in light of Jacobi's intervention in the Atheism Controversy of 1799 – which cost Fichte his professorship at Jena – and the later polemic against Schelling, *Von den Göttlichen Dingen und ihrer Offenbarung* (1811), spurred in part by Schelling's address *Über das Verhältnis der bildenden Künste zu der Natur* (see Chapter 5).[4] Yet before the later animosity, in the early 1790s, both Fichte and Schelling expressed admiration for Jacobi's work. Fichte, while acknowledging the difference between his transcendental idealism and Jacobi's realism, sought the latter's approval by attributing a common commitment to both sides toward emphasizing the practical and moral character of human being (see the letters to Jacobi dated August 30, 1795 and April 26, 1796 in Fichte, 1988: 411–414). In the same spirit, Schelling states in the essay *Vom Ich* that he desired 'Plato's gift of language or that of his [Plato's] kindred spirit, Jacobi, in order to be able to differentiate between the absolute, immutable being and every kind of conditional, changeable existence' (1980: 109/I, 216).[5] However, unlike Jacobi, Fichte and Schelling go to great lengths to defend the importance of theoretical reason. Schelling's system will attempt to incorporate Jacobi's emphasis on an immediate insight, Spinoza's third kind of knowledge and Fichte's absolute I into systematic philosophy through the principle of intellectual intuition.

Though the *Doctrine of Spinoza* begins with a biographical account of Lessing's discussions with Jacobi, the stakes of the book are philosophical.

Jacobi makes it clear that the principle issue is the doctrine of Spinoza, which, as his dialogue with Lessing reveals very early on, is the highest (Lessing), or at least the most consistent (Jacobi) expression of philosophy.[6] Thus, to confront Spinoza is to contest the strongest account of philosophy and the power of reason. Jacobi summarizes his argument against philosophy as such:

1. Spinozism is atheism.
2. The Leibnizian-Wolffian philosophy is no less fatalistic than the Spinozist philosophy and leads the persistent researcher back to the principles of the latter.
3. Every avenue of [philosophical] demonstration ends up in fatalism.
4. We can only demonstrate similarities. Every proof presupposes something already proven, the principle of which is *Revelation*.
5. Faith is the element of all human cognition and activity (1994: 233–234).[7]

As this summary shows, Jacobi takes philosophical demonstration and moral action as mutually exclusive: philosophical demonstration necessarily results in atheism and materialism, of which Spinoza is the most consistent expression, and therefore moral action requires a foundation in faith. At issue is Jacobi's understanding of the principle of sufficient reason – that each condition comes about through a necessary set of previous conditions. For Jacobi this is expressed in Spinoza's principle that 'nothing comes from nothing' (*ex nihilo nihil fit*), and, conversely, that 'something must necessarily come from something else.' The principle of sufficient reason, Jacobi then claims, requires an immanent, infinite cause to the world that must be mechanistic: 'If there are only efficient, but no final causes, then the only function that the faculty of thought has in the whole of nature is that of observer; its proper business is to accompany the mechanism of the efficient causes' (1994: 189). The mechanistic and determined chain of efficient causes, if followed consistently, does not permit for morality and freedom, because all human action is determined from without by the infinite chain of causes. Therefore, the argument for the pure immanence of God and nature (the Spinozist '*Hen kai pan*') excludes, according to Jacobi, the possibility of a personal God; instead, it must be, if consistent, an argument for 'pantheist' naturalism (i.e. atheism) and a materialism that dismisses human freedom as an illusion. Lessing, according to Jacobi, espouses this naturalism when he 'insisted on having everything *addressed to him in natural terms*,' while Jacobi stressed 'that there cannot be any natural philosophy of the supernatural' (1994: 196). A personal God, for Jacobi, must be extra-mundane and possess will.

After arguing that Spinozism and faith in revelation are incompatible, Jacobi accuses all modern philosophy (including Leibniz and Wolff) of fatalism and atheism, due to its reliance on the principle of sufficient reason.[8] According to Jacobi, there is a fundamental choice between two exclusive positions: either a personal God of faith or a philosophical system. This was a damning criticism in 18th century Germany. By connecting Leibniz to Spinoza, Jacobi implies that, at the heart of the German Enlightenment, there is a fundamental misrecognition. It is one thing to claim that the difficult work of Spinoza is fatalistic, and it is another thing to claim that Lessing casually acknowledged that the metaphysical foundations of Enlightenment philosophy were, all claims to the contrary, also fatalistic.[9] The challenge for critical philosophy after the Pantheism Controversy was to develop a theoretical philosophy compatible with freedom. Fichte and the young Schelling attempted to show that practical reason and theoretical reason were compatible by grounding both in the action of the self-positing subject.

In contrast to Spinoza (and, as he will claim, all theoretical reason) Jacobi offers an account of moral action grounded on faith and revelation. For Jacobi, human cognition is grounded in an immediate experience of certainty, 'which not only needs no proof, but excludes all proofs absolutely' (1994: 230). As Jacobi states, the original, immediate certainty reveals an I and a Thou (which is God), a revelation that grounds all other experiences (1994: 231). All subsequent demonstrations can only show the similarity of a new thing or proof to this original certainty. His position, then, conflates the experience of things (the sensible) with divine revelation (the supersensible) through a loose use of the term faith: both the experience of things and the experience of revelation rely on the original experience of immediate certainty.

Later in the text, Jacobi adds a historicist dimension to his argument (1994: 238–251).[10] Not only does all demonstration rest on faith, but people's beliefs and actions are determined by their historical situation: 'one ought not to derive the actions of men from their philosophy, but rather their philosophy from their actions; that their history does not originate from their way of thinking, but rather, their way of thinking from their history' (1994: 239). Yet the polemical effect of Jacobi's claim is effective only insofar as it does not apply to faith and revelation.[11] As it turns out, history cannot be a medium for reform, only faith and religion can. A truly historicist position would require that the concepts or experiences of faith and revelation would also be subject to the contingencies of history – in other words, it would require that Jacobi recognize his own position as conditioned by his historical situation. However, Jacobi does not allow this possibility; instead, his digression on historical circumstances ends in an overwrought defense of 'rectitude, patriotism, love of mankind [and] fear of the Lord' against the moral lassitude of his age (1994: 241). Jacobi's apparent historicism is limited by the ahistorical 'truth' of religion: 'from time immemorial all the nations' have held the conviction that religion is the only means for moral education and reform (1994: 242–243).[12]

Regardless of his conclusions, Jacobi's polemic had a profound and lasting effect on the development of early German Idealism. In the wake of the *Doctrine of Spinoza*, Schelling struggled to demonstrate the compatibility and ultimate *unity* of theoretical philosophy and practical freedom. Hence while Jacobi strictly rejects theoretical reason as the ground of practice in favor of faith, Schelling – initially following Fichte – argues that practical reason is the ground of theoretical reason, but also that theoretical reason provides the concepts for the practical subject's self-reflection, by showing how the human being is essentially a self-determining subject. Once a person is aware of his or her freedom, free practical action follows. As Schelling states in *Vom Ich*, 'Give man the awareness of what he is and he will soon learn to be what he ought to be. Give him the theoretical self-respect and the practical will soon follow' (1980: 67/I, 157). Schelling will argue that intellectual intuition can unify this 'theoretical self-respect' and practical freedom. But we must first turn to Fichte.

1.3. Fichte's Science of Knowledge

Although we began our study with a discussion of Jacobi's influence on Schelling, Fichte's influence on the younger philosopher's work should not be underestimated. In a letter to Hegel dated January 6, 1795, Schelling writes, with characteristic bombast,

> *Fichte*, when he was last here, said that one must have the genius of Socrates to fathom Kant. Every day I find this more true. – We must still go further with philosophy! [. . .] *Fichte* will raise philosophy to a height at which most of the current Kantians will dizzily stagger. [. . .] Would I be so lucky to be one of the first to salute the new hero, Fichte, in the land of truth! Blessed be the great man! (AA, III/1: 15–16)

What Schelling found most immediately appealing in the work of Fichte is the emphasis on freedom. The reference to Kant should serve as a reminder that Fichte's own thought was worked out in an attempt to unify the Kantian distinction between the practical and theoretical faculties – a unification suggested by Kant in the *Critique of Practical Reason* – and as a response to the skeptical challenges to the critical philosophy of Kant and Reinhold.[13] Though we cannot develop these themes here, Fichte's early work attempts to derive both theoretical and practical reason from a common principle, which, in turn, will allow critical philosophy to overcome the skeptical objections leveled at it.[14] This principle is the absolute I.

Yet this interpretation of Fichte cannot be granted as obvious. There is much contention in Fichte scholarship regarding the aims and accomplishments of Fichte's *Science of Knowledge*. It has been argued that the first principle – the absolute I – of the *Wissenschaftslehre* is primarily theoretical (Henrich, 2003: 231–262, 279; and Pippin, 1989: 42–59), primarily practical (Mandt, 1984: 127–147), both practical and theoretical (Beiser, 2002a: 273–288; and Breazeale, 1996: 47–64), or, finally, that it cannot be decided if the first principle is practical or theoretical if one only consults the text of 1794 (Neuhouser, 1990: 44–45). I will argue that, whether successful or not, Fichte articulated a version of his first principle that was intended to be both theoretical and practical: he provides a theory of practical action grounded in a practical subject who infinitely strives to realize the regulative ideal of an absolutely unconditioned self, which in turn demonstrates the ideal foundation of theoretical reason.

This section will focus on the exposition found in the first part of the *Science of Knowledge*, where Fichte posits the fundamental principles of what he claims is a complete system of critical philosophy.[15] The premier part is notoriously difficult and condensed, due in part to Fichte's writing style, but also to the fact that his principles have methodological, ontological, ethical, and epistemological consequences: he details the dialectical method to be utilized in the subsequent parts of the work, postulates the existence of the self-determining subject, and argues that the absolute I [*Ich*] has a regulative status, as an ethical ideal, within the system and not a constitutive status. In addition, he attempts to ground formal logic within his transcendental logic and to deduce several of the Kantian categories in establishing the three principles of the system.[16] Despite the obscurity, Fichte himself conceived of the project of the *Wissenschaftslehre* as, in Frederick Beiser's words, a 'dialectic of consciousness by which the ego comes to recognize for itself what has been postulated and hypothesized by the philosopher' (Beiser, 2002a: 247). As Fichte writes in *Concerning the Concept of the Wissenschaftslehre*, 'We are not the legislators of the human mind, but rather its historians. We are not, of course, journalists, but rather writers of pragmatic history' (1988: 131/I, 77).

To discover the first principle of the *Wissenschaftslehre*, Fichte attempts a regressive transcendental analysis, which leads from a fact of consciousness to the condition that makes such a fact possible. As such, the first principle cannot be found among the facts of consciousness, but it must ground any possible fact. The first proposition, which demands universal assent, is the principle of identity: A=A. The principle is asserted absolutely, for no proof can be given for it. Nor does A=A assert the existence of A; Fichte states that the principle of identity is expressed in the conditional tense: if A then A. Thus, as conditional, A=A cannot serve as the first principle of philosophy. But as conditional, it establishes a necessary connection (designated as 'X') between the antecedent and consequent, which is absolute. The next step in Fichte's argument inquires into the condition in which A would exist. The importance of the principle of identity becomes clear at this point. The inquiry regarding the necessary connection 'X' is a judgment that takes place in self-consciousness. The necessary connection 'X' can only be posited in the self and by the self as a law, and because this law 'is posited absolutely and without any other ground, the I must be given by the I itself' (1982: 95tm/I, 94).

Therefore the principle of identity has no other basis than the I or self [*Ich*].[17] It is the self that makes the judgment of identity (the necessary connection 'X'), and A is posited in the self insofar as 'X' is posited. That is to say that A exists insofar as it is posited in the judging self, and that within the self there is something uniform and enduring: 'hence the X that is absolutely posited can also be expressed as I = I; I am I' (1982: 96/I, 94). In positing the principle of identity, the self posits a principle of uniformity and sameness. However, the principle of identity (A=A) is not the same as the proposition I = I. Fichte argues that contrary to appearances, the principle of identity is grounded in the activity of the self, that is, the self's activity of positing itself. This opens Fichte's argumentation to charges of circularity, because the principle of identity was first proposed as the starting point in the search for the first principle (I = I), which he now claims is grounded in self-identity. And Fichte acknowledges the circularity at the outset. But a sympathetic reading – without which we will never get to Schelling – would grant that the transcendental self's activity grounds all particular activities of empirical consciousness, so Fichte chose 'the shortest road' to demonstrate the positing self (1982: 94/I, 92). As absolutely self-posited, the 'I am' posits 'the pure character of activity as such, in abstraction from its specific empirical conditions' (1982: 97/I, 96). The self-positing itself is both the agent and product of activity. Here Fichte breaks with philosophical tradition: the self is an act and not a substance; the self is a being 'whose being or essence consists simply in the fact that it posits itself as existing' (1982: 98/I, 97).

Fichte understands this first principle to be an advance over both dogmatic philosophy and Kantian philosophy. First, dogmatic philosophers, such as Spinoza, ground the self in a thing outside the self (in this case God). According to Fichte, in attributing the 'highest unity in human cognition' to God, Spinoza sought to prove a practical need through theoretical reason. This point underlines the regulative status of the absolute I in the *Wissenshaftslehre*: the absolute self is a regulative ideal to be sought in practical action. Spinoza's mistake occurred when 'he claimed to have established something as truly given, when he was merely setting up an appointed, but never attainable, ideal' (1982: 101/I, 101). We will return to the contrast between criticism and dogmatism after elucidating Fichte's other two principles.

Second, Fichte sees his position as an advance over the 'letter' of Kant by providing the systematic unity sought by Kant but never explained (we are concerned at this point with how Fichte sees his own project; we must leave aside the fact that, in developing the *Wissenschaftslehre*, Fichte also breaks with the 'spirit' of Kantian philosophy). This unity is found in the absolute I: one can derive the complete system from the first principles, and by conceptualizing the self in terms of practical action, one also unifies the faculties; finally, the justification for this first principle is moral, insofar as it provides an ideal for the striving subject.

But to complete the 'logic' of the *Science of Knowledge*, Fichte provides two additional principles: that of opposition, and that of grounding. According to Fichte, these principles are already presupposed in the first principle, and though as an act of self-consciousness they are simultaneous, they can be distinguished through philosophical reflection (1982: 108/I, 109). The principle of opposition is unconditioned in form and conditioned in content. Fichte again begins with a fact of consciousness that should be universally accepted: '~A is not equal to A.' If one asserted that '~A=~A' then the proposition would only be a variation of the principle of identity, and it could not explain the *act* of opposition in its form. Instead, the act of opposition is absolute and unconditional in its form. But the content of the second principle relies on the first already being posited. The content is conditioned by the first principle because it is counter-positing a term to A. That is, one can only oppose a term to A if A is already posited.[18]

As in the first principle, the proposition '~A is not equal to A' is not the proposition of the principle, just as 'A=A' is not 'I am I.' Just as the positing of A requires the act of self-positing, the positing of ~A in opposition to A requires a transcendental basis: the not-I or not-self [*Nicht-Ich*]. Formally, the not-self is in absolute opposition to the self, but in content, it relies on the self. According to Fichte, the not-self grounds the principle '~A is not equal to A,' which in the dialectical method is the principle of opposition, and as a specific activity of self-consciousness, provides the category of negation. Yet the not-self cannot be abstracted from representations, but must first be grounded in the self before any object can be opposed to the self. As Fichte states, 'in order to set up something as an *object*, I have to know this already; hence it must lie initially in myself, the presenter, in advance of any possible experience' (1982: 105/I, 105). Therefore, the content of opposition cannot be represented without the positing of the self. But this puts Fichte in a predicament regarding the unconditional form of the principle of opposition: the not-self must be absolutely opposed to the self. To resolve this difficulty, Fichte introduces the third principle, the grounding principle.

The form of the third principle is determined by the first two principles, but its content is unconditioned. Thus the content of the third principle will provide the first synthetic judgment of the *Wissenschaftslehre*. In Fichte's terms, the task for action is provided by the first two principles, but its resolution is not (1982: 106/I, 105–106). I have already alluded to the problem posed by the first two principles; if the not-self is posited, then the self cannot be posited, and vice versa. But the not-self can only be posited insofar as the self posits itself. This presents the problem to be resolved by the third principle, because, in their form, both the self and not-self are unconditional, positing the not-self annuls the self, and yet, the not-self requires the self in order to be set in opposition. Without a third principle, it seems that there are only two possible conclusions: (a) in positing the not-self, the self is nullified; or, (b) in positing the not-self, the self must already be posited, which nullifies the not-self.

It appears that to accept both conclusions, the self must be equal to the not-self, which then eliminates the identity of consciousness. If this is the case, the absolute foundation of philosophy is negated. Therefore, the task for action is to find a relation 'by means of which all these conclusions can be granted as correct, without doing away with the identity of consciousness' (1982: 107/I, 107). The third principle resolves the task by introducing a synthesis of the first two principles through limitation: they act on each other by mutual limitation. If both the self and not-self are limited, then they can both be posited in the self; the self is not posited in the measure that the not-self is also posited. Hence the form of the grounding principle is expressed by Fichte as such: 'A is in part = ~A' (1982: 110/I, 111).

The third principle answers the primary question of Kant's *Critique of Pure Reason* ('how are synthetic judgments possible a priori?') by demonstrating a synthetic judgment through positing the mutual limitation of the self and not-self. All further synthetic judgments will be methodologically grounded in the first synthesis in order to be established as valid. The task of the remainder of the theoretical discourse of the science of knowledge is to find the point of conjunction between opposites on a higher ground (a synthesis), which is itself grounded in a higher synthesis. The one exception is the original thesis of self-positing consciousness. Therefore, the dialectical method applied in Part One of the *Science of Knowledge* differs from the remainder of the deductions in one important regard: in opposing a not-I to the absolute I, the latter is 'degraded into a lower concept' (1982: 116/I, 119). Every other synthesis will be grounded in a higher synthesis. The form of the system is based on this highest synthesis, and the possibility of the system is based on the absolute thesis (1982: 114/I, 115).

In establishing the foundation of the *Wissenschaftslehre*, Fichte has foreshadowed the necessity of practical philosophy. By introducing a limitation into the self, he has put the identity of the self into question; the limited self is not identical to the absolute self. It is practical action which will attempt to resolve this contradiction within the self – the finite self *ought* to strive for absolute unconditionality. Again, despite the format of his presentation, Fichte claims that practical reason makes theoretical reason possible. Theoretical reason is no less important, however, as practical reason relies on the theoretical in order to conceptualize practical principles (1982: 123/I, 126). But, the absolute I is not *only* theoretical *or* practical, it is both the ground of theoretical reason and, as a regulative ideal, a practical principle.[19]

With the foundational principles established, we can now turn to the differences between criticism and dogmatism. Fichte understands dogmatism and criticism as the only two possible systems of philosophy. Each system is monistic, as it proceeds from an exclusive first principle; that is, philosophy cannot explain the possibility of experience from both an absolute self and a thing in itself. Criticism, including the spirit of Kant's philosophy, posits the absolute self as the first principle of philosophy while dogmatism goes beyond the self and posits the thing in itself as the ground of the self.[20] In other words, criticism proposes a principle immanent to the self, while dogmatism proposes one transcendent to the self (1982: 117/I, 120). Fichte does not admit skepticism as a philosophical stance: it is self-refuting insofar as it categorically denies the possibility of systematic philosophy.

Fichte's treatment of dogmatism vacillates between showing how it is either inconsistent or skeptical and showing how it is a step toward idealism. First, Fichte accuses dogmatism of being unable to justify the thing in itself (the not-self) as absolute. Because the thing in itself transcends the self, the dogmatist can only presuppose that the thing is absolute, but cannot defend this presupposition. But then, as suggested above, dogmatism posits the thing in itself out of practical need: 'the feeling that, insofar as it is practical, our self depends upon a not-self that is absolutely independent of our legislation, and is to that extent free' (1982: 118/I, 121). The dogmatic solution to the feeling of necessity, for Fichte, contains a crucial mistake: because it attempts to solve the problem of the feeling of necessity in theoretical reason instead of practical reason, it subordinates the self to an absolute object of theoretical reason, thus abolishing the activity of the self.

However, Fichte follows this critique by stating that such criticism is unfair to dogmatism. Dogmatism has not gone *beyond* the absolute self; instead, it has never *attained* the absolute. Spinozism, the most consistent dogmatic system, has advanced only to the second and third principles of the *Wissenschaftslehre*, but only critical idealism can reach the first principle. Criticism surpasses dogmatism because it recognizes the first principle as a regulative ideal grounded in practical action, and not as an object of theoretical reason. Fichte surprisingly states, in this account, that the theoretical section of the *Science of Knowledge* (save the acknowledgment of the absolute self), which is developed from the second and third principles, is 'Spinozism made systematic' (1982: 119/I, 122). Critical philosophy completes theoretical philosophy through the addition of a practical ground. By 'including' Spinozism within the theoretical section of the *Science of Knowledge*, Fichte implies that idealism presents a higher realization of self-consciousness. In other words, Fichte argues that dogmatism is a necessary step to the higher system of criticism, thus subordinating the former to the latter.[21] Demarcating these differences between dogmatism and criticism allows Fichte to respond to Jacobi's charges that theoretical reason necessarily leads to fatalism. By arguing that practical reason and theoretical reason have a common principle, Fichte shows that freedom and systematic philosophy are not mutually exclusive. As George di Giovanni states,

Fichte was only trying to demonstrate that, far from being detrimental to the cause of freedom, [philosophical reflection] was on the contrary its

UNIVERSITY OF WINCHESTER
LIBRARY

best expression, and a philosophy based on it the clearest manifesto of
the primacy of action and existence over theory that Jacobi had promoted
from the beginning. (1994: 114)

Yet, as I have argued, where Jacobi's account of practical action was
marred by an inconsistent historicism, Fichte argues for a universal and
moral ideal – the self-determining subject as the ground of free action.

1.4. The Practical Rivalry of Dogmatism and Criticism

Now that we have examined the Pantheism Controversy and Fichte's
Wissenschaftslehre, we can turn to Schelling's *Letters*, which offers an early
glimpse into his philosophical differences with Fichte.[22] While their contemporaries often viewed Fichte and Schelling as engaged in *Fichte's* project, we can now see that Schelling was seeking to produce a much more
extensive philosophy out of Fichte's critical idealism. I think it is central to
Schelling's philosophy that he understood the most extensive philosophy
as the most true – that is, a true system could account for the full development of reason as it is expressed throughout the history of philosophy.[23]
While Fichte was notorious for claiming that he was not interested in
engaging with those who did not understand his system, or those who made
strong claims against it from other philosophical perspectives, we see in
Schelling's work a willingness to include opposed philosophies to adju-
dicate their competing claims. Even though Jacobi, Spinoza, and Fichte are
opposed on first principles, Schelling subsumes each of their principles
under the idea of intellectual intuition in order to render an account of
the advantages and disadvantages of each.

   This, I think, is the result of Schelling's desire to incorporate Spinoza's
reference to intellectual intuition while preserving the critical emphasis
on freedom. A month after his letter to Hegel praising Fichte, Schelling
writes again to Hegel (the letter is dated February 4, 1795) to inform him
that he has become a Spinozist:

   For Spinoza the world (the absolute object in opposition to the subject)
   was all, for me the *I* is all. The essential distinction between critical and
   dogmatic philosophy appears to me to lie therein, that one proceeds
   from the absolute I (not yet conditioned through any object), the other
   from the absolute object, or not-I. The latter, in its highest consequence
   leads to Spinoza's system, the former to Kant's. Philosophy must proceed

from the *unconditional* [*Unbedingten*]. Now it is only a question of wherein this unconditional lies: in the I or not-I? If this question is decided, everything is decided. For me the highest principle of all philosophy is the pure, absolute I; that is, the I insofar as it is the bare I [*bloßes Ich*], not yet conditioned through any objects, but rather posited through *freedom*. The Alpha and Omega of all philosophy is freedom. (AA, III/1: 22)

This letter anticipates several themes that appear in the *Letters*. Most importantly, Schelling presents the difference between the two systems as a difference in principles, and draws the conclusion that once a decision is made regarding principles, the system follows. Nevertheless, it is difficult initially to see how this makes him a Spinozist when he states that the 'Alpha and Omega of all philosophy is freedom,' which echoes the primacy of freedom found in Fichte's *Wissenschaftslehre*. But, to foreshadow a bit, Schelling also cites in the *Letters* two passages from Spinoza's *Ethics* that support the self-caused freedom of God's nature (1980: 189/I, 330–331).[24] The differences between Fichte and Schelling become clearer, though, if we see that when Schelling interprets criticism and dogmatism as two opposed philosophical systems, this higher standpoint above criticism implies that the absolute is beyond the subject and object. But Schelling also maintains, like Fichte, that criticism is superior to dogmatism by recognizing absolute freedom as a regulative ideal for practice.

While part of the *Letters* reflects Schelling's own attempt to reconcile his affinities with both criticism and dogmatism, the text, in its epistolary form, along with the Spinozist position of Schelling's anonymous interlocutor, appears to be a response to the Spinozism of his friend Hölderlin (who we will also discuss in Section 2.6). In the fragment now entitled 'Urtheil und Seyn,' Hölderlin argues that the absolute I cannot be its own ground:

Where subject and object are absolutely, not just partially united, and hence so united that no division can be undertaken, without destroying the essence of the thing that is to be sundered, there and not otherwise can we talk of an *absolute* Being, as is the case in intellectual intuition.

But this Being must not be equated with identity. When I say: I am I, the subject (I) and the object (I) are not so united that absolutely no sundering can be undertaken, without destroying the essence of the thing that is to be sundered; on the contrary the I is only possible through this sundering of I from I. How can I say 'I' without self-consciousness? But how is self-consciousness possible? Precisely because I oppose myself to myself; I sunder myself from myself, but in spite of this sundering

I recognize myself as the same in opposites. [. . .] So identity is not a
uniting of subject and object that takes place absolutely, and so identity
is not equal to absolute Being. (1972: 515–516tm/*HSA*, IV, 226–227)

It has often been assumed that Hölderlin is criticizing Fichte, but Manfred
Frank argues that this fragment is a response to Schelling's *Vom Ich*, wherein
he conflates the absolute I with all Being. As Frank summarizes their
central point of contention:

The material unity of that as which we experience ourselves in self-
consciousness is thus contradicted by the duality of the form of judgment
we use to express this unity. But there *is* such an experience of unity (and
not only the duality of judgment). And so we *must* presuppose a unified
Being, and we can render the epistemic self-*relation* as *self*-relation
comprehensible [. . .] only if we think of it as the reflex of this unified
Being. (Frank, 2004: 107)[25]

While Frank hesitates to identify Hölderlin's 'Being' with Spinoza's substance (he claims that 'Being' is not a first principle like Fichte's absolute I;
in this Fichte would be in agreement)[26], it is possible that Schelling did
identify the two. If the *Letters* is a response to Hölderlin, it is difficult to tell
whether Schelling took Hölderlin's position to be positing an absolute that
grounds both subject and object, but which itself *is* neither (for, here,
we are on the path to absolute idealism; see Chapter 4), or as another
Spinozist objection to criticism. We can find both possible interpretations
in the *Letters*: when Schelling argues that criticism is *practically* superior
to Spinozistic dogmatism, it is because critical practice infinitely strives to
realize the absolute, which is (implicitly) neither subject nor object.

  To rehabilitate Spinoza, Schelling distinguishes Spinoza's work from
other types of dogmatism.[27] According to Schelling, Spinoza recognized the
primacy of praxis, despite presenting a systematic philosophy that has
the thing in itself (the absolute object) as its first principle. So, while the
Leibnizian-Wolffian School also posits the object as first principle it does
not recognize the primacy of praxis, which is why, Schelling argues, it was
refuted by the *Critique of Pure Reason*. But more pernicious than this form
of dogmatism is that of the Tübingen *Stift*, which included the professors
Gottlob Christian Storr and Johann Friedrich Flatt, the so-called proponents of criticism who used Kant to reintroduce the relics of precritical
philosophy.[28] Schelling had firsthand experience with this tendency, as he
was in residence there as he wrote the *Letters*, which no doubt explains

why their original publication was anonymous. As he writes from Tübingen to Hegel, on January 6, 1795, 'All possible dogmas have now been stamped as postulates of practical reason, and where theoretico-historical proofs are lacking, there practical (Tübingenian) reason cuts the knot' (AA, III/1, 15). These 'philosophical heroes,' as Schelling calls them, have combined the superstitions of positive and 'so-called' natural religion with Kantian philosophy. With obvious sarcasm, he calls it a 'pleasure' to watch them 'pull the string of the moral proof; before you know it the *Deus ex machina* springs forth, the personal, individual Being (*Wesen*) who sits up there in Heaven!' (AA, III/1: 16).

Schelling's central objection is that the Tübingen School misuses the practical postulate of God; instead of interpreting the idea of God as an 'object of action,' they understand it as an object 'considered as true' (1980: 159/I, 288). But the acceptance of truth can only take a theoretical form. Therefore, they have confused the domains of theoretical and practical reason. From practical need, they reintroduce theoretical truth. As Klaus Düsing notes, they 'weakened and falsified the concept of [Kant's] practical postulates in that they declared every possible claim containing theoretical, even empirical, representations to be a postulate of practical reason merely insofar as a moral-practical interest or need was served thereby' (1999: 203–204). This, according to Schelling, is inconsistent with both the theoretical and practical perspectives: first, it reintroduces absolute causality into theoretical reason; second, it introduces an absolute object into practical reason.

The latter objections are adapted from Kant. In the preface to the second edition of the *Critique of Pure Reason*, Kant addresses the inclusion of the practical postulates within the domain of theoretical reason. There he states that it is not possible to postulate God, freedom, and the immortality of the soul for practical reason without simultaneously depriving theoretical reason 'of its pretension to extravagant insights' (1998: 117/Bxxx). Since theoretical reason only deals with objects of possible experience, attempting to introduce the practical postulates into theoretical reason would reduce them to mere appearances. The importance of the postulates is that they are not just appearances but morally necessary. So Kant draws the conclusion that the dogmatic inclusion of practical reason within theoretical reason is the 'true source,' not of faith, but of unbelief.

Yet morality is also endangered by introducing the cognition of the postulates into practical reason. As Kant states in the *Critique of Practical Reason*, if human subjects had theoretical knowledge of the postulates, then 'God and eternity in their awful majesty would stand unceasingly before our eyes,' and the reason for moral action would be constantly present and external (1956: 152/V, 147). Practical action would no longer be autonomous, or done for the sake of the moral law, but would be done predominately out of fear. Kant draws the striking conclusion, against dogmatism, that if direct knowledge of God were possible, all human action would be reduced to 'mere mechanism,' that is, to necessity and fatalism.[29] Here we can see why Schelling objects to introducing absolute, objective causality into practical action, as positing God's causality extinguishes the subject's free causality. After these criticisms of this dogmatic tendency, however, Schelling's accord with Kant reaches its limit, as Schelling refutes the other forms of dogmatism in order to rehabilitate Spinoza as the most consistent proponent of a dogmatic system of action that can be opposed to criticism. With this opposition, Schelling opens a practical contest between the two opposed systems over human freedom.

Schelling's appropriation of the *Critique of Pure Reason* is intended to situate the conflict between dogmatism and criticism. This orientation requires overlaying his concerns, Kant's own concerns, and the debates over the status of the thing in itself within the *Critique of Pure Reason*. To defend Kant, proponents of critical philosophy were required to navigate between two claims: first, by limiting the understanding to the cognition of appearances, Kant was only repeating Berkeley's idealism; or second, that Kant's utilization of the thing in itself was not justified by the tenets of his own critique (the restriction of the inquiry to objects of possible experience). Therefore, the inclusion of the thing in itself within critical philosophy is itself dogmatic.

Schelling's interpretation of the *Critique of Pure Reason* breaks with this dilemma, and the defense of criticism articulated by Kant and Fichte. Instead of defending Kant's critical system as a *system*, Schelling explains his predecessor's inconsistencies by claiming that, far from establishing one system of knowledge, the *Critique of Pure Reason* 'prepares' a canon for both criticism and dogmatism:

> the *Critique* is destined to deduce from the essence of reason the very possibility of two exactly opposed systems: it is destined to establish a system of criticism (conceived as complete), or, more precisely, a system of idealism as well as and in exact opposition to it, a system of dogmatism or of realism. (1980: 169/I, 302)

For Schelling, the absolute I serves as the first principle of criticism, and the thing in itself serves as the first principle of dogmatism. As already mentioned, Kant distinguishes critical philosophy and dogmatic philosophy (which Schelling calls 'dogmaticism' – the metaphysics of the Leibnizian-Wolffian school) by way of method: the latter utilizes pure reason without inquiring into its limits. Thus Kant views neither the transcendental subject nor the thing in itself as the exclusive first principle of one of two opposed philosophical systems. Though the transcendental unity of apperception grounds the possibility of objective experience, it must be noted that, for Kant, consciousness of this unity is derived from the representations of inner sense (time) and not from an absolute act (1998: 236–237/A116–117, and the rewritten sections found in the second edition, 1998: 248–251/ B136–140). And although Kant introduces the thing in itself in opposition to the transcendental subject, the former remains a 'boundary concept' within critical philosophy (1998: 362/A255/B310–311). The thing in itself, as a concept, serves to limit the domain of sensible intuition to appearances: though it can be thought without contradiction, it cannot be cognized; instead, it functions as a limit to cognition, restricting the understanding to appearances (phenomena) while remaining agnostic on the ontological status of the noumenal world. Yet, in later sections of the *Critique of Pure Reason*, Kant himself seems to overstep his own critical boundaries when he attributes causality to the transcendental object (1998: 381/A288/B344).[30]

Fichte attempts to resolve the problematic status of the thing in itself in his 'Review of Aenesidemus,' a response to an anonymous critique (written by Gottlob Ernst Schulze, a professor at Helmstadt) of Kant's and Reinhold's critical philosophy from the standpoint of Humean skepticism.[31] Schulze's criticisms of Kant and Reinhold forced the young Fichte to develop his own critical approach later realized in the *Wissenschaftslehre*. The primary contention against Kant (we will leave Reinhold aside) was the accusation that Kant's introduction of the noumenal world, by attributing causality to the subject (as a subject who represents) and the thing in itself (as the external cause of representations) violated critical philosophy's explicit limits.

Fichte resolves the problematic status of the thing in itself by subordinating it to the subject (the I), the self-consciousness which accompanies all representation. Ascribing causality to self-consciousness is defensible because the autonomy of the self is valid *for itself*; to ask whether this autonomy could be *in itself*, as Schulze demands, extends beyond possible knowledge (1988: 70–71/I, 16). Then Fichte removes the thing in itself from critical philosophy, claiming that the concept of a thing *in itself* not *opposed to* consciousness is self-contradictory. Thus, he states, the structure of consciousness is oppositional: consciousness of the self requires something (the not-I) to be thought. While this reply seems to confirm the accusation that Kant's philosophy falls into Berkeley's idealism, Fichte dismisses this possibility by noting that Berkeley was refuted in the 'Transcendental Aesthetic' of the first *Critique*, where Kant argues that space and time are not appearances but pure intuitions that ground all possible experience.[32]

By contrast, Schelling explains Kant's inconsistencies by claiming that the first *Critique* necessarily had to establish a common point of reference between criticism and dogmatism: from the perspective of theoretical reason, Kant provides a negative refutation of dogmatism, but being limited to the cognitive faculty, the *Critique of Pure Reason* could proceed no further; the resolution to the conflict must be sought within practical action. Before turning to the practical solution proposed by Schelling, in which criticism triumphs through the recognition of human freedom, it is necessary to introduce the solution's metaphysical ground, found in neither Kant nor Fichte. For the latter two, criticism is a higher stage of cognition, in which reason recognizes the limits ignored by dogmatism. For Schelling, the two systems are mutually opposed, and the choice of a system requires a decision which itself imposes a theoretical framework. So criticism's superiority is demonstrated through its self-recognition of human freedom. However, in setting the two systems in direct opposition, Schelling implies a common point of dispute that requires a system more extensive than Fichte's *Wissenschaftslehre*.

The common point between the two systems, which is a 'necessary consequence of the concept of philosophy' itself, according to Schelling, is the original opposition resulting in the departure from the absolute (1980: 163tm/I, 293). The original opposition provides the respective first principles of the two systems. Schelling is careful to note that Kant's *Critique* proceeds from the fact of the opposition between the subject and object, and that it does not – and cannot – 'ascend' to the absolute, as the latter is a regulative ideal of practical reason. However, as the common ground of both dogmatism and criticism, the absolute is not the absolute subject postulated in Fichte's *Wissenschaftslehre*. The *fact* of opposition, for Schelling, orients the inquiry of the *Critique of Pure Reason*. Schelling rephrases the Kantian question of 'how synthetic judgments are possible a priori' to ask how the first principle of a philosophical system proceeds toward its opposite: 'How do I ever come to egress from the absolute, and to progress toward an opposite?' (1980: 164/I, 294). The common point between dogmatism and criticism is this original synthesis. At this point, criticism can demonstrate its theoretical superiority. But it cannot confute dogmatism through theory, because the ultimate tribunal is that of practical reason.

Criticism can refute dogmatism (although not decisively) through the theory of synthetic judgments. Criticism proves, Schelling states, that once the subject judges objectively, it must judge synthetically. However, dogmatism cannot show how absolutely objective cognition is possible, that is, how an absolute object can judge synthetically. Therefore, all cognition is possible only under the condition of the subject (1980: 165/I, 296). Yet the *Critique of Pure Reason* does not end with the theory of synthetic judgments; it also demarcates the boundaries of pure reason. Kant uses the Transcendental Dialectic to show how pure reason overextends its boundaries when it enters the domains of rational psychology, cosmology, and theology. In Schelling's terminology, theoretical reason cannot achieve the absolute thesis (the unconditional ground of the conditional) demanded by pure reason. Or, as Schelling phrases it, in reference to Jacobi, the transition from the infinite to the finite is prohibited by philosophy (which, as we will see in Chapter 4, becomes a central problem of Schelling's absolute idealism). The absolute, as unconditional, falls outside the limits of theoretical reason because anything that can be said about it is not synthetic but analytic. If synthesis ended in a thesis, it would have to eliminate all that is conditional. But synthesis requires the condition of opposition between subject and object. Theoretical reason seeks an unconditional ideal which it cannot realize: 'having formed the *idea* of the unconditioned, and, as *theoretical reason*, being unable to realize the unconditioned, it therefore *demands* the *act* through which it *ought* to be realized' (1980: 167/I, 299).

Therefore, insofar as we must resolve these demands, we must move from theoretical to practical philosophy. Here, too, Schelling will argue for criticism's superiority over dogmatism. Before moving to the practical domain, we should complete Schelling's interpretation of the *Critique of Pure Reason*: his ultimate claim is that the *Critique* establishes the practical postulates for both criticism and dogmatism. This is why Kant includes the thing in itself within transcendental idealism, despite the implication that the thing in itself exists as noumenon. This inclusion is only inconsistent if Kant had aimed to found only a system of criticism. However, Schelling claims that the first *Critique* establishes an exhaustive canon for both systems that comprises the genuine *Wissenschaftslehre* (which implies that Fichte's system is not a complete doctrine of science). Yet, according to Schelling, Kant also establishes that a complete system of philosophy is not an object of knowledge but a goal of practical activity (1980: 171/I, 305).

Thus in demonstrating that the realization of a system is the goal of activity, Schelling further claims that Kant deduces the ground of the spontaneous activity of philosophy: every philosopher guided by the ideal of a system – whether consciously or unconsciously – practices the realization of his or her system. As Schelling argues each philosopher – Spinoza is his explicit example – lives his or her system. But a system can only be an ideal for gradual approximation, for a completed system would vanquish free activity. We should pause here to underline that freedom is explicitly conceived as *creative*: if a philosopher believed his system to be completed, at that 'very moment he would cease to be *creator* and would be degraded to an instrument of his system' (1980: 172tm/I, 306). It is this idea of creativity that Schelling will continuously elevate above the formalism, as he will say later, of practical reason.

From *creativity* to the necessity of two opposing systems: a permanent resolution of their opposition into a complete and actual system of philosophy would extinguish the freedom 'lived' in a system of action (1980: 172/I, 302). This is yet another criticism of Fichte's claim to have arrived at a complete and systematic doctrine of science. However, it is important to clarify the conceptual status of this freedom, including its relation to the opposition between dogmatism and criticism. It is in the realm of practice that the philosopher can answer the question of 'how the absolute could come out of itself and oppose to itself a world' (1980: 174/I, 310). Dogmatism and criticism provide two different answers: the latter asserts the subject's causality through the individual's self-recognition of freedom, while the former ascribes absolute causality to the object, thereby subsuming individual activity under necessity. The original free act takes place in the choice between systems. Yet the free act is not voluntarist or irrational; for Schelling, the relationship between the choice and the system is an 'inevitable circle': theoretical reason serves as an anticipation of practical reason. It is practical reason that, through its creative powers, gives reality to theoretical propositions. As Schelling states,

> If we want to establish a system and, therefore, principles, we cannot do it by an anticipation of the practical decision. We should not establish those principles unless our freedom had already decided about them; at the beginning of our knowledge they are nothing but proleptic assertions, or, as Jacobi expresses it somewhere – wryly and awkwardly enough, as he says himself, yet not quite unphilosophically – they are *original insuperable prejudices* [*Vorurteile*]. (1980: 176/I, 312–313)

The reference to Jacobi both establishes his influence on Schelling and serves to distinguish their positions: one cannot assert the dignity of theoretical reason and the importance of Spinoza without reprimanding Jacobi. While for Jacobi, the experience of faith grounds all knowledge, for Schelling practical action imposes a theoretical framework by creating the reality of its principles. At the point of this free choice, the critical philosopher would hold not only that 'I act freely' and that 'I will act freely' but also that 'I will have acted freely.' This shows the practical superiority of critical philosophy, as the dogmatist misrecognizes the initial free choice as conditioned by objective necessity.

Fichte's implicit response to Schelling in the *First Introduction to the Science of Knowledge* (1797) has often been cited as a more radical formulation of the choice between dogmatism and criticism, because Fichte interprets this choice as a consequence of pre-systematic interests and inclinations:

> What sort of philosophy one chooses depends, therefore, on what sort of man one is; for a philosophical system is not a dead piece of furniture that we can reject or accept as we wish; it is rather a thing animated by the soul of the person who holds it. A person indolent by nature or dulled and distorted by mental servitude, learned luxury, and vanity will never raise himself to the level of idealism. (1982: 16/I, 434)

Yet the claim that one chooses a system according to inclination is not more radical than Schelling's vertiginous circle of theoretical anticipation and practical action. Instead, Fichte pits the cool and rational disposition of the idealist against the passions and animosity of the dogmatist. Opposing rationality to passion is, as is well-known, a fairly standard discursive trope in Enlightenment and post-Enlightenment philosophy. And after deploying this trope, Fichte claims that the ultimate danger for the idealist would be to break character and show contempt for the dogmatist's inability to recognize the superiority of criticism. By contrast, Schelling risks the irresolvable conflict of two rival practical systems.

Yet in the seventh, eighth, and ninth letters, Schelling still argues that the dogmatist misrecognizes the initial free choice of practical action through a misinterpretation of the principle of intellectual intuition. The terminology itself should indicate that he has not returned the first *Critique* to the bookshelf in order to retrieve the second. Instead, Schelling turns to a modified Fichtean account of practical action (as found in the *Science of Knowledge*) with the addition of the principle of intellectual intuition.

At the time of the publication of the *Letters* Fichte had yet to publicly develop this principle. Until 1797, the 'Review of Aenesidemus' was the only published text by Fichte to mention 'intellectual intuition.' Though explicitly prohibited by Kant, Schelling introduces intellectual intuition in *Vom Ich*. There he argues that the absolute I can be grounded neither in a concept nor an object, but as self-determined in an intellectual intuition, which is the self-attribution of absolute freedom (1980: 84–86/I, 180–183). This self-attribution of freedom grounds the identity of the absolute subject, despite the fact that empirical consciousness is constantly threatened by the ineluctable flux of change:

> Self-awareness implies the danger of losing the I. It is not a free act of the immutable but an unfree urge that induces the mutable I, conditioned by the not-I, to strive to maintain its identity and to reassert itself in the undertow of endless change [. . .] But that striving of the empirical I, and the consciousness stemming from it, would itself not be possible without the freedom of the absolute I, and absolute freedom is equally necessary as a condition for both imagination and action. (1980: 84/I, 180–181)

In the *Letters*, intellectual intuition is still an absolute act but it is now the common practical principle between the two systems, and it seems to have its origins in his reading of Fichte, Jacobi's immanent feeling of faith in revelation, and Spinoza's intellectual intuition of the infinite. For Spinoza, recall that there are three kinds of knowledge: the kind arising from sensation or imagination, the kind arising from reason and concepts, and the third (intellectual intuition) which proceeds from adequate knowledge of the infinite (God) to the essence of finite things (see the *Ethics*, Scholium 2, prop. 40, Part III and prop. 25, Part V; 1992: 90, 214). Because Schelling holds (1980: 177/I, 314), like Jacobi (1994: 188), that philosophy is prohibited from speculating about the transition from the infinite *to* the finite, intellectual intuition offers the practical principle that intuits the infinite *in* the finite (thus reversing Spinoza). But now, the danger of losing the absolute I is not found in the transitory nature of things, but in the enthusiasm of dogmatism. Hence there are two different accounts of intellectual intuition between *Vom Ich* and the *Letters*: in the former, intellectual intuition is the Archimedean point preventing the subject from losing itself in the constant changes of the world; in the latter, it runs the risk of losing the world by abstracting from the opposition of subject and object.

Dogmatism, and, Schelling adds, all religious enthusiasm (*Schwärmerei*) and madness, misinterprets intellectual intuition as an intuition of an absolute object. That is, dogmatism ascribes absolute causality to an object beyond the self, rendering the self passive to the object's causality. Schelling provides Spinoza as an example. Spinoza holds, through a practical decision, that the 'finite world is nothing but a modification of the infinite, finite causality merely a modification of infinite causality' (1980: 178–179/I, 316). Had the limitations of finite causality been overcome, then the finite would become identical to the infinite. To live this ethics one would have to lose oneself in the absolute, relinquishing one's subjectivity to the causality of external necessity. Schelling claims that this could only be bearable to the dogmatist because he or she falls prey to the delusion that identifies the individual's ego with that of the deity. Even the dogmatist, he claims, cannot annihilate the self when objectifying self-intuition, and so the dogmatist self-identifies with the absolute object (1980: 182/I, 320–321).

This misidentification is not entirely the fault of the dogmatist, for intellectual intuition is abstracted from all objects, allowing for an 'infinite expansion' of the self, which risks losing the self. This is not a danger for the empirical self, which finds resistance among a world of objects, but it is for intellectual intuition, abstracted from all sensuous intuition. It therefore remains a danger for criticism as well, if criticism attempts to make the object identical to the subject. Therefore, for criticism itself to avoid the reproach of enthusiasm it must explain the transition from the finite to the infinite while prohibiting the accomplishment of absolute identity between subject and object. Just as dogmatism demands the loss of the subject in the absolute object in the transition from the finite to the infinite, criticism demands the dissolution of the object in the subject. Both of these demands have the same consequence, the resolution of the opposition between subject and object in absolute identity. There 'Absolute freedom and absolute necessity are identical' (1980: 189/I, 330–331).[33]

To represent the absolute as realizable, or as an object of knowledge, through practical action leads to enthusiasm (the identification of the finite self with the infinite). We have already seen that Schelling attributes this error to dogmatism. Because criticism shares its practical goal (of attaining an absolute thesis) with dogmatism, it too runs the risk of enthusiasm. However, criticism avoids this risk, and demonstrates its practical superiority over its systematic rival by positing the absolute as a regulative ideal for practical action. That is, critical praxis realizes, and recognizes, itself in an infinite striving toward its goals. It is through infinite striving that the free subject expands its freedom in the world. Through one's own way of being, one can exercise practically one's philosophy. Thus Schelling argues for a different, more extensive conception of the philosophical vocation than Fichte. Where Fichte sought to subordinate the intellectual allure of Spinoza in the theoretical section of the *Wissenschaftslehre* to the domain of practical reason, Schelling opened a contest between rival philosophical systems as the *agon* for practical action. Yet after establishing this rivalry, the *Letters* formulates a defense of the spirit of critical idealism, that is, a defense of freedom, even if it does not adhere to Fichte's doctrines. This is the context in which we should read the discussion of Greek tragedy in the tenth letter.

1.5. The Sublime of Greek Tragedy and the Interest of Reason

In the tenth letter, Schelling returns to the theme of an aesthetic side to philosophy, which was introduced in the first. More specifically, Schelling asks if Greek tragedy can provide a model for a system of ethics. Peter Szondi argues that Schelling breaks with the modern tradition of poetics based on Aristotle, and in Germany, Lessing, 'by not focusing on the effect that the tragic has on the audience' (Szondi, 2002: 1–3, 7) but on the idea of tragedy. However, as Szondi rightly notes, while a philosophy of tragedy, as opposed to a poetics of tragedy, becomes possible after Schelling, the *Letters* remains committed to the affirmation of practical reason (we will return to absolute idealism and tragedy in Chapter 4).

In the *Letters*, Schelling attributes the demonstration of this identity between freedom and necessity (as fate) to the *content* of Greek tragedy, but he evaluates this content according to the dictates of practical action, specifically the disjunction between the first principles of criticism and dogmatism. Greek tragedy, he concludes, cannot be proposed as a system of practical action because it reintroduces an objective power to limit the absolute freedom *demanded* by critical philosophy. In terms more appropriate to Sartre, we might say that an avowal of tragedy as a system of action allows for the emergence of bad faith through the denial of one's freedom. This caveat, prohibiting the use of Greek tragedy for a system of action, introduces ambiguity into Schelling's praise for Greek tragedy, which several recent commentators minimize (Krell, 2005: 183–187; Distaso, 2004: 105–110). Both Theodore D. George and Jason M. Wirth omit it altogether (George, 2005: 135–146; Wirth, 2003: 146).[34] But the exclusion of Greek tragedy as a model for practical action should be understood through Schelling's defense of the practical aspects of critical philosophy, that is, the defense of freedom as conceived by criticism.[35]

In the first letter, Schelling affirms the implied position of his interlocutor – that it is greater to struggle against fate than to flee to the safety
of a moral God. Yet Schelling quickly differentiates his affirmation from
the dogmatism of his addressee. Although consistent dogmatism has an
aesthetic side, it is not of struggle against fate but a 'Quiet abandonment to
the immeasurable' (1980: 157/I, 284), because any thought of resistance
to fate through the self-assertion (*Selbstmacht*) of freedom 'comes from a
system better than dogmatism,' namely, criticism (1980: 157/I, 284). The
inner principle of art, Schelling claims, is ultimately opposed to the
mechanism of dogmatism. He foreshadows the further development of the
Letters in this dense passage:

> True art, or rather, the divine (*theion*) in art, is an inward principle that
> creates its own material from within and all-powerfully opposes any
> sheer mechanism [and] aggregation of stuff from the outside lacking
> inner order. This inward principle we lose simultaneously with the
> intellectual intuition of the world, an intuition which arises in us by means
> of an instantaneous unification of two opposing principles and is lost
> when neither the struggle nor the unification is any longer possible in
> us. (1980: 157tm/I, 285)

The passivity of the subject and the necessity of fate implied by dogmatism
stands opposed to the inner principle of the artwork. However, this inner
principle is also lost when criticism tries to end the conflict with dogmatism
by attempting to actualize its unconditional causality. The principle of
art is grounded in either the unification of, or struggle between, fate
and freedom.

This opposition to both systems is made explicit when Schelling returns
to the question of the work of art in the tenth letter. Again he affirms a
conviction of his interlocutor: that, despite being dispelled by the 'light of
reason,' it remains to be seen if there is an objective power that threatens
human freedom. This knowledge, though 'banished' from theoretical
reason, remains possible for Greek tragedy, which he calls the highest art.
Greek tragedy demands the free struggle of the protagonist against the
powers of fate, a struggle in which the protagonist must suffer in a testimony to human freedom. Thus in the 'conflict between human freedom
and the power of the objective world . . . the mortal must succumb *necessarily* if that power is superior, if it is fate. . . . That the malefactor who
succumbed under the power of fate was punished, this tragic fact was
the recognition of human freedom; it was the *honor* due to freedom'

(1980: 192–193tm/I, 336). Thus Greek tragedy realizes what neither criticism nor dogmatism can, the presentation of the absolute (we will return to this point in Section 4.4). Yet despite presenting the identity of freedom and necessity, Greek tragedy cannot propose a tenable system of action; it would 'presuppose a race of titans, and . . . without this presupposition, it would turn out to be utterly detrimental to humanity' (1980: 194/I, 338). Properly speaking, this knowledge of freedom and necessity is neither theoretical nor practical, but sublime, motivating reason to think the identity and conflict of freedom and fate. Though the Greeks are the most faithful to the sublime essence of human freedom, their tragedies cannot provide a system of ethics.

Yet the sublime aspect of tragedy motivates reason to resolve the conflict between freedom and necessity. It is in the interest of reason, Schelling claims, to search out all self-imposed limitations on freedom. In this regard, even Greek tragedy must not be allowed to lull philosophy back into a dogmatic slumber.[36] As he states,

'Reason must renounce either an objective intelligible world, or a subjective personality; either an absolute object, or an absolute subject, freedom of will.' This antithesis once definitely established, the interest of reason demands also that we watch with the utmost care that it be not obscured again by the sophistries of moral indolence, in a veil which would deceive humanity. It is our duty to uncover the whole deception, and to show that any attempt at making it acceptable to reason can succeed only through new deceptions which keep reason in constant ignorance and hide from it the last abyss into which dogmatism must inevitably fall as soon as it proceeds to the last great question, which is, to be or not to be. (1980: 194/I, 338–339)

The choice of practical reason is between an objective supersensible world and the subject's freedom. Admitting an objective limit to freedom acts against the self's activity and threatens the self (which is interpreted as the modification of absolute object or God) with moral ruin (*Untergang*) (1980: 194/I, 339). By contrast, criticism demands the self to act, to 'Be!' (1980: 192/I, 335). It is in the interest of freedom to renounce the supersensible powers of the objective world and assert humanity's capacity for freedom. The task of philosophy, for Schelling, is to expose self-imposed limitations of freedom, and critical idealism's superiority over dogmatism is revealed in its insistence on the autonomy and freedom of the subject.

Thus Schelling turns, in closing, from the discussion of art to the critical demand that humanity reclaim the creative powers it once 'sought in the objective world' (1980: 195/I, 339). Although Greek tragedy provides the rule (*Regel*) for all art (1980: 193/I, 337), it is in the interest of reason to promote human freedom. Thus, in the *Letters*, tragedy and practical freedom remain in conflict. It is only later, in the *System of Transcendental Idealism*, that Schelling fully acknowledges the superior character of artistic production, in distinction to practical action. However, in this latter text, Schelling's interest shifts from the *content* of Greek tragedy – the mortal struggling against fate – to the *form* of productive activity exhibited in artistic creation. The *Letters*, though, remains conflicted between a defense of Spinoza's legacy, the practical tenets of critical idealism, and the sublime power of Greek tragedy. As a consequence Schelling argues for a more extensive account than Fichte of what a doctrine of science (*Wissenshaftslehre*) can achieve. Soon he will develop a systematic account of a system of transcendental idealism, a nature-philosophy, and a philosophy of art. The *Letters* anticipates this tripartite structure by evaluating the advantages and disadvantages of criticism, dogmatism, and Greek tragedy for the free and creative life.

Chapter 2

From Nature-philosophy to the 'Mythology of Reason'

2.1. Nature-philosophy and the Beginnings of the Philosophy of Art

In 1809 Schelling begins his *Philosophical Investigations into the Essence of Human Freedom* with a two-pronged critique of modern philosophy from Descartes to Fichte and, it is safe to assume, Hegel. On the one hand, modern philosophy lacks a true philosophy of nature (2006: 26/VII, 356), while on the other, it has only produced a formal account of freedom (2006: 21/ VII, 352). Overcoming these problems, according to Schelling, requires unifying these one-sided presentations of idealism and realism within a 'living whole' grounded in a common creative principle (2006: 26/VII, 356).

We have already seen in the first chapter that Schelling's interest in the creative capacity of freedom is present as early as the *Letters*, and we will see over the next few chapters how he turns to a philosophy of art to overcome the formal character of practical reason as it is conceived by Fichte and Kant. In this chapter, we will outline how, in 1797 and 1798, Schelling extends the domain of critical idealism to include a nature-philosophy, a philosophy of history, and a philosophy of art. The unprecedented development of nature-philosophy was Schelling's first distinct contribution to, or most notorious liability within, the field now recognized as German idealism.[1] In the annals of German idealism it is well-known that Fichte and Schelling irrevocably split over the status of nature-philosophy in Schelling's system. Yet what is lesser known, though no less important, is that Schelling initially developed his nature-philosophy as a concrete application of theoretical reason within critical idealism, and that Fichte initially approved of these innovations (see Erich von Berger's letter, dated October 6, 1797, quoted in Tilliette, 1999b: 48). Claude Piché notes that the two philosophers' early views on organic nature are compatible, although Fichte maintains, unlike Schelling, an instrumental view of nature (2004: 211–237). Their differences, however, will become more profound as Schelling progresses toward grounding the self's activity in nature, which is the most important step toward absolute idealism (see Chapter 4). It is significant that Hegel forced the break between Fichte and Schelling in the *Difference Between Fichte's and Schelling's System of Philosophy* (1801), where he argues that Fichte exhibits 'nature as an absolute effect and as dead' (1977a: 143), because it is also Hegel's attack on nature-philosophy in the *Phenomenology of Spirit* and his subsequent work that bears much of the responsibility for the negative reception of Schelling's contribution to philosophy.[2]

No matter its reception, we must discover some of the origins of nature-philosophy.

Schelling draws on a variety of sources to develop it, and many of these sources have been well documented. Some commentators have shown how Schelling criticizes the reliance on the principle of sufficient reason or mechanical explanations of nature in interpreting the world, through the scientific research of his contemporaries, and in dialogue with Kant's *Metaphysical Foundations of Natural Science*. These commentaries also make a significant effort to demonstrate how nature-philosophy, at least initially, adhered to many of the scientific practices of the late 18th and early 19th centuries (see Esposito, 1977; and Friedman, 2006). Some recent literature has traced the development of nature-philosophy to Schelling's early study of Plato's *Timaeus* (Baum, 2000; Distaso, 2004: 37–47). More recently, Iain Hamilton Grant, in his *Philosophies of Nature after Schelling* (2008), argues that Schelling revives a Platonic physics that overcomes the dualisms inherent in Kantian, Aristotelian, and post-Kantian philosophy in general.[3]

I will use a different approach – which argues that Schelling pieced together the various fragments of a nature-philosophy from Spinoza's monism, Leibniz's concept of inner purposiveness, and Kant's concept of teleology, while defending the critical position concerning the primacy of practical reason – to underline the connection between his early nature-philosophy, practical reason, and the philosophy of art. The approaches listed above are not mutually exclusive: each highlights an important aspect of Schelling's work, and they are compatible because Schelling worked from the premise that a truly universal philosophical system will encompass the largest variety of perspectives and experiences.

All these elements, which are rendered in a more or less systematic form in the *System of Transcendental Idealism*, are found in the *Allgemeine Übersicht der neuesten philosophischen Literatur* (hereafter referred to as the *Survey*; it was published over the course of 1797–1798 in Immanuel Niethammer's and Fichte's *Philosophisches Journal*) and the *Ideas for a Philosophy of Nature* of 1797.[4] In these two texts, Schelling develops, from contemporaneous scientific discoveries and what we might call the fragmentary antecedents found in Spinoza, Leibniz, and Kant, a general task for investigating nature: to justify and demonstrate philosophically both an organic idea of nature as a totality and to show how the self acts *within* the world and not *opposed* to it. This task requires both (1) showing how nature cannot be reduced to a mechanistic series of causes and effects and (2) demonstrating the falsity of the dualism between the self and world, which is persistent within philosophy – whether, for example, it appears as the division between thought and extension (Descartes) or noumena and phenomena (Kant). These are the central problems facing a program of nature-philosophy. When Schelling writes in the *Ideas* that 'Nature should be Mind made visible, Mind the invisible Nature,' the prescriptive character is telling: philosophy has yet to demonstrate, or render visible, the common origins of self-consciousness and nature, but it *should*, if it is to be a complete and systematic philosophy (1988: 42/II, 56).

While the influence of Spinoza and Leibniz on Schelling has been duly noted, there is very little commentary that focuses on the respective deductions of the *Survey* and the *Ideas*. Admittedly, these deductions are brief, incomplete, and at first glance, puzzling, but this does not mean that they are not important. I think by reading these two texts together it is possible to reconstruct how Schelling systematically develops his own philosophical approach, later presented in the much more involved deductions of the *System of Transcendental Idealism*. Although Schelling, in 1797–1798, reiterates his commitment to the primacy of practical reason, he departs from Fichte's approach in a significant manner: the 'history of self-consciousness' (1994a: 90/I, 382) and the 'natural history' (*Naturlehre*) of the mind (1988: 30tm/II, 39)[5] offer genetic accounts of the natural conditions of self-consciousness that bypass the problem of circularity confronted by Fichte in the *Science of Knowledge*. The primary task of this chapter, then, is to show how Schelling deduces the natural and historical conditions of subjectivity. It is no coincidence that these deductions extend his work to new vistas beyond Fichte's epistemological and practical concerns.

Admittedly, Schelling has some difficulty making all the antecedents to his nature-philosophy fit together into a unified whole. To make these difficulties visible to the reader, I have divided this chapter according to Schelling's concerns. In Section 2.2, I show how Schelling reenters the debate about the Kantian thing in itself in order to show the limits of theoretical philosophy and to make room for an 'applied' theoretical science, which is nature-philosophy (1988: 3/II, 5). This explains why, as I show in Section 2.3, Schelling appropriates the monism of Spinoza's 'doctrine of the attributes' and Leibniz's 'inner purposiveness' as supplements to nature-philosophy: both provide concepts for Schelling's argument that, just as self-consciousness is purposive, both the body and other natural beings can be intellectually intuited as purposive. In Section 2.4, I argue that Spinoza's and Leibniz's influence is important to understanding Schelling's sketch of the 'history of self-consciousness,' when he discusses the organic nature of the self. In Section 2.5, I turn to Schelling's 'natural history of the mind' to show how self-consciousness arises both through intersubjectivity, and through organic purposiveness. Schelling turns to Kant's concept of teleology to underline that all purposiveness is organic and without intention. If there is any kind of 'intention' within nature, it is that of humanity, which develops within nature itself. Schelling holds to the demand that 'Nature should be Mind made visible, Mind the invisible Nature' (1988: 42/II, 56).

As Schelling works out these problems, he continues to extend the range of his philosophy. By the final installment of the *Survey*, published in 1798, Schelling adds that a philosophy of art will overcome the divisions between practice and theory, and between freedom and necessity (I, 465). I will evaluate, in Section 2.6, Schelling's brief references to art and aesthetics in the period from 1797–1798, which culminate in this claim. Then I will close this chapter with a reading of another document from this time period that claims that art can unify philosophy and even humanity: the 'Älteste Systemprogramm des deutschen Idealismus.' This curious document outlines the general program that anticipates some of Schelling's later positions. I will not argue that Schelling is necessarily the author of this document, but I would like to show how this text presents several ideas that will be found in the *System of Transcendental Idealism*: the author of the 'System Program' argues that beauty – taken in a Platonic sense – is the 'supreme act of reason' because it unites all ideas, suggesting that an aesthetic sense is highest expression of the self's activity, a kind of *ethos* beyond mere free activity. In addition, the author argues that this recognition of beauty as the highest idea returns poesy to a higher dignity. The art of poetry, the author writes, possesses a utopian potential insofar as it can dissolve the fractured state of humanity and the conflict inherent in history and philosophy through a mythology of reason that renders philosophy sensuous, so that its truth is recognizable to all. These claims will reappear later in a philosophy of art that bears Schelling's signature.

2.2. Fichte, Kant, and the Thing in Itself

Both the *Survey* and the *Ideas* continue to defend the primacy of practical reason, but in doing so they extend Schelling's critique of the thing in itself to open a theoretical field for nature-philosophy. In the *Letters*, Schelling had ventured an original appropriation of the *Critique of Pure Reason*, which, he claimed, set the terms of the rivalry between criticism and dogmatism by forcing philosophers to choose between two exclusive first principles, either the self or the thing in itself. By reinterpreting the thing in itself as the ground of the system of dogmatism, Schelling removes the primary target of Kant's skeptical critics from his system. According to Schelling, post-Kantian philosophers must either explain the thing in itself in reference to the self (as did Fichte) or the self in reference to the thing in itself (Spinozist dogmatism). All other systems are skeptical or inconsistent, or are what Schelling calls dogmaticist (they do not distinguish between theoretical and practical philosophy).

Yet a year later, in the *Survey* and the *Ideas*, Schelling's critique of the concept of the thing in itself appears to have returned to a more Fichtean position: instead of pursuing the conflict between the two systems found in the *Letters*, Schelling criticizes the use of the thing in itself within critical idealism as being unjustified. Certainly the *Survey* includes argumentation pointing toward a defense of practical reason along Fichtean lines. So, in places, Schelling argues that Kant cannot provide the principle for the thing in itself because he can only symbolize the supersensible ground of the sensible with the expression 'things in themselves,' which is a contradiction because it demands that one think the unconditioned [*das Unbedingte*] through the conditional [*ein Bedingtes*] (1994a: 106/I, 406). While Schelling does not criticize the restrictions that Kant places on theoretical reason with respect to the thing in itself, he argues (like Fichte before him) that the problem of the supersensible ground of representation should be solved in practical philosophy. Kant initiates this step by arguing that the autonomy of the will through freedom provides the principle of the self's activity, but he does not complete the solution by showing that the thing in itself is grounded in the self's activity insofar as he continues to speak of the thing in itself as providing 'the substance' for our representations (1994a: 108/I, 409).

Yet this line of argument is only one side of Schelling's critique; the benefit of reading the *Survey* in tandem with the *Ideas* is that the latter illuminates the other side: there it becomes clear that he also interprets the thing in itself as representing a thing absolutely external and opposed to the *Ich*, a *Nicht-Ich* that is its own substance. An absolute distinction between I and not-I 'makes that separation between man and the world *permanent*, because it treats the latter as a *thing-in-itself*, which neither intuition nor imagination, neither understanding nor reason, can reach' (1988: 11/II, 14). To be more precise: Schelling is attempting to overcome the dualism between self and world that neither Kant nor Fichte avoid. In fact, Fichte explicitly affirms it. In the *First Introduction to the Science of Knowledge* (1797), he writes that 'Intellect and thing are thus two exact opposites: they inhabit two worlds between which there is no bridge' (1982: 17/I, 436).[6] There is no bridge because the intellect acts through free causality while things are subject to mechanism. By contrast, Schelling seeks to show how the self and nature share a common ground. As Iain Hamilton Grant summarizes,

> The thing-in-itself therefore becomes the weakest point not only in the metaphysics of transcendental idealism, but in the physics underlying it: insofar as I can have no access to nature beyond my representations of it, the 'thing-in-itself' poses not merely the *formal* problem of limiting the validity of empirical cognition, but also the problem of a nature *real* in itself. (Grant, 2008: 76)

Thus Schelling extends his critique of the thing in itself to open a theoretical field for a philosophy of real nature, an account that shows how the self emerges within an organic and dynamic nature (even if he struggles to render this account consistent). While Schelling presents arguments that resemble those of Fichte, he also criticizes the thing in itself to prepare his nature-philosophy. It becomes clear that his arguments against empiricism are a rejection of mechanistic explanations of nature:

> Before Kant, things in themselves were hardly conceived in the particular sense in which *he* speaks of them. They were merely supposed to constitute the *check* [*Anstoss*] that would first rouse the reader from the slumber of *empiricism*, the [philosophy] that presumes to be able to explain experience with experience [and] mechanics with mechanics. (1994a: 106/I, 407)

The point common to both sides of Schelling's critique (the epistemological and physical flaws of the thing in itself) is a rejection of dualism: the critical task, he argues, it to pursue Kant's suggestion that 'it might well be that the *intelligible substrate of matter and thinking were the same*' (1994a: 107/I, 407).[7] Fichte's merit, Schelling notes, is to have unified theoretical and practical philosophy in one principle, the absolute self; the 'real object' can be known because it is derived from the self-activity of the subject.

Yet in a step beyond Fichte, Schelling then seeks to discover how a self comes to self-consciousness within nature. As Dieter Sturma argues, this allows Schelling to ground the self's activity in the organic totality of nature rather than the 'logic of immanent circularity that attaches' to Fichte's account of self-consciousness (Sturma, 2000a: 219). In addition, as I will show, Schelling attempts to demonstrate how self-consciousness arises within nature and how thinking and matter have a common origin. In these texts, Schelling appropriates Kant's concepts of purposiveness and teleology in his argumentation, but also incorporates important themes from precritical philosophy; like Spinoza, Schelling argues that thinking and matter are two expressions of the same substance (but for the latter, it is the absolute I), and, more surprisingly, he draws on Leibniz's discussions of inner purposiveness in order to characterize nature's own activity. By acknowledging Schelling's debts to these 'dogmatic' philosophers it becomes possible to understand his brief deductions of the 'history of self-consciousness' and the 'natural history of the mind' found in the *Survey* and the *Ideas* respectively. In these two sketches, Schelling incorporates the insights of Leibniz and Spinoza within the becoming of self-consciousness.

2.3. Appropriating Spinoza and Leibniz

It is important to be precise about Schelling's project, and what he thinks Spinoza and Leibniz offer to post-Kantian philosophy. Schelling's project of including nature-philosophy in transcendental philosophy is intended to show how the self emerges within nature. But, as we will see, this project is plagued by the difficulty of maintaining the self's activity as the first principle of philosophy while at the same time showing how the self emerges in nature as an embodied and organized (and innerly purposive) being. Schelling's temporary solution, which he holds through to the *System of Transcendental Idealism*, is to deduce the self's natural organization as a necessary condition for consciousness even though its productivity never comes to consciousness. On this basis, he then proceeds to deduce a concept of natural teleology (so we intuit organization in nature, but we do not cognize it). Therefore Spinoza and Leibniz are introduced as his predecessors because they too argue that the self is productive. Schelling *appropriates* Spinoza's doctrine of the attributes to reconceptualize the self and its activity, and *appropriates* the work of Leibniz to provide a concept of inner purposiveness. Both are monist precedents to his project; for in rejecting the thing in itself, Schelling rejects any attribution of passivity to the self. The only alternative is to explain the self through its own activity (1994a: 85–89/I, 376–382; and 1988: 24/II, 32), which can already be seen in Spinoza's realism and Leibniz's idealism. The task of nature-philosophy is to unify these one-sided presentations.

In contrast to the *Letters*, we now find approbation instead of rejection regarding Spinoza, 'who, with complete clarity, saw mind and matter as one, thought and extension simply as modifications of the same principle' (1988: 15/II, 20), because Spinoza's doctrine of the attributes proposes that the ideal and the real should be explained as affectations and determinations of ideal reality.[8] Thus 'no separation could occur between actual things and our representations of them. Concepts and things, thought and extensions, were, for this reason, one and the same for him, both only modifications of one and the same ideal nature' (1988: 27tm/II, 35).[9] The problem for Schelling is that the 'one and same ideal nature' is not the absolute self but the infinite One-All.

Spinoza's first principle is still the point of contention, but Schelling's criticism hinges, as it did in the *Letters*, on the status of intellectual intuition: the 'third' kind of knowledge beyond experience and reason. For Schelling, intellectual intuition names the primordial, free activity of the absolute self. For Spinoza, intellectual intuition is externalized in the One-All; it 'proceeds from the adequate idea of certain of God's attributes to the adequate knowledge of the essence of things' (*Ethics*, Proposition 25, Part V; 1992: 214). Spinoza's problem is that he cannot explain how a self can become conscious of itself amidst the constant succession of representations. According to Schelling, it is only possible to make Spinoza intelligible by substituting the absolute self for the infinite substance.[10] Schelling's idealism begins with the self's activity because the idea of an infinite substance explains neither the connection between the finite and infinite nor any transition from the infinite to the finite.

By contrast, Schelling claims, Leibniz attempted to explain the identity of subject and object by proceeding from the finite individual to the Infinite (God). The revival of Leibniz, whose system is Kant's primary target in the *Critique of Pure Reason*, is one of the more surprising features of the *Ideas*.[11] Schelling explicitly dismisses the Kantian criticisms of Leibniz:

There is nothing from which Leibniz could have been more remote than the speculative chimera of a world, which, known and intuited by no mind, nevertheless affects us and produces all our representations. The first thought from which he set out was [in Schelling's paraphrase]: 'that the representations of external things would have arisen in the soul by virtue of her own laws *as in a particular world*, even though nothing were present but God (the infinite) and the soul (the intuition of the infinite).' (1988: 16tm/II, 20)

Schelling neglects to mention that the 'intuition of the infinite' is precisely what Kant argues is beyond finite cognition (that is, beyond constitutive claims about knowledge), and this stands as a division between the philosophy of Kant and the philosophies of Fichte and Schelling. The latter two include an intellectual intuition of the self as the first principle of all philosophy. Now, Schelling turns to Leibniz to reinforce the character of the self's absolute activity, and the division between activity and passivity. Schelling's paraphrase, quoted above, is drawn from the 'New System of the Nature of Substances and Their Communication, and of the Union Which Exists Between the Soul and the Body (1695),' where Leibniz argues that the capacity for representation has its origin in the individual's own activity, and cannot be attributed to external things (Leibniz, 1998: 150). Kantians, according to Schelling, are wrong to have attributed to Leibniz a world of things in themselves outside perceptual beings. He argues that Leibniz saw that no external cause can be the origin of the mind's activity, and thus all modifications and representations arise from inner purposiveness. Because Leibniz recognized the monad's (individual self's) inner purposiveness, he could not hold that things were actual in themselves, but that they are only actual through the self's mode of representation. Leibniz stands in distinction to Kantians who want both the self and things in themselves: 'if among ourselves it is said that no representations could arise in us through external causes, there is no end of astonishment. Nowadays it is valid in philosophy to believe that the monads have windows, through which things climb in and out' (1988: 16/II, 21).[12]

As we will see, Schelling uses this concept of inner purposiveness to argue that the self's activity is itself organically organized in a process of overcoming its own self-imposed limitation. Yet, ultimately, Leibniz's account of the self's purposiveness is limited, Schelling argues, by the fact that Leibniz still explains the intersubjective nature of the world through a principle external to the self; preestablished harmony, Schelling argues, *asserts* that the world is intersubjective (all monads necessarily experience the same series of representations), but does not *explain* it (i.e. through reference to the self's activity, but through an external principle). In other words, Leibniz interprets the relationship between the self and the world in its being and not its becoming: he explains the relationship as it is, but does not demonstrate how the self becomes conscious of the series of representations as its own activity (1988: 29–30/II, 38–40). In terms we have already employed: Leibniz grounds his principle in a theoretical principle (God) and not in a practical principle. When Schelling develops an account of intersubjectivity in the *Ideas*, the concept has a practical basis. It is questionable how much the references to Leibniz add to Schelling's characterization of the self's faculties, especially once the 'pre-established harmony' is removed as an explanation of intersubjectivity. However, Leibniz lends support to the principle that inner purposiveness – and not just mechanism – characterizes all organized beings in nature. Schelling will fortify these arguments, however inconsistently, with reference to Kant's concept of teleology.

We are now in a position to show how Schelling appropriates the insights of Spinoza and Leibniz in both the *Survey* and the *Ideas*. Schelling will adapt their respective insights – the unity of thinking and matter, which we will now specifically refer to as embodiment, and the self's purposive character – by placing them within the becoming of self-consciousness. In doing so, we can show that these two texts share the common concern of elucidating Schelling's early nature-philosophy within the framework of critical philosophy.

2.4. The History of Self-consciousness

In the *Survey*, Schelling introduces what he calls a 'history of self-consciousness,' which provides a genetic account of the self's activity from intellectual intuition to the will (1994a: 90/I, 382). This departs from Fichte's approach in a significant manner: the 'history of self-consciousness' and the 'natural history of the mind' offer genetic accounts ('Philosophy becomes genetic'; see 1988: 30/II, 39) of the natural conditions of self-consciousness that bypass the problem of circularity confronted by Fichte's *Wissenschaftslehre* (see also Section 1.3). Dieter Sturma succinctly summarizes their differences:

There is absolutely no need to discover ever new metaphorical ways of supposedly overcoming the logic of immanent circularity that attaches to self-consciousness. In Schelling's eyes, all that is required is to interpret the transcendental conditions of subjectivity in a developmental and historical fashion. If it is indeed possible to grasp the given and the conditions of subjectivity in terms of a systematic and developmental prehistory of the fact of subjectivity itself, then there can be no pure self-relation on the part of subjectivity in the first place. According to this perspective, human subjectivity is not condemned ceaselessly to move solely within a closed circle of its own. (2000a: 219)

The difference between Fichte and Schelling is precise: while Fichte, who refers to himself as the 'pragmatic historian' of the mind, struggles with the relationship between reflection and the circularity of consciousness (1988: 131/I, 77; and 1982: 93–94/I, 92), Schelling turns to the productivity of the self, which includes its natural history: 'transcendental philosophy aims by its very nature at the *becoming* and the *living*, for its first principles are *genetic*, and the mind becomes and grows together with the world' (1994a: 104tm/I, 403).

Before turning to the organic nature of the self, we will sketch an outline of Schelling's deductions leading from sensation to will. Although the 'history of self-consciousness' begins with an immediately sensible intuition, it would be a mistake to equate the epistemologically prior and the transcendentally prior: though each successive intuition increases the sphere of the self's activity, and thus, its sphere of cognition, the deduction regressively leads to the transcendentally unconditional ground, which makes possible all other intuitions – the will presented in an intellectual intuition. While the will is the last in the series of deductions, Schelling argues that intellectual intuition is the highest stage of intuition because it is the only unconditionally free act. All previous stages do not form a temporal sequence, but reciprocally interact within consciousness (but not consciously), and are only divisible by the analyses of the transcendental philosopher (1994a: 98/I, 394). Only willing breaks this reciprocal interaction by an absolutely free act. The latter turns the subject away from objects and toward its self-determination and will as such, constituting the 'supreme condition of self-consciousness' that grounds both theoretical and practical philosophy (1994a: 98/I, 395).

We are primarily interested in Schelling's deductions of organization and inner purposiveness, in which the self intuits itself as purposive, self-organized, and embodied within nature. As we have mentioned, these arguments provide an inventive attempt to overcome the dualisms that plague modern philosophy (mind/body, self/world, thought/extension) while simultaneously arguing for the primacy of the will within systematic philosophy. Although the *System of Transcendental Idealism* will first make it explicit, the unconscious identity of mind and nature in the self is sundered for the self in reflection and judgment when the self becomes conscious, requiring, for epistemological reasons, a concept of teleology. So to fill in the next piece of our puzzle, after the 'history of self-consciousness' we will turn to Schelling's development of teleology in the *Ideas*. The standpoint of reflection needs teleology, but in intellectual intuition, Schelling states, the 'external world lies unfolded for us, so that we may rediscover within it the history of our mind [*Geistes*]' (1994a: 90tm/I, 383).

The self, Schelling argues, is defined by its productive activity and its constant striving to overcome the limitations of its activity. Therefore, limitations of the self's activity are not one of kind (like, he would claim, the Kantian thing in itself or Fichte's *Nicht-Ich*), but one of degree; the stages of consciousness follow the expansion of the sphere of the self's activity until it attains self-consciousness. In the *System of Transcendental Idealism*, he will specifically refer to this activity of the self as unconscious, because the self is not conscious of this activity, although it can be deduced transcendentally (see Section 3.2.1).

The first limitation of the self is sensation, and the self strives to overcome this limitation by separating itself from the present. In doing so, it intuits itself within a succession of time (and, also, in space). At this stage of the intuition of space and time, the self intuits itself as 'nothing but a flux of representations' (1994a: 91/I, 384). However, these representations are not understood as contingent but external to the self, and as external, they are considered mechanically. The self intuits itself as limited by this external succession. In striving against this mechanical succession of representations, the self intuits itself as active within the succession. It is at this stage that Schelling introduces the concepts of purposiveness and organization. After the self intuits its striving as productive – but before it becomes self-conscious of its willing as such – it intuits its embodied, organic nature. The self, he claims, not only intuits the succession of representations in time, but also itself as productive within time, that is as cause (producing) and effect (which is the product, or the self's representations). This self-productivity shows that the self's activity is of an organic nature.

The question remains, however, how the self recognizes nature as living and organic. The *Survey*, it seems to me, struggles with conceptual confusion between precritical and Kantian philosophy: it has not yet overcome its Kantian limits. Schelling's 'doctrine of the attributes,' as it were, shows how the self intuits itself as embodied in order to collapse the modern distinction between mind and body, or self and world: the self's own productive activity is intuited as both purposive and embodied within nature. The self's production is not mechanistically determined, but freely determined for itself. In this intuition 'the mind is lost in matter [and] no differentiation between the two is possible' (1994a: 94tm/I, 389). This intuition of embodiment serves as the pivot between the self and the world, but it does not answer how the self comes to self-consciousness. As he states, this stage of consciousness does not explain how the self comes to recognize its body as its own, and as 'governed by its own representations' (1994a: 95/I, 390).

Schelling's argument is similar to Spinoza's doctrine of the attributes, in which thought and matter are two attributes of the same substance. However, Schelling substitutes the self for substance. The self intuits itself as embodied and in nature, but as it proceeds through the additional stages of abstraction, judgment, and will, mind and matter are reflectively separated. These steps in the deduction require that Schelling introduce a concept of natural teleology for epistemological purposes, which we will see below in the *Ideas*.

In the process of arguing for the purposiveness of the self's activity, Schelling provides a brief sketch of nature-philosophy, which grasps nature as organic and productive, irreducible to mechanistic laws. He claims that nature's tendency toward organization reveals a universal productive force that aims to express itself in the archetype of the pure form of the mind (1994a: 92–93/I, 386–388). Like the self, the totality of nature expresses a principle of inner activity, of organization. An object that contains this inner principle is a living being. As living, each organized being is 'virtually removed' from the mechanistic series of cause and effect. Each living being, such as a plant, is its own 'united world' developing according to its own inner purposiveness, although 'according to Leibniz,' a confused representation of the world (1994a: 93/I, 387).

The self is distinguished from other living beings because it recognizes itself and *acts* according to inner purposiveness, and as such, the self is the highest expression of nature. Other living beings, to return to Leibniz, are 'confused' due to their passivity in only being freely acted upon ('Monadology,' §49, in Leibniz, 1998: 274). For Schelling, the self and the world are living, and while the inner purposiveness is exhibited in the self through its productive capacity, purposiveness is exhibited in the products of living nature: 'life constitutes the visible analogue of the mind [*Geist*]' (1994a: 93tm/I, 388). At one point, Schelling attributes both a universal *Geist*, and an infinite drive to realize this archetype to nature. In Kantian terms, he argues that the universal *Geist* and productive drive are not just regulative, but constitutive for our experience of the world. Schelling will continue to struggle with the status of nature as either, in

Kantian terms, constitutive of the self or as a regulative idea for knowledge until he prepares his system of absolute idealism (see Chapter 4). However, in the *Ideas*, Schelling addresses the question of how the self recognizes nature as living and organic with explicit reference to Kant's concept of teleology.

2.5. A Natural History of the Mind

In the *Ideas*, Schelling sketches a 'natural history [*Naturlehre*] of the mind' (1988: 30tm/II, 39) to make more explicit the interconnection of the self and nature, while arguing that nature-philosophy – as a philosophy of the natural world as totality, which is populated by living, organic (organized) beings – is possible within a system of critical idealism. This includes defending the concepts of purposiveness and teleology, which he draws from Kant's *Critique of the Power of Judgment*. In the third *Critique*, Kant introduces teleological judgments to supplement the 'inadequacy' of the use of mechanical laws in the cognition of nature. Kant, as a belated participant in the Pantheism Controversy, would know the pitfalls of articulating a purely mechanistic philosophy of natural science. While his *Metaphysical Foundations of Natural Science* is restricted to grounding Newtonian physics in an a priori science based in mathematics,[13] the 'Critique of the Power of Teleological Judgment' in the third *Critique* argues that critical philosophy does not result in a reductively mechanistic account of nature.[14] Teleological judgments allow the subject to ascribe purposiveness and unity to nature. However, Kant specifies that the use of the concept of purposiveness in researching nature is regulative and not constitutive; that is, purposiveness in nature does not refer to objects themselves, but to subjective judgment. If it were constitutive (determining objects, even as phenomena), the addition of purposiveness to mechanical laws would introduce a special causality into nature. Instead, the principle of purposiveness serves as a regulative ideal for research into nature, and more specifically, for the subsumption and unification of the manifold of natural laws under universal laws, including the judgment that nature is a totality, which cannot be discovered a priori or through experience. While the pure understanding determines the a priori laws for natural science, it lacks a guideline with which it could discover a 'thoroughgoing lawfulness of nature or of its unity in accordance with empirical laws' (2000: 258/V, 386). The principle of purposiveness provides a maxim for the reflective power of reason, and not an objective principle for the understanding.

UNIVERSITY OF WINCHESTER
LIBRARY

Schelling utilizes many of the same arguments, but draws especially on the concept of natural end, or self-organizing being. A thing can be considered a natural end if it is the cause and effect of itself (note that Schelling uses these terms in the *Survey* as well). A self-organizing being cannot just be conceived as an aggregate of parts but requires that we recognize the whole as greater than a sum of parts. Purposiveness is important to Schelling for understanding individual natural organisms and the idea of nature as a whole. The unity of nature, and of individual organisms, cannot be derived from matter. Schelling phrases his point to show the limits of mechanistic explanation: unity

> is absolutely inexplicable in terms of *matter*, as such. For it is a unity of the *concept*, a unity that exists only in relation to an intuiting and reflecting being. For there is absolute individuality in an organism, that its parts are possible only through the whole, and the whole is possible, not through assembling, but through interaction, of the parts, is a *judgement* and cannot be judged at all save only by a mind, which relates whole and part, form and matter, reciprocally. (1988: 31–32/II, 41–42)[15]

Here, Schelling defends Kant's claim that purposiveness is possible only in relation to subjective judgment. Schelling will push this claim further, by claiming that a judgment of purposiveness is not only a judgment of logical possibility, but is also accompanied by a feeling of necessity. He will then ask why the self feels constrained by this judgment (that is, why one natural object seems purposive while other objects do not). This problem will ultimately set the task for nature-philosophy. But first, Schelling, like Kant before him, must refute the dogmatic assumption that teleology implies intentionality – in other words, the assumption that purposiveness in nature requires a deity. This way of phrasing the problem allows us to show where Kant and Schelling differ. For the dogmatist, teleology is constitutive; purposiveness is often identified with intelligent causality or design. For Kant, the central problem of the 'Dialectic of the Teleological Power of Judgment' in the *Critique of the Power of Judgment* is to establish the legitimacy of teleology as a regulative ideal, even if it cannot be used to make constitutive claims about purposiveness. This position undercuts the dogmatic assumption that teleology requires a special kind of constitutive causality distinct from mechanism. While not a dogmatist, Schelling sometimes seems to assert that organization implies a constitutive causality distinct from mechanism, but just as often he explicitly states that judgments of purposiveness are regulative and not constitutive. We will return to this problem below.

Schelling argues against ascribing purposiveness to an external creator, who imprints final causes into things. The external creator is often conceived as an artist, but then the natural product would, like a work of art, have its purpose imputed to it from without (1988: 33/II, 45). If teleology is external to nature then it contradicts any sense of inner purposiveness.[16] The addition of an external creator to nature does not advance the philosophical understanding of teleology; a finite creator external to nature is not a creator at all, and the idea of an infinite creator external to nature lapses into the quandary Schelling ascribes to Spinoza: the latter cannot explain the transition from the infinite to the finite. An unexpected objection, since Spinoza attempted to refute teleological conceptions of the world, unless we keep in mind that Schelling's alternative to an infinite creator is a producer *within* nature – the self.

Thus the failure to explain purposiveness externally opens the path to Schelling's alternative: it can be explained through the transcendental subject. After arguing that teleology and purposiveness are not contrary to transcendental inquiry, Schelling attempts to ground these ideas in the transcendental subject in a manner similar to the *Survey:* organic nature (purposive nature, in opposition to a purely mechanistic account of nature) is grounded in life, which in turn is grounded in – or has, as its highest principle – the practical subject. But the practical subject is embodied and not essentially separate from nature. In a being organized by such a higher principle, we find the

> absolute unification of Nature and freedom in one and the same being. The living organism is to be a product of *Nature:* but in this natural product an ordering and coordinating *mind* is to rule. These two principles shall in no way be separated in it, but most intimately united. In intuition the two are not to be distinguishable at all; there must be neither *before* nor *after*, but absolute simultaneity and reciprocity between them. (1988: 36/II, 48–49)

Here again Schelling reiterates the importance of showing how the self is embodied. The self must be a product of nature, but it must also raise itself through self-consciousness and freedom 'above' nature. While Schelling acknowledges that the soul is the name for the mind considered as the principle of life, this gets the philosopher no closer to understanding how we come to the idea of the connection between the soul and the body. Note that the question of *how* the two are connected is dismissed for the same reason that both mechanistic accounts of life and the principle of the life-force are rejected: Schelling holds that it is impossible to provide

physical accounts of mental acts (1988: 37–38/II, 49–51). While from a
practical view, distinguishing between the two is illegitimate, Schelling
holds that they can still be theoretically separated; although the body
cannot explain mental acts, the capacities of thinking and willing explain
how I can come to experience the body as *my* body. The reason is that self-
consciousness is known through intellectual intuition. Curiously, Schelling
gives a Cartesian demonstration of this principle (even calling it an immediate experience), presenting this intuition in the rhetoric of an immediate
first-person experience.[17] He writes

> if there is in me life and soul, the last as something distinct from the body,
> I can become aware of either only through *immediate* experience. That
> I *am* (think, will, etc.) is something that I must know, if I know anything
> at all . . . because I am immediately aware of my own being, the inference
> to a soul in me, even if the conclusion should be false, at least rests on *one*
> indubitable premise, that I *am, live, imagine, will.* (1988: 39/II, 50–51)

Although presenting an argument for the immediate character of the intellectual intuition of the absolute self, Schelling manages to open himself to
charges of materialism: even if the inference from the immediate premise
of self-consciousness (I am, live, imagine, will) to the soul (now, interestingly, not equated with the principle of life) is shown to be false, the premise remains indubitable. I cannot but read this caveat as a defense of
transcendental philosophy regardless of the truth of the metaphysic-
religious idea of the soul. Yet if transcendental philosophy can explain how
self's activity is natural, Schelling again asks how an immediate intuition
can be acknowledged in other beings. For other humans, this acknowledgment is ethical: I am practically compelled to acknowledge others, and
through this my moral existence acquires purpose (1988: 39/II, 53–54).[18]
    At this point, Schelling's argument takes a curious turn. He asks if the
same ethical acknowledgment does not apply to other natural things (that
is, whether or not they have self-consciousness like humans), but he does
not provide a clear answer. It is worth noting that this passage is changed in
the second edition of the *Ideas.* In the first, he argues that one can only
judge those like him, while in the second he argues that it is impossible to
have mediated knowledge of something that can only be valid as immediate
(1988: 40, II, 54).[19] In any case, while animals are experienced as natural
beings it is impossible to know if they are conscious like humans. From this
question, Schelling transitions from the recognition of the self's moral
existence back to the question of the self's natural existence: how should

we think the idea of nature as totality? To answer Schelling returns to the opposition of purposiveness to mechanism. Like Kant before him, Schelling claims the two principles are not exclusive: if mechanism ('a regressive series of causes and effects') and purposiveness (simultaneity of causes and effects) are united, 'the idea arises in us of a purposiveness of the whole; Nature becomes a circle which returns to itself, a self-enclosed system' (1988: 40/II, 54). By drawing a connection between the theoretical problem of the division of mind and matter and the regulative problem of the distinction between purposiveness and mechanism as explanations of nature, Schelling is blurring the Kantian distinction between faculties, and between regulative and constitutive principles. This is not to criticize Schelling, but to note how he works toward overcoming the limitations of Kantian philosophy.[20] Schelling demands that purposiveness should be shown to be necessary, and not only logically possible. Because we necessarily think nature as purposive, the task of nature-philosophy is to show that nature necessarily corresponds to the laws of thought, namely, that nature realizes the purposiveness recognized by our thought. As he states,

> what we want is not that Nature should coincide with the laws of our mind *by chance* (as if through some *third* intermediary), but that *she herself*, necessarily and originally, should not only *express*, but *even realize*, the laws of our mind, and that she is, and is called, Nature only insofar as she does so.
>
> Nature should be Mind made visible, Mind the invisible Nature. Here then, in the absolute identity of Mind *in us* and Nature *outside us*, the problem of the possibility of a Nature external to us must be resolved. The final goal of our further research is, therefore, this idea of Nature. (1988: 41–42/II, 56)

Nature-philosophy becomes applied theoretical philosophy based on a demand: 'Nature *should* be Mind made visible' (my emphasis). This demand is similar to the Fichtean demand of practical reason that reality *ought* to conform to the self's activity. However, Schelling takes an additional step to separate himself from Fichte's instrumental interpretation of nature. The task of philosophy – a search for a Schellingian doctrine of the attributes – is to show the identity and isomorphism between mind and nature. This will later trouble Fichte, for both its apparent materialism and its denial of the primacy of the absolute self. When their debate about nature-philosophy goes public in 1801, Schelling explicitly cites Spinoza as his paradigmatic predecessor (see Section 4.2). If Schelling's early thought is an attempt to balance the insights of Fichte and Spinoza, the scale begins to tilt as early as 1797.

2.6. Toward a Philosophy of Art

Despite extending critical idealism into the field of nature-philosophy, Schelling remains committed to the primacy of freedom through 1797. As the introduction to the *Ideas for a Philosophy of Nature* affirms, philosophy 'is throughout a work of freedom' (1988: 9/II, 11). Nevertheless we should detail how this freedom is expressed in the system. In the *Ideas*, Schelling announces a dual system of theoretical and practical reason, grounded in freedom, with each side divided in turn between pure and applied sciences: theoretical philosophy, when applied, becomes nature-philosophy, and applied practical philosophy becomes a philosophy of history (1988: 3–4/II, 4–5). This, Schelling states, will embrace the whole of applied philosophy.

Nevertheless, by 1798, in the final installment of the *Survey*, he announces a philosophy of art to unify the philosophy of history (freedom) and nature-philosophy (necessity) (I, 465). Although Schelling does not develop the philosophy of art until the *System of Transcendental Idealism*, he does sketch a philosophy of history that ends with a passage that discusses the development of mythology. The purpose of this section is to investigate any precedents to the final part of the *Survey*.

I think the 'Älteste Systemprogramm des deutschen Idealismus' could be that document.[21] The authorship of the 'System Program,' which is written in Hegel's hand (and has been dated between spring 1796 and early 1797), has generated much dispute in the literature concerning Schelling, Hegel, and Hölderlin. Since its publication, it has been attributed first to Schelling (by Franz Rosenzweig, who published the document in 1917), then to Hölderlin (by Wilhelm Böhm in 1926), and finally to Hegel (by Otto Pöggeler in 1965),[22] which emboldened H. S. Harris to claim it for Hegel (1972: 249–257) and discouraged Xavier Tilliette, who deleted a discussion on the 'System Program' from his *Schelling, Une philosophie en devenir*. In 1973 Tilliette published a forceful rejoinder to Pöggeler (Tilliette, 1973: 35–52), and more recently Manfred Frank has attributed – with several precautionary remarks – this document to Schelling (1982: 153–155).

I myself initially hesitated to include the 'System Program' in the development of Schelling's philosophy of art, plagued by the same doubts that Tilliette recalls. However, I now think that we should remain agnostic regarding the document's authorship. Thus it is not my intent to prove decisively the authorship of the 'System Program,' which would require refuting Hegel and Hölderlin as alternatives. Instead, I would like to present the 'System Program' as an intermediate step in the development of Schelling's philosophy of art. I will argue that the latter half of the document sketches *in nuce* significant parts of the system developed in the *System of Transcendental Idealism.*

It might have been possible, and it would be less controversial, to attribute the development of the philosophy of art to biographical details in his life, except that the editors of the *Historisch-Kritische Ausgabe* of Schelling's work have established that the final installment of the *Survey* was written before his involvement with the Jena circle and his visits to the galleries in Dresden. When he arrives in Dresden, one gathers that these experiences only confirmed his philosophical intuitions, when he describes, in a letter to his parents, the 'divine paintings of Raphael and Correggio' and the 'vivid [*lebendigen*] statues of the ancient world' (the letter is dated September 20, 1798. AA, III/1: 191).

If he began working through a philosophy of art before his visit to Dresden and before his acquaintance with the Jena Romantics, we should again consider his interactions with Hölderlin. In the last chapter we saw how Hölderlin influenced Schelling's metaphysics. Now we will turn to the development of their ideas in relation to art and philosophy. Aside from their correspondence, Hölderlin and Schelling met in July–August 1795 and December 1795 in Tübingen, and Frankfurt in 1796. We can establish that Hölderlin, through the influence of, and in response to, Friedrich Schiller, sought to develop an aesthetic solution to the problems of Kantian and Fichtean critical philosophy as early as October 1794 (see the letter to Neuffer, dated October 10, HSA, VI, 149–150). Then, on February 24, 1796, he writes to Immanuel Niethammer:

I want to discover the principle which explains to me the divisions in which we think and exist, yet which is also capable of dispelling the conflict between subject and object, between our self and the world, yes, also between reason and revelation, – theoretically, in intellectual intuition, without our practical reason having to come to our aid. For this we need an aesthetic sense [*ästhetischen Sinn*], and I will call my philosophical letters 'New Letters on the Aesthetic Education of Man.' Also, I will move in [these letters] from philosophy to poetry and religion.

And then, I think not incidentally, he continues:

Schelling, whom I saw before my departure, is happy to participate in your journal and to be introduced by you to the learned world. We did not always speak in agreement, yet we agreed that the new ideas can be presented most appropriately in letter form. As you will know, he has shifted to a new road with his new convictions before he would have reached the goal on the worse one. (Hölderlin, 1988: 132–133/HSA, VI, 219–220)

We can see that Hölderlin's concept of aesthetic sense is more than likely responsible for the discussion of Greek tragedy in the final epistle of the *Letters* (see Section 1.5). And, while Schelling rejects Greek tragedy as a model of practical action, he returns to the idea of an aesthetic for philosophy in the *Survey*. There, Schelling suggests that the entirety of philosophical inquiry

> belongs properly to aesthetics [. . .] For this science [aesthetics] opens *access* to all of philosophy, because it is only by means of [aesthetics] that we can explain what the philosophical *spirit* [*Geist*] is. To philosophize without it is no better than to exist outside of time or to write poetry without imagination. (1994a: 103tm/I, 402; the *Historisch-Kritische Ausgabe* dates composition of this section in Summer 1797; AA, I/4: 28ff.)

Through an aesthetic sense (although he does not use the term), one has access to the spirit of philosophy beyond the letter. Yet the role of the aesthetic is not obvious at this point. Schelling could, for instance, be making an observation like Fichte, in *Concerning the Concept of the Wissenschaftslehre*, that a philosopher needs a sense of genius like a poet; just as the 'latter needs a sense of beauty; the former needs a sense of truth' (1988: 128/I, 74). An aesthetic sense would explain how one could follow the spirit of philosophy in contrast to the letter, which is what both Fichte and Schelling claim inspires their readings of Kant.

Schelling's other reference to aesthetics in the early part of the *Survey* concerns the problem of presenting ideas in philosophy. He states that it is only through inconsistent or contradictory expressions that the philosopher can present an idea. It takes an aesthetic sense to grasp the idea within a contradictory expression; 'unaesthetic minds' are not adequate to the Idea: 'Plato *exhausts* himself trying to express that the *ideas* contain a *Being* that reaches far beyond all *empirical existence*. Nevertheless, even in our days we encounter "proofs" that show how Plato's ideas are *real substances* no less than Kant's things in themselves' (1994: 106/I, 406).

These references are not quite the aesthetic sense that proceeds without 'our practical reason having to come to our aid,' as Hölderlin states. This will only come later, in the *System of Transcendental Idealism* (1978: 14/III,

351). In the meantime, Schelling only introduces the idea of a philosophy of art (I, 465) to overcome the challenge that Hölderlin saw in the search for a principle 'capable of dispelling the conflict between subject and object, between our self and the world, yes, also between reason and revelation' (Hölderlin, 1988: 132–133/HSA, VI, 219–220). Schelling's suggestive remarks may anticipate a passage in the final installment of the *Survey*, near the conclusion, where he writes:

> for us all becomes history that we cannot determine a priori. Thus it also does not depend on whether something has a mechanistic determination or occurs according to determinate laws, but on whether we *observe* this mechanism, and can *state* its laws. *Accordingly*, for example, the poet can intentionally make into history what is not history, a necessary event that he exhibits as contingency (not related to general natural mechanism). Thus one permits the historical writer (who is more and more also a *poet* [*Dichter*]) a kind of superstition; then where he understands his art he will not take lightly a natural event in history, without thereby suggesting more than bare nature (a higher but also secret hand). – In all the sciences, history preceded theory. So Greek mythology was (wherever its birthplace may be) originally nothing other than a historical schema of nature (that one had not yet begun to explain). So every doctrine of the things of a supersensuous world turns into history (because we do not have any natural laws for this world); and every religion that is theoretical crosses over into mythology, and will and should always be mythology and never something else (because it can really only have poetic truth, and only as mythology is it true). (I, 472)

Let us begin with the context of this passage. The importance of a history a posteriori is that it affirms the causality of freedom within human history. A history a priori would, like dogmatic philosophy, posit the absolute as realized outside of us, which results, philosophically speaking, in fatalism (as Schelling already mentioned in the *Letters*), and aesthetically speaking, in a state as boring as 'the performance of a play in which only perfected beings appear, or reading a novel – such as [Samuel] Richardon's – where ideal people (*IdealMenchen* [*sic*]) appear, or a Christian epic in which angels – really the most boring of all beings – play the leading roles' (I, 473).[23] By contrast, a history a posteriori includes human freedom within history, and allows for an infinite striving. This passage, as we will see in the next chapter, anticipates Schelling's remarks on revelation in the *System of Transcendental Idealism*.

What is also interesting about this passage is the emphasis on history as the basis for philosophical discussions on the objects of the supersensuous world (such as found in Kant: freedom, God, and the immortality of the soul) and the relationship between the theoretical content of religion and mythology. We will confine our remarks to mythology. Although brief, Schelling's remarks anticipate his position in the *System of Transcendental Idealism*, where the truth of philosophy is manifested for all in poetry and mythology. If so, the importance of mythology in the *Survey* derives from the same idea that all people will have access to the truth of religion through its mythico-political content. The difference, in comparison to the *System of Transcendental Idealism*, is that Schelling there proposes a specifically philosophical mythology, oriented around the philosophy of art (the relationship between religion and art is again taken up in Schelling's *Philosophy of Art* from 1802–1803; see Chapter 4).

Yet this idea of a philosophical mythology may have an antecedent in the 'System Program.' In fact, many elements of the *System of Transcendental Idealism* appear in the rough outline of this short text. Because the first page is missing, the 'System Program' begins midsentence with 'an ethics' grounded in the idea of freedom, which is the 'sole true and conceivable *creation out of nothing*' (in Krell, 2005: 23). With freedom the whole world arises, and the author claims that this creation *ex nihilo* requires a new physics to satisfy the 'creative spirit' of the new philosophy of freedom. To convey both the idea of freedom and the new physics, the philosopher must possess an aesthetic sense and an aesthetic force (*Kraft*): 'The philosopher must possess as much aesthetic force as the poet. Those human beings who are devoid of aesthetic sense [*ästhetischen Sinn*] are our pedantic philosophers. The philosophy of spirit is an aesthetic philosophy' (in Krell, 2005: 24).

Such aesthetic force is granted by beauty, in the Platonic sense, which, no matter who the author is, reveals the influence of Schiller via Hölderlin.[24] Beauty is the goal of an ethic of aesthetic sense, which unites all the ideas; it addresses the entirety of a human being, who often, as Schiller points out in his *On the Aesthetic Education of Man*, is only considered as a fragment of one's whole self (see the Sixth Letter, 1982: 31–43). From this point on, the 'System Program' sets out a program that is very close to the closing pages of the *System of Transcendental Idealism*: the aesthetic sense of philosophy, properly realized, returns poesy [*Poësie*] to a higher dignity and it opens the possibility of dissolving the conflict inherent in history and philosophy. Only the art of poetry [*Dichtkunst*] will remain (in Krell, 2005: 25). This occurs because poetry will open onto a new mythology, a 'mythology of reason,' which will serve, for the philosopher, the ideological function of transmitting philosophical ideas to the people. It presents the ideas in sensible form for the use of the people [*Volk*]:

> Thus the enlightened and unenlightened must at long last clasp hands; mythology must become philosophical, and the people rational, while philosophy must become mythological, in order to make philosophers sensuous. Then eternal unity will prevail among us. (in Krell, 2005: 25–26)

The new mythology will be, according to the author, the expression and realization of freedom and egalitarianism; it will liberate the people from the superstitions of priests and sages. This manuscript also presents the most revolutionary version of the idea of a new mythology, which is explicitly opposed to the mechanism of the state. In considering the 'works of mankind,' the author argues that there is no idea of the state, just as there is no idea of a machine (in Krell, 2005: 25). By contrast, the rest of the 'System Program' teems with ideas: among them freedom, beauty, and a new mythology. In contrast to the mechanism of the state (and, we might suppose, the mechanism of the 'old' physics compared to the organicism of the 'new' physics), the author presents the new mythology as an organic work of humanity (for an account of the political implications of the various presentations of the new mythology, see Section 5.4). This initial reference to a new mythology is the first appearance of one of the *Three Conditions* set out in the Introduction,[25] and if we suppose that the ethics of the 'System Program' is preceded by a discussion of theoretical philosophy, we can see, in rough sketch, a series similar to the *System of Transcendental Idealism*, which progresses from theoretical philosophy, to practical philosophy and a philosophy of art that unifies the system and that shows how they can be presented in sensible form.

Whoever the author, these passages suggest the strong influence of both Hölderlin and Schelling, which has led many to admit that the 'System Program' is an act of symphilosophy between Schelling, and Hölderlin, or/with Hegel. Of course, it is difficult to reconcile this with the author's proprietary remark that 'I shall speak here of an idea [namely, the "new mythology"] that, as far as I know, no human mind has ever entertained' (in Krell, 2005: 25). Who would relinquish his discovery of the idea of the new mythology to Schelling without comment, if it were not from Schelling himself?

One more comment: the striking invocation of the 'Monotheism of reason and of the heart, polytheism of the imagination and art' (in Krell,

2005: 25) is, according to Tilliette, unique to the 'System Program,' and as he puts it, 'falls out of the clouds' (Tilliette, 1973: 45). Nevertheless, this invocation might point both forward and backward in Schelling's development. In the *Letters*, the 'monotheism of reason' can be glimpsed when Schelling rejects Greek tragedy as a model of action in favor of the ideas of reason, demanding that the affirmation of freedom not be compromised. But the 'polytheism of the imagination and art' appears under the sublime power of Greek tragedy, even if Schelling rejects it as a model for a system of ethics. Although imagination [*Einbildungskraft*] is not mentioned in the final letter, let us recall that for Kant, in the *Critique of the Power of Judgment*, the sublime arises from the imagination. The dynamical sublime arises from the 'all-powerfulness of nature,' but only because at the same time, we recognize our independence and superiority over nature (2000: 145/V, 261–262). Schelling appropriates Kant's remarks in his discussion of tragedy, although he, unlike Kant, holds that art can produce a feeling of the sublime. Schelling elides Kant's distinctions by identifying nature, fate and necessity in distinction to human freedom. Greek tragedy is all the more terrible when its heroes succumb to fate. This power of tragedy is sublime because it requires us to think that in freedom one only realizes fate (and that not even the gods can elude fate). As we have seen, Schelling struggles with tragedy before rejecting it in favor of the ideas of reason, yet now, the author of the 'System Program' attempts to reconcile philosophy and the power of art and imagination.

Then, in the *System of Transcendental Idealism*, imagination and aesthetic intuition play a central role in the system and in grounding the self's activity. The imagination is central to the system because it unifies the totality of the self's products, but more importantly, aesthetic intuition is the activity that drives artistic production, which, because it produces the work of art, reconciles the opposition between freedom and necessity, and opens the possibility for a future mythology. This insight into aesthetic intuition, it seems, had its origins in the discussions between Hölderlin and Schelling sometime between 1795 and 1796, and appears in a systematic expression in the *System of Transcendental Idealism*, which is the concern of the next chapter.

Chapter 3

Artistic Activity and the Subversion of Transcendental Idealism

3.1. The System of Subversion

The first two chapters have outlined the prehistory of Schelling's philosophy of art, in which his concept of critical idealism is extended to include a philosophy of nature that can account for necessity, a philosophy of history to account for freedom, and finally, the search for a principle that can unify both. With the *System of Transcendental Idealism* (hereafter *ST*), Schelling makes good on his proposed philosophy of art in order to reconcile the separation of freedom and necessity, the self and nature. This chapter will reconstruct how, in the *ST*, he proceeds to construct the schema of the relationship between theoretical-, practical- and art-philosophy, which, as I will argue, Schelling maintains through 1807 despite the changing metaphysics of his systems. I will also argue that the primacy of the philosophy of art in the *ST*, and its principle of aesthetic intuition, subverts the primacy of practical reason found in Fichte's *Wissenschaftslehre*.

These two interrelated tasks both require clarification regarding how we are to read the *ST* and its philosophy of art. In fact, the more controversial claim of the two I have made above is that the philosophy of art remains an important aspect of Schelling's philosophy through 1807, a contention which is at odds with the standard interpretation of Schelling's philosophical development. According to this interpretation, Schelling first glimpsed the idea of absolute idealism with the idea of aesthetic intuition in the *ST*, and having reached the absolute in its final section, he could then surpass the *ST*'s subjective idealism and its philosophy of art. Although not all the commentators are explicit about the basis on which they reach this conclusion, there is a general argument for this interpretation that I will reconstruct in two parts.

The first step is based on Schelling's own interpretation of his earlier works found in the lectures given nearly three decades after its publication, and posthumously published as *On the History of Modern Philosophy*. This self-interpretation has played an important role in subsequent interpretations of Schelling's *ST*, including those of Jähnig (1969: I, 133ff. and 155ff.), Schulz (1992: xxv–xxx), Bowie (1990: 84–88), and Fackenheim (1996: 60–65). According to this interpretation Schelling sought, despite the Ficthean exterior, to provide an account of the history of self-consciousness wherein the objective I is led by the subjective (or philosophizing) I to recognize both its origins in nature and its ground in freedom through a kind of anamnesis. The relationship between the subjective I and the objective I, who are two distinct individuals, is compared to

> the pupil and the master in the Socratic dialogues. In the objective I *more* was always posited in a developed way than it itself knew; the activity of the subjective, of the philosophizing I now consisted in helping the objective I itself to knowledge and consciousness of what is posited in it, and of finally bringing it in this way to complete knowledge of itself. (1994b: 112–113/X, 98)

The purpose of the *ST*, according to the self-interpretation of the later Schelling, is to dispel the self's illusions through the dialectical method of this 'Socratic dialogue.' As Schulz notes, Schelling's claim to a dialectical method is clearly aimed at showing how Hegel's method derives from his own (Schulz, 1992: xxvii; see Schelling, 1994b: 111/X, 96). It is also clear that this interpretation, in which the *ST* becomes a kind of *Bildungsgeschichte*, or 'history of cultivation,' of the *Ich* (W. Marx, 1984: 48) is attractive to later commentators because it offers a clear distinction between Schelling's contributions to German philosophy and those of Fichte's subjective idealism. However, this reading is completely at odds with Schelling's own stated methodology and purpose as it is found in the *ST*, and it has also allowed later commentators to minimize the importance of the philosophy of art in his thought.

Thus the second step in the standard interpretation is to apply this *Bildungsgeschichte* to Schelling's own philosophical development in order to explain the transition from subjective idealism to absolute idealism. That is, once Schelling grasps the absolute identity in artistic activity, he then takes the next step and posits the absolute beyond the subject in the *Darstellung meines Systems der Philosophie* (1801), without the subjective or heuristic principles found in the *ST*. This argument also has a basis in Schelling's later self-interpretation (1994b: 110–113/X, 95–98). It seems to be assumed by many of the commentators (to whom we can add Lawrence,

1988: 11 and Velkley, 1997: 159–160), although it has been brought to explicit formulation by Antoon Braeckman, who argues that absolute idealism rests on 'the transposition of the inner structure of the work of art . . . to the inner structure of absolute reason in the *Darstellung*' (Braeckman, 2004a: 551). A response to this standard interpretation requires refuting both steps: this chapter will argue against the first step, while Chapter 4 will refute the second step by showing the continuity of the philosophy of art between the *ST* and the lectures collected as the *Philosophy of Art* (1802–1804) from the period of absolute idealism. The key to the subversive aspect of the *ST* is Schelling's subordination of practical reason to the philosophy of art. The true sting derives from how Schelling turns the infinite striving of the self into an insurmountable limitation: the self can only *strive* to realize its object (the categorical imperative), while aesthetic intuition realizes itself in the artwork.

While this critique is developed fully in the final section of the *ST*, let us turn to how it is anticipated in the sections on the preliminary division and organ of transcendental philosophy found in the 'Introduction.' Here the philosophy of art is introduced to resolve the contradiction between theoretical philosophy and practical philosophy: while theory seeks to explain the necessary conformity of representations to objects, practical reason seeks to transform these objects through freedom. The 'highest task of transcendental philosophy' is to think both necessity and freedom, that is, to reconcile them (1978: 11/III, 348). Schelling proposes two possible answers: teleology and the philosophy of art.

This is the point where Schelling's concept of productivity becomes central. He argues that both the objective world and the will are productive, and so must share a common principle. We can discover this productivity both in nature (including its products) and in the self's activity in aesthetic intuition. The question of how teleology or aesthetic intuition can resolve the contradiction between theory and practice comes down to whether or not productivity is realized with consciousness. With teleology, nature and its products appear (*erscheinen*) as 'consciously engendered' or purposive at the same time they appear as the product of blind mechanism (1978: 12/III, 349). While teleology, Schelling states, is the 'point of union' between theoretical and practical philosophy, it does not express this activity of production from the identity of subject and object. To close the circle of transcendental philosophy, this activity must be shown to be the product of the self, which he calls aesthetic intuition.[1] Aesthetic intuition produces from the identity of subject and object, of conscious (free) and unconscious (natural) activity; it is 'intellectual intuition become objective' through the work of art (1978: 229/III, 625). The ground of the system is the 'aesthetic act of the imagination,' and its proof the work of art. Thus aesthetic intuition is the 'organon' of transcendental philosophy (1978: 13/III, 351) and art the 'only true and eternal document of philosophy' (1978: 231/III, 627).

It is clear, then, that the *ST* is not a history of the self's cultivation, but rather that the 'standpoint of the transcendentally philosophizing ego is the one that performs the reconstruction of reason's original self-constitution by disclosing the conditions for the constitution of self-consciousness' (W. Marx, 1984: 48) through the 'free imitation' (Schelling, 1978, 48/III, 396–397) of the self's productivity. The *ST* does not present a path of cultivation or anamnesis, but a transcendental reconstruction of the conditions necessary for the self to recognize itself as producing objectively. As Werner Marx notes, if it were a case of cultivation of self-consciousness, each time the self encountered a transcendental illusion (such as, according to Schelling, freedom), this would require surpassing the illusion for a true idea or concept (W. Marx, 1984: 49). Instead, Schelling argues that the only responsibilities philosophy has to common understanding are to account for its claims and expose the 'inevitability of its delusions' (1978: 14/III, 352). As we will see, freedom itself is a product of an illusion.[2]

This chapter reconstructs the contours of Schelling's system as it progresses from theoretical philosophy and practical philosophy (Section 3.2), thought teleology (Section 3.3) to the philosophy of art (Section 3.4). Though we give priority to the structure of the *ST*, we must also discuss the *Introduction to the First Outline of a System of the Philosophy of Nature* to show how, at this stage, nature-philosophy still conforms to the concepts of transcendental idealism. Both sciences arise when the philosopher must explain the identity of subject and object that grounds all knowledge. To explain the identity of subject and object, one must start with either the subjective or objective, and with each respective first principle the philosopher attempts to explain the possibility of knowledge of its opposite, and how they concur in representation. For transcendental idealism, the subject is primary, which gives rise to the problem of how an object can be known; and for nature-philosophy, the object is primary and the question is how the subjective (intelligence) can be added to it (1978: 5–6/III, 340–341 and 2004a: 194/III, 272–273).

The systematic separation of these two sciences recalls Schelling's outline of the confrontation between criticism and dogmatism found in the *Letters*, although the system of realism is no longer the fatalist system of dogmatism but that of nature-philosophy. The two respective systems that begin with either subject or object are no longer two competing approaches to practical philosophy but two sciences within the framework of transcendental idealism. However, in the *ST*, Schelling has added a third branch to the system to unify them, which is the philosophy of art.

We will close by discussing the socio-political aspects of the philosophy of art. The importance of artistic production extends beyond its systematic purpose. It also holds out collective promise in the future. Art, through the medium of poetry, will bring about a new mythology, 'which shall be the creation, not of some individual author, but of a new race, personifying, as it were, one single poet' (1978: 233/III, 629). Not only does artistic production present the unity of conscious and unconscious activity, of freedom and necessity; it also offers the possibility of reconciling the individual and society through the intersubjective production of a new mythology. Like the 'System Program,' the *ST* proposes that the aesthetic force produced by the proper relationship between philosophy and poetry can unite humanity under free activity through a mythology 'in service to ideas,' which becomes 'a mythology of reason' (quoted in Krell, 2005: 25). Art is the 'eternal document' of philosophy because it produces, or makes actual, what philosophy can only intuit in the ideal. The *ST* sets out the features that I have identified as the *Three Conditions* of the philosophy of art (see the Introduction). These conditions are the basis of my determination that Schelling gives a continuous priority to the philosophy of art from 1800–1807. The next two chapters will argue that they remain present in Schelling's philosophy, no matter the metaphysical ground of his system. In the next chapter, in particular, I will show that, despite the shift to absolute idealism, the philosophy of art still plays a central role in Schelling's thought.

3.2. The Limits of Theory and Practice

How Schelling reaches primacy of the philosophy of art cannot be understood apart from the structure of the *System of Transcendental Idealism*. Hence it is necessary to discuss the principles of Schelling's theoretical philosophy before moving on to his practical philosophy. Theoretical philosophy is concerned with the possibility of objectivity and the necessary correspondence of representations and objects. These conditions of possibility include showing how the self becomes limited, the deduction of logical categories, and, unique to Schelling, how the self 'becomes' conscious within nature. These deductions, which Schelling claims follow from the self's productivity, remain unconscious, which is why self-consciousness does not intuit them. Practical philosophy, which in the *ST* marks the emergence of self-consciousness, is primarily concerned with intersubjectivity, history, right and most importantly for us, the limitations of a formal account of freedom. It is Schelling's emphasis on these limitations that opens the way for the philosophy of art.

3.2.1. Theory

The theoretical section of the *System of Transcendental Idealism* attempts to demonstrate the unconscious production of the self. Because Schelling holds that subject and object are mutually exclusive principles, the deductions in the *ST* are limited by the requirement that all explanations of objectivity must be derived from the self's subjective activity, which Schelling calls productivity.[3] The concept of productivity, which is ultimately grounded in the productive imagination (*Einbildungskraft*), allows him to orient transcendental idealism around a continuum of the self's activity, from intellectual intuition to aesthetic intuition. Productivity, then, is supposed to overcome the Kantian separation of the faculties by unifying them under a common concept.[4] But this leads to what appears to be an extreme version of idealism. Schelling makes claims such as: 'nothing external can operate upon the self *qua* self,' or 'The self is a completely self-enclosed world, a monad, which cannot issue forth from itself, though nor can anything enter it either, from without' (1978: 36–37/III, 380–381). Such stringent idealism is, Schelling argues, balanced by his nature-philosophy (of Spinozistic realism), but then it becomes all the more important that his philosophy of art reconcile these two extremes. However, it could also be said that the concern of transcendental philosophy is strictly epistemological. In this case, Schelling's position is that all knowledge is the result of the self's activity, and that all intuition requires such activity to become objective. Yet if intellectual intuition inaugurates this process of self-positing, and objectivity is the result of the self's activity, Schelling must explain why objects seem necessarily external. He does this by arguing that the feeling of necessity is a result of these processes remaining unconscious; they never obtain consciousness.

The use of the term 'unconscious' (*Bewußtlos*), for many readers, suggests a connection to Freud (Marquard, 2004: 13–29). This is not entirely unreasonable, although the connection is fairly distant. Dale E. Snow suggests that the introduction of the unconscious implies Schelling's recognition of an irrational element in existence and even within the system (Snow, 1996: 125–128). However, this obscures the fact, as Werner Marx argues, that the deductions of the theoretical part of the system concern the self as governed by natural laws; that is, the philosopher follows how the self's (the intelligence's) activity becomes objective. Schelling is describing 'the unconscious lawfulness of intelligence in its process of becoming conscious' (W. Marx, 1984: 37). As I will argue, Schelling holds that nature exhibits a rational structure, with human activity at its apex. In any case, there is, I think, a degree of equivocation in the *ST* regarding the unconscious, because the section on art implies a kind of agency of nature as compulsion in the artist's activity (referred to as the 'unfathomable depth' granted the artist by nature – see 1978: 224/III, 619), which is not the same kind of 'unconscious' as developed in either theoretical philosophy or nature-philosophy. This is probably because the philosophy of art has a broader reach than the epistemological concerns of the earlier sections of the book. In Chapter 5, we will see that Schelling's concept of the unconscious in *Über das Verhältnis der bildenden Künste zu der Natur*, when he associates it with the natural passions that must be sublimated in the production of art, is much closer to Freud's.

For the moment, let us return to the *ST*. The general task of transcendental inquiry, according to Schelling, is to show how the activity of the self can explain objectivity, and he divides this explanation into three 'epochs': intuition, production, and reflection. The first two epochs, intuition and production, include important passages dedicated to showing the emergence of consciousness with nature, and so they will be the focus of our reconstruction of Schelling's theoretical philosophy.[5] After establishing the first principle of intellectual intuition Schelling deduces the self's original limitation, which is sensation or feeling (*Empfindung*). This, he argues, is to show how the self's activity remains ideally infinite (because its ideal limitations can be overcome) at the same time it is limited in the real. Because Schelling restricts the deduction to the self's activity, without permitting an external principle, he must show how the self produces both subjectivity and objectivity at the same time it does not recognize itself as ground. This limitation of the self's intuition is feeling/sensation (*Empfindung*), which includes both a sensation of externality or objectivity and a feeling of necessity that accompanies the representations thereof. The presence of self-consciousness is only possible through a feeling of necessity or objectivity, although it is not conscious of this production of necessity as its own. The self intuits this necessity as a feeling of limitation that is an unrecoverable past:

> the self in its present action is limited *without its consent*, but that it finds itself so limited is also the whole of what is contained in sensation, and is the condition of all objectivity in knowledge. So in order that the limitation shall appear to us as a thing independent of ourselves, provision is made for this purpose, through the mechanism of sensation, that the act whereby all limitation is posited, as the condition of all consciousness, does not itself come to consciousness. (1978: 58/III, 409)

From this initial limitation Schelling constructs all objectivity from the self's productivity. These deductions are similar to those of the *Survey*, but in the *ST* they are much more developed, and their connection to nature-philosophy is much stronger. In the first epoch, the transition from sensation to productive intuition makes this clear. When deducing the three dimensions of matter – which, Schelling notes (1978: 86/III, 444), had not been previously explained – he does so by utilizing the dynamic processes of nature (as a speculative physics) rather than by assuming a philosophy of mathematics. Hence the three dimensions of matter are only possible as products of natural processes: magnetism, electricity, and chemical processes (1978: 86–93/III, 444–454). Schelling underlines that they are not external moments but intrinsic to the 'history of self-consciousness': 'the three stages in the construction of matter really do correspond to the three acts in the intelligence' which are intuition, limitation, and production (1978: 92/III, 453).

The next step in Schelling's argument that the laws of the mind and the natural world emerge together can be found in the second epoch, or the transition from productive intuition to organization. Organization appears twice in the *ST*: first in theoretical philosophy, then in Part 5, which is dedicated to teleology (see Section 3.3). Teleology answers the epistemological question of how the subject can think a self-producing nature that exhibits a conscious production which cannot be cognized by the self, while organization as dealt with in theoretical philosophy shows how the self intuits itself as an agent within the constant change of succession. The presence of consciousness restricts succession to 'a specific circle' (1978: 121/III, 490). This circle is the relationship of reciprocity between the self (substance) and succession (accident). However, this reference to the categories is not intended to establish their purely logical validity, but to show how they are valid through the 'higher potency' (*Potenz*) of natural organization (1978: 126/III, 495). Organization is the self's intuition of itself as active within succession as the reciprocity of cause and effect, producer and production. Organization is the point in which the 'intelligence must appear to itself as an organic individual' (1978: 125/III, 495). With it comes the 'physics' of organization: the organism persists against the constant change of succession through the activities of sensibility, irritability, and the formative urge (*Bildungstrieb*). Organization also provides a concept of nature, in which all individuals become in themselves accidents and nature as totality becomes substance (1978: 126/III, 495). Nevertheless, even if organization is the pinnacle of natural processes, the nature of the self remains unconscious, and because it is unconscious, the production of subjectivity and objectivity as found in theoretical philosophy cannot close the series of activities. There remains the deduction of reflection, the emergence of self-consciousness and freedom in practical philosophy, the investigation into natural teleology, and the condition that makes the entire system possible, the philosophy of art.[6]

3.2.2. Practice

In his practical philosophy, Schelling shows how the self becomes conscious of itself as *really* productive within a world, and yet he also argues – in a move that subverts the primacy of the practical reason found in Fichte – that this practical activity does not obtain the absolute identity of subject and object. At its basis, practical activity divides the identity of subject and object that grounds the self's productive activity, but this separation has important positive consequences for the system: practical activity becomes the basis for consciousness, individuality, empirical time, and the separation of the in itself from appearances in representation. In more Romantic terms, this separation results in the divided nature of the self: 'Man is forever a broken fragment, for either his action is necessary, and then not free, or free, and then not necessary and according to law' (1978: 216/III, 608). Practical activity can only approach the identity of freedom and necessity through infinite progress toward the ideal (the categorical imperative) but can never objectively realize this identity (thus the actions appear as either free or necessary). However, as Schelling argues, along the way, the self changes the world by making its activity objective.

I will underline two important aspects of Schelling's account of the ground of practical reason: first, Schelling focuses on the intersubjective basis of practice, which introduces a second free act of the self as ground;

and second, his account stresses that the imagination provides the continuity of the self's productive activity, which connects it to both theoretical philosophy, and later, to aesthetic intuition. Practical philosophy begins with a second act of the self. Like the initial act of intellectual intuition, it must be an act of freedom, but unlike intellectual intuition, it is the beginning of self-consciousness, individuality, and empirical time. Schelling argues that the first act of self-consciousness takes place within an intersubjective world, and that it constitutes the origin of the *real* limitations of the self.[7]

His argument encounters several problems in this regard, which he only superficially confronts. Despite his previous insistence that all activity of the self must have its origin within the self, the original act of practical philosophy, which is an act of willing, is 'indirectly grounded' by the activity of other selves. It is not intersubjectivity that is problematic but Schelling's presupposition that all activity and objectivity arise from the self. By contrast, recall that Fichte's 'not-I,' for all its ambiguity, could still be interpreted as qualitatively different from the self, a negation of the self's sphere, and even as another subject: 'the not-self [is] simply the counterpart of the self and nothing more. No Thou, no I: no I, no Thou' (1982: 172–173/I, 188–189). However, for Schelling, the structure of the system will not allow for an external *object* to *cause* the self's activity, because the Object is the first principle of the other side of the total system, nature-philosophy.

Hence, in the argument concerning intersubjectivity, Schelling holds that the activity of other intelligences must be recognized as *subjects* and not as *objects*, which he claims dispenses with the heretofore prohibited influence of externality. This, he states, is possible through a 'pre-established harmony' of the universal conditions for the possibility of any subject whosoever: 'such a harmony is conceivable only between subjects of equal reality, and hence this act must have proceeded from a subject endowed with just the same reality as the intelligence itself' (1978: 161/III, 540).[8] In any case, this concept of an intersubjective practical world has the advantage of explaining the real limitations of the self's activity by the rightful domain of the free action of other selves, and not by objectivity. Additionally, intersubjectivity constitutes the condition for freedom in both its origins and its realization within history as a universal rule of law.[9] We will return to the historical aspect of practical reason and its relationship to mythology in the final section of this chapter.

While the intersubjective interaction of other intelligences 'elicits' the self's free activity, this does not remove the first practical act from the entire succession of acts leading from intellectual intuition to the objective result of aesthetic intuition (which is the artwork). However, Schelling's deductions show how, at its basis, practical action sunders the identity between subject and object at the basis of the self's activity. In this regard, Schelling returns to the fundamental problem found in his *Letters*: how it is 'possible to have a transition from the subjective into the objective' (1978: 182/III, 566), that is, the problem of the relationship between the self's infinite free activity and the finite world.

Schelling's deduction of practical action, again, rests on the postulate that the subjective can never be determined by the objective. As mentioned in the theoretical exposition of the *ST*, objectivity is grounded in the self's productivity, though this productivity is unconscious. Willing, as Schelling defines it, is activity directed toward an external object, and thus cannot be identical to this object. Therefore, at its very basis, freedom cannot realize the identity between practical activity and producing; there must be a difference between the will's activity and the object. Thus practical reason cannot fulfill the demand that philosophy discover the act in which the self becomes conscious of absolute identity – Schelling must still show how practical reason fails to do so.

In practical action there arises the contradiction between the infinite capacity of the will and the finite 'compulsion to represent,' or between infinite activity and particular objects (1978: 176ff./III, 558ff.). This contradiction is resolved, Schelling argues, by the activity of the imagination, which 'wavers' (*Schweben*) between infinity and finitude, and which serves as the connection between theoretical reason (the activity of representation) and freedom. As we will see, the power of imagination extends the continuity of the self's activity to aesthetic intuition as well. The products of imagination are Ideas, which have their origin in reason itself, not in the understanding. Moreover, just as Schelling proposes the imagination as the mediator between the will and representation, he proposes the ideal as the mediator between the Idea and the object. The opposition between ideal and object 'engenders the drive to transform the object as it is into the object as it ought to be' (1978: 177/III, 559). Because the self is divided between the unconscious producing of representation and conscious willing, the demand to realize the ideal in the intuited object gives rise to the drive 'directly bent upon restoring the lost identity of the self' (1978: 177/III, 560). Yet even if the self can realize the ideal by transforming the object, its attempt to restore the lost identity can only be realized in a *progressus ad infinitum*, while the ideal can be actualized in the present, the Idea remains infinite.

Yet this infinite progress leaves 'man a broken fragment' because of the difference between the intuiting self (as productive) and the practical self (as willing). As Schelling argues, in practical philosophy the distinction between the in itself and appearance obtains. Because Schelling begins with the presupposition that the entire transcendental system rests on the self's activity (including both representation and freedom), he reaches the conclusion that free action is only an appearance to the self; or, in a word, an illusion. This illusion is a consequence of the difference between the intuiting self, which is both ideal and real, and the practical self, which acts ideally.[10] In itself, the self is both intuitant and active; both the external object and freedom are grounded in the self's activity. However, all practical action is that of modifying the intuiting self's production of objects. Because the self's production is unconscious, it appears to be grounded in external objects.

The problem is that for ordinary consciousness the self acts freely in a world of natural objects, while according to the transcendental standpoint, the self 'can never be anything other than it is, namely subject and object at once, that is, productive' (1978: 184/III, 569), though blindly productive. Although the identity of subject and object as the basis of production is not a problem for theoretical philosophy, where this identity obtains but is unconscious, it is a problem for practical philosophy. Between the two, we are presented with the contradiction between the self's activity as free, or as necessary, but in itself, the self is both productive and free.

Like Fichte, Schelling holds that this transcendental illusion is necessary because the reality of representation is grounded in the self's practical activity; only insofar as the self acts do its representations become objectively real. 'If the objective world is a mere appearance, so too is the objective element in our acting, and conversely, only if the world has reality, does the objective element in action also possess reality' (1978: 185/III, 570). Free action is, at its basis, an intuition, but it does not appear as such because free activity is confined to the laws of intuition, to natural laws. As stated at the outset, this identity will not obtain for self-consciousness; it 'cannot be evidenced in free action itself, since precisely for the sake of free action . . . it abolishes itself' (1978: 213/III, 605). Thus we see that practical action cannot bring the identity of subject and object to self-consciousness. Freedom qua action appears, but in itself, such action stands under the necessity of natural laws. And as previously mentioned, the task of transcendental idealism is to explain how the identity of subjectivity and objectivity becomes objective. This will require a third branch of philosophy to resolve this central problem, which is reserved for the philosophy of art.

This opens the path to what I have called the *first condition* of the philosophy of art: what philosophy constructs in the ideal, art produces in the real. Thus artistic activity is the highest human vocation because practical philosophy can only approximate its object, which is the moral law.

But before considering the philosophy of art, Schelling proposes an examination of teleology and nature. He will argue that nature-philosophy can show how organisms are productive but without intention. While this provides an account of nature that is productive and not merely mechanistic, Schelling will also argue that nature-philosophy requires the philosophy of art to show how the identity of freedom and necessity becomes objective through an activity that includes self-consciousness.

3.3. Teleology and Nature-philosophy

The discussion of teleology is not the only time that Schelling considers the relationship between nature and the self in the *System of Transcendental Idealism*. In the first two epochs of the theoretical section, Schelling argues that the laws of the mind and laws of natural processes are both internal to the 'history of self-consciousness,' even if they later appear to self-consciousness to be external. Schelling notes that 'insofar as the intelligence produces unconsciously, its organism is immediately identical with it, in such a way that what it intuits externally is reflected by the organism without further mediation' (1978: 129/III, 499). However, confined to the theoretical section, this natural aspect of the self remains unconscious. Hence, because practical action sunders this identity, the system requires a theory of teleology in order to secure the epistemological status of organic nature *for* the self.

The principles of teleology demand that the self thinks nature as *appearing* as purposive, but *not* purposive in·its production. This position is similar to the *Ideas* (which appropriated Kant's concept of teleology; see Section 2.5), but now Schelling holds that mechanism and organic nature are incompatible. Thus organic nature – in either the particular or nature as totality – must be considered as producing through 'blind mechanism.' Literally, nature is unconscious. So while nature *appears* as both the product of conscious forces and unconscious forces, the task of transcendental idealism is to explain how the self grasps this identity for itself. Teleology exhibits the identity of subject and object, but only in the object, and not in the self. In addition, Schelling gives this problem a twist: it is only possible for the self to grasp the teleological character of nature if it has already intuited the identity of subject and object. This is only possible through aesthetic intuition.

Yet, while the principles of teleology are limited within transcendental idealism, they are not exhaustive of nature-philosophy. By the time the *System of Transcendental Idealism* had been published, Schelling had already published the *First Outline of a System of the Philosophy of Nature* (1799) and its separate *Introduction to the First Outline of a System of the Philosophy of Nature*,[11] the latter of which sets out the formal principles of a realist 'speculative physics,' or, 'Spinozism of physics,' subordinated to the task of explaining the ideal (subject) through the real (object) (2004a: 194/III, 273). While Schelling prohibits all acts of the self from being explained by objective causes in the *ST*, in the *First Outline*, he argues that nature is the medium in which 'self-consciousness can take place,' and suggests that reason could be a 'mere play of higher and necessarily unknown natural forces' (2004a: 194–195/III, 273–274). This claim is not meant to reduce humanity to the 'most unfortunate, most delicate, most evanescent beings' as Nietzsche would have it (1954: 43), but to demonstrate how reason is a law giving force for nature itself, which leads to the highest potency of nature's productivity: self-consciousness. For Schelling, the higher determines the lower; the most perfect provides the rule in human activity and in nature. This suggests that an aesthetic intuition underlies nature-philosophy.

Despite Schelling's claims to the contrary, nature-philosophy, like the *ST*, is riddled with inconsistencies. While Schelling claims to demonstrate a system of speculative physics (which is realist), nature-philosophy maintains a transcendental framework and is thus also grounded in the principles of transcendental idealism, which concludes with a philosophy of art. In fact, nature-philosophy contains many formal structures which are iso-morphic with transcendental idealism. In the *ST*, Schelling himself draws the parallel: 'Precisely as the intelligence, by means of succession, constantly tries to depict the absolute synthesis, so likewise will organic nature con-stantly appear as struggling towards universal organism and at war against an inorganic nature' (1978: 125/III, 494). Nature-philosophy begins with an original identity between productivity and product, which is sundered in order to make empirical nature possible, just as the identity of the self is split in transcendental idealism in order to explain the possibility of the objective. Each side of the system requires a principle that can unite the two.

For the first principle of nature-philosophy, Schelling posits nature as productive and not just as a totality of empirical objects. But nature is not just assumed, as in the teleological investigations of the *ST*, to *appear* as a totality; instead, Schelling argues in the *First Outline* that nature *is* an organic, productive totality. Nature-philosophy is a Spinozist physics:

> Insofar as we regard the totality of objects not merely as product, but at the same time necessarily as productive, it becomes *Nature* for us, and this *identity of the product and productivity*, and this alone, is implied by the idea of Nature, even in the ordinary use of language. *Nature* as mere *product* (*natura naturata*) we call Nature as *object* (with this alone all empiricism deals). *Nature as productivity* (*natura naturans*) we call *Nature as subject* (with this alone all theory deals). (2004a: 202/III, 284)

Again, Schelling's appropriation of the concepts of *natura naturata* and *natura naturans* shows a desire to reconcile both the thought of Spinoza with Fichte (although Spinoza's influence is becoming more explicit), and more importantly human being and nature. This attempt at reconciliation is one of the factors restricting nature-philosophy to a transcendental framework, which here involves resolving the contradiction between nature as productivity and nature as product. His solution, like that of practical philosophy, will be that nature is possible only insofar as it infinitely approaches the identity of absolute productivity or absolute product: nature cannot be absolute productivity or else there would be no products, and conversely, it cannot be absolute product because this would extinguish all productivity. Thus, while at its very basis, nature is 'originally only productivity' (2004a: 202/III, 284), it must be thought as the duplicity of productivity and product (limitation).

According to Schelling, nature must, like the self, become an object to itself: 'Nature must originally be an object to itself; this change of the *pure subject* into an *object to itself* is unthinkable without an original diremption in Nature itself' (2004a: 205/III, 288). Therefore, nature is at the same time productive and limited, infinite and finite. Yet it is precisely around the question of explaining the limitation of nature's productivity that the *First Outine* perpetually circles. There are explanations and deductions involving the mathematical continuum, galvanism, and the metaphor of a whirlpool, the latter of which is particularly *à propos* of Schelling's conceptual struggle – continuing through the period of absolute philosophy – with the transition from absolute productivity (infinite nature) and limitation (determinate products):

> Suppose, for illustration, a stream; it is *pure identity*; where it meets resistance, a whirlpool is formed; this whirlpool is not an abiding thing,

but something that vanishes at every moment, and every moment springs up anew. – Originally, in Nature there is nothing distinguishable; all products are, so to speak, still in solution, and invisible in the universal productivity. It is only when retarding points are given that they are thrown off and advance out of the universal identity. – At every such point the stream breaks (the productivity is annihilated), but at every step there comes a new wave which fills up the sphere. (2004a: 206/III, 289)

As with the image of the whirlpool, Schelling proposes various kinds of limitations through dynamic processes but does not deduce the principle of limitation itself until he shifts, in the concluding pages of the *First Outline*, to a more aphoristic and axiomatic style. Transcendental methods of inquiry into nature such as found in the *Ideas* are abandoned for the elucidation of the axioms of his speculative physics. Yet, strikingly, the explanation follows the same structure as that of practical action: specifically, nature is a *striving*, out of duplicity, for the identity of productivity and product. But if this identity is actualized in nature as totality, all difference collapses, it falls into indifference (*Indifferenz*), a concept central to his later philosophy of identity, which is the focus of the next chapter. Individual natural objects, obtain as relative points of indifference, but they are only possible insofar as nature *in toto* infinitely strives toward the absolute point of indifference (2004a: 224/III, 315).

Although Schelling's inquiry formally abandons the method of transcendental idealism because of his use of axioms (recalling Spinoza), nature-philosophy remains grounded in the activity of the self. Despite the introduction of terms such as *Indifferenz* and the first appearances of the Schelling's use of the concept of the potency (*Potenz*) (which we will discuss in Chapter 4; we have already highlighted the use of *Potenz* in the *ST*), the system has not yet arrived at absolute idealism. As Jean-François Marquet emphasizes, the opposition between productivity and product is based on the opposition in the self between intuition and reflection (Marquet, 2006: 170–174). The absolute continuity of productivity 'exists only for intuition' while 'all the laws of mechanics, whereby that which is properly only the object of the productive intuition becomes an object of reflection, are really only laws for reflection' (Schelling, 2004a: 203/III, 285–286). This last claim, we can add, holds for Schelling's criticisms toward the capacity of reflection to explain the productivity of the self. The upshot, however, is that nature as productivity (*natura naturans*) can also be grasped by intellectual intuition, as Schelling claims in the introduction to the *ST*. However, absolute identity, sought in the early pages of the *ST*, is only proved indirectly in nature, while, as he notes, for both self-consciousness and philosophy, it 'is *directly* proved in the case of an activity at once clearly conscious and unconscious, which manifests itself in the productions of *genius*' (2004a: 193/III, 271). There is only one more step to the *second condition* of the philosophy of art, which we will address in the next section: while both the natural organism and the artwork embody the same identity of real and ideal, of necessity and freedom, the work of art overcomes these oppositions through the identity of conscious and unconscious production, whereas the organism's activity is unconscious.

3.4. From Aesthetic Intuition to the New Mythology

So far we have focused on the limits of theory and practice. The remainder of this chapter will be dedicated to showing how Schelling's philosophy of art reconciles the opposition between theoretical reason and practical reason by demonstrating that the activity of artistic production overcomes the separation of freedom and necessity through the production of the work of art. We will conclude with a commentary on the political role played by the promise, found in the 'System Program' and the *System of Transcendental Idealism*, of the 'mythology of reason.'

Schelling's use of the concept of genius to overcome the separation of freedom and nature is not without precedent: the close proximity of art and nature can be found in the central figures of the *Sturm und Drang*, Romanticism, and even in Kant. Take, for example, Goethe, who was no small figure in Schelling's life: in a passage from *The Sorrows of Young Werther*, the protagonist reflects on the relationship between nature and artist and resolves 'in future to rely on nature alone' as a basis for art, as it 'alone is infinitely rich, and it alone forms the great artist' (2004: 16).[12] Or, take Kant, who acknowledges genius as 'the inborn predisposition of the mind (*ingenium*) through which nature gives the rule to art' (2000: 186/V, 307). Even Fichte, as we noted in Section 2.6, hinted at a connection between philosophizing and a kind of genius like that of artists and poets.

A further comparison with Fichte is illustrative. In his *System of Ethics*, Fichte writes that the aesthetic point of view 'makes the transcendental point of view the ordinary point of view' (2005: 334/IV, 353–354).[13] The *ST* makes similar statements, but there is a crucial difference: Fichte's consideration of aesthetics is didactic because practical reason maintains priority over artistic production. Although the aesthetic point of view regards the relationship of the self's activity to the moral law as one of freedom, 'our ultimate end, however, is the self-sufficiency of reason' (2005: 335/IV, 354). For Schelling, by contrast, artistic production – what he calls aesthetic intuition – is the *real* expression of reason; it objectively produces what philosophy can only address ideally with intellectual intuition. It also has higher priority than nature-philosophy because artistic production pro-duces out of the identity of subject and object *with consciousness*. Schelling stands out from his predecessors by the conceptual priority given to the activity of genius and artistic production, for it alone (qua *praxis*) has the capacity to overcome the contradiction between freedom and necessity, conscious and unconscious activity. Thus Schelling overturns the Fichtean priority of practical philosophy. In addition, insofar as artistic production reconciles the central contradiction between freedom and necessity, it concerns both epistemology and being of the self as a 'whole person.'

Therefore Schelling breaks with the Enlightenment tradition by eliminat-ing reference to external standards of art such as taste, morality, or aesthet-ics (as a science of sensation). Instead, Schelling's focus is the search for the idea produced through art, that is, the truth of art.[14] This ultimate truth is produced through beauty. The task, for us, remains to show how Schelling's philosophy of art deposes practical philosophy from the pinnacle of transcendental idealism. Or, in Schelling's terms, the task is to show how intellectual intuition becomes objective, which occurs through the activity of genius, through aesthetic intuition. Aesthetic intuition presents the absolute identity of subject and object through the production of the artwork. Thus, Schelling undertakes a transcendental inquiry to deduce aesthetic intuition as the ground of the possibility for the artwork, which is the product of both free (conscious) and necessary (unconscious) production.

To do so, Schelling deduces the product (the artwork) and then the act of production that makes the product possible. The product will unite the conscious activity (like freedom) and the unconscious production of nature. It is the opposition of freedom and necessity that drives this activity, although Schelling gives two different accounts of how the activity begins. On the one hand, he argues that genius sets out from freedom and ends in the necessity of the artwork's inner harmony; genius is an activity 'freely granted by [the artist's] own nature' (1978: 223/III, 617). Yet, on the other hand, he also claims that artistic production arises due to inner conflict, and that this 'can be justifiably inferred already from the testimony of all artists, that they are involuntarily driven to create their works and that in producing them they merely satisfy an irresistible urge of their own nature' (1978: 222/III, 616).[15] These two accounts seem to beg the question. The difficulty, I think Schelling would argue, is that the philosophical account of artistic production requires dividing and analyzing that which is not separated in activity. Let us recall that Fichte's positing of the absolute I also exhibited circularity, and Schelling, it seems, has displaced this circularity on to the activity of genius, with the difference being that, according to Schelling, that genius produces an objective proof – the artwork – for absolute identity.

Interestingly, the artist-genius revives the figure of the tragic hero discussed in the *Letters*. Recall that the tragic hero, the 'man of destiny,' acts freely but is ultimately condemned by fate to be punished for the unforeseen consequences of his actions. Unlike in the *Letters*, this figure is no longer confined to the past of Greek mythology:

> Just as the man of destiny does not execute what he wishes or intends, but rather what he is obliged to execute by an inscrutable fate which governs him, so the artist, however deliberate he may be, seems nonetheless to be governed, in regard to what is truly objective in his creation, by a power which separates from all other men, and compels him to say or depict things which he does not fully understand himself, and whose meaning is infinite. (1978: 223/III, 617)

Instead of being excluded from a system of freedom, the activity of the artist (who exhibits the same characteristics as the tragic hero) is now the basis of both practical and theoretical philosophy. However, the identity of conscious and unconscious activity is not expressed in the activity but the product: the work of art.

The work of art is the centerpiece of Schelling's system, because, as Andrew Bowie points out, 'we only ever "see" products, not the productivity' (Bowie, 1993: 50). The subordination of practical philosophy to the philosophy of art occurs because the infinite striving of practice can never be completely objective, and it itself relies on the separation of subject and object in appearances, while aesthetic intuition results in the artwork, which presents [*darstellen*] the infinite in finite form (1978: 225/III, 620). The infinite characteristic of art is based in (1) the lack of an external rule leading to its creation, meaning that the artwork presents its own rule; and (2) the cessation of striving, resulting in 'calm, and silent grandeur.' In less technical terms, the artwork exhibits both infinite beauty and harmony. But the artwork is also superior to natural objects because, (1) they only exhibit the appearance of intelligence (whether we are talking about the teleology of the *ST* or the concept of *natura naturans* in nature-philosophy), and (2) the art product resolves the central contradiction of the system, overcoming the separation of subject and object in the self's activity. Artistic

UNIVERSITY OF WINCHESTER
LIBRARY

production confronts a human being not as a fragment, but as a whole. Finally it presents what philosophy can only show in ideal form:

> art is at once the only true and eternal organ and document of philosophy, which ever and again continues to speak to us of what philosophy cannot depict in external form, namely the unconscious element in acting and producing, and its original identity with the conscious. (1978: 231/III, 627–628)

Art is paramount in a dual sense for Schelling. First, aesthetic intuition is intellectual intuition become objective: aesthetic intuition removes the objection that the absolute self (its producing from the identity of subject and object) is a kind of subjective deception by presenting its objective truth in the product of the artwork. Remember that Schelling holds that freedom is a necessary illusion for the self because practical philosophy rests on the separation of subject and object. By contrast, the subjective element of activity is unified with the objective (unconscious) in aesthetic intuition, resulting in the artwork.

It is important to pause on this statement regarding the relationship between philosophy and artistic activity, because some of the secondary literature grants to artistic activity sovereignty or autonomy over philosophy, a sovereignty that is lost in the period of absolute idealism (see Beiser, 2002a: 584–585; 2002b: 73–87).[16] To claim that artistic production is sovereign over philosophy severs the unity between intellectual intuition and aesthetic intuition. For Schelling, intellectual intuition and aesthetic intuition are unified by the imagination (*Einbildungskraft*) (1978: 230/III, 626); the former is expressed ideally while the latter is expressed in the real, objectively as the work of art. Because art is produced objectively, it leads the self itself 'up to the very point where we ourselves were standing when we began to philosophize,' verifying the transcendental inquiry (1978: 232/III, 628–629).

It is the concept of the imagination that allows Schelling to unify theoretical-, practical-, and art-philosophy. As I mentioned earlier, the imagination is the basis for the continuity of activity in the self's productive activity: in thought, the imagination allows the philosopher to think and combine what is contradictory – for example, the identity of subject and object – and in artistic activity, it produces the inner harmony of the artwork: hence 'that which appears to us outside the sphere of consciousness, as real, and that which appears within it, as ideal, or as the world of art, are also products of one and the same activity' (1978: 230–231/III, 626).

In philosophy this activity is intellectual intuition; in art, this activity is aesthetic intuition, the production of beauty. Schelling refers to artistic production as the highest potency (*höchsten Potenz*) of the imagination, which confirms the continuity of Schelling's art-philosophy between the *System of Transcendental Idealism* and the *Philosophy of Art*, because this is exactly what he argues in the latter text (which is the focus of Chapter 4).

Second, art plays a significant socio-political role for Schelling. Not only does art close the circle of transcendental philosophy; the philosophy of art opens the possibility of returning philosophy to its origins in poetry and mythology. This mythology will also, as mentioned in the 'System Program,' play a utopian role within community: it 'shall be the creation, not of some individual author, but of a new race, personifying, as it were, one single poet,' which could arise 'in the future destinies of the world, and in the course of history to come' (1978: 233/III, 629). Despite these difficulties, art plays an ideological role; it embodies the results of transcendental philosophy and presents these results for all; the philosopher and non-philosopher both recognize the universal character of art.

This role of mythology was anticipated, as we saw, in both the *Survey* and the 'System Program' (see Section 2.6). Because this account of the *System of Transcendental Idealism* is close to that of the 'System Program' (and because this document's author remains in question) we will focus on the differences with the *Survey* and the problems they present: there mythology appeared within the philosophy of history as the poetic truth of religion. I argued that Schelling's general point concerned the role of revelation, as the role of human freedom in bringing about the absolute as an infinite task. At no point in history is freedom (qua absolute) perfectly realized, or else all free action would be nothing but necessity (I, 473; and 1978: 210/ III, 602). In the *Survey*, Schelling states that such an absolute state of reason (*VernunftZustandes* [*sic*]) would be as boring as watching a play where only 'perfected beings appear' (I, 473).[17] By contrast, Schelling's system argues that an infinitely progressive revelation is revealed through freedom. Schelling returns to the metaphor of theater:

> if the playwright [i.e. God] *were to exist* independently of his drama, we should be merely the actors who speak the lines he has written. If he *does* not exist independently of us, but reveals and discloses himself successively only, through the very play of our own freedom, so that without this freedom even he himself *would not be*, then we are collaborators of the whole and have ourselves invented the particular roles we play. (1978: 210/III, 602)

He provides three progressive stages of revelation: destiny, natural law, and providence (my argument follows 1978: 211–212/III, 603–604). Schelling argues for a historical development of consciousness itself; each era's self-conscious point of view is transformed by a later era, so the sense of the preceding era changes. In this progress that which appears as destiny then appears as natural law and then as providence. Hence the first period, of destiny, is that of blind fate. He calls this era the 'tragic age,' which is that of antiquity and its glories and downfall, which itself appears as tragic. The second is that of natural law, beginning with the Roman Empire and that, Schelling implies, still holds sway through his era, in which freedom operates under a 'mechanical conformity to law.' The final stage is providence, which has yet to come. Schelling writes that the 'the third period of history will be that wherein the force which appeared in the earlier stages as destiny or nature has evolved itself as *providence*, and wherein it will become apparent that even what seemed to be simply the work of destiny or nature was already the beginning of a providence imperfectly revealing itself' (1978: 212/III, 604). It is with the concept of providence, which is 'to come' (to borrow a phrase from Derrida), that Schelling's philosophy of revelation shows its inconsistencies.

A primary inconsistency becomes manifest in the system because the philosophies of history and revelation are contained within the practical philosophy of the *ST*, indicating that the realization of providence has some relationship to the 'gradual realization of the rule of law' within a league of nations (1978: 203/III, 593).[18] However, while this was the outcome of Kant's 'Idea for a Universal History from a Cosmopolitan Point of View,' Schelling closes the *ST* with the invocation of a higher revelation, that of poetic mythology. He seems less content than Kant with providence being equated with the realization of a universal rule of law (Kant, 1988: 424/VIII, 30). Schelling argues that the state functions as a legal mechanism to guarantee the realization of individual freedom, although this mechanism lacks any moral force. Any attempt to realize the state as a moral force, Schelling claims (most likely with the French Revolution in mind), leads to despotism. Thus 'although the legal system performs the same office, *materially* speaking, that we expect, in fact, from providence, and is altogether the best theodicy that man is able to contrive, it still does not do this in *form* . . . with judgment and forethought' (1978: 196/III, 584). This indicates, for Schelling, that the epoch of providence is yet to come, but also suggests that, in overcoming the age of natural right, society must also be transfigured. Yet we are still presented with the problem of the relationship between providence and the new mythology, which Schelling himself

leaves unresolved. There are two options to solve this problem. If we decide
to abandon the distinction between practical philosophy and the philosophy of art against the letter of Schelling (and we will not), to combine
providence and the new mythology (see White, 1983: 69–70), this risks
removing the systematic priority of artistic production, because the philosophy of revelation deduced within practical philosophy could plausibly
render the philosophy of art either redundant or superfluous. If, however,
we take this separation seriously, as we have, these tasks 'to come' – the
universal rule of law, revelation, and mythology – are inconsistent.

In any case, in a broader historical and political sense, Schelling's utopian
mythology presents an alternative ideal to the developments of capitalism
in the 18th century. Schelling specifically contrasts artistic production with
economic production, arguing that artistic production presents a sense of
dignity and value above and beyond exchange value (what Schelling calls
'the useful'). This contrast allows us to symptomatically read Schelling's
concern, shared by his Romantic contemporaries, with the separation of
human beings from nature as a crisis engendered by capitalism: the greater
the progress of economic development, the more the natural 'quality' of
human being recedes. As Karl Marx notes, some of the benefits of capitalist
development were the end of traditional feudal relations of domination
regulating people's lives, which includes the strictures of morality. The
urbane German, of course, lived with some of the cosmopolitan benefits of
these transformations; this includes Schelling's unconventional living situation with Caroline Böhmer Schlegel, who was then wife of August Schlegel.
But these transformations, as the Romantics recognized, also denigrated
the dignity and aesthetic dimensions of nature through its exploitation. In
response, Schelling proposed the revival of the mythology, in a philosophical
form. Hence the importance of the Greeks, who in the *Letters* Schelling called
more 'natural' than the moderns, and who exhibited (or so the German
tradition thought) an organic totality in society. In the *System of Transcendental Idealism*, they are the exemplar of the infinite meaning of art:

> the mythology of the Greeks, which undeniably contains an infinite
> meaning and a symbolism for all ideas, arose among a people, and in a
> fashion, which both make it impossible to suppose any comprehensive
> forethought in devising it, or in the harmony whereby everything is united
> into one great whole. (1978: 225/III, 619–620)[19]

What Schelling did not recognize is that this image of Greek mythology was
an ideological projection of German social relations onto those of ancient

Greece (which were neither 'organic' nor autochthonic). The danger of this position lay in the potential obfuscation of the truth of art, as expressing something fundamental about human activity, and art's ideological function in mythologizing political relationships (the mythologization of these relationships as an organic community has dangerous political connotations when connected to a proto-nationalist project. We will return to this subject in Chapter 5). Nevertheless, the idea of a philosophical mythology or religion remains a constant feature within Schelling's thought, and through 1807, he held that it was the task of an artistic renewal through a new mythology. This is the *third condition* for Schelling's philosophy of art: artistic production has a socio-political task, because it aims to overcome the fragmentary condition of modernity through a new mythology and artistic renewal.

If much Schelling literature is split between interpreting him as a protean thinker endlessly shifting in his philosophy (see Fackenheim, 1996: 50–74; and Bowie, 1990: 104), or a philosopher restlessly unfolding the consequences of one fundamental intuition, I agree with the latter. Often this fundamental intuition is seen to be a commitment to explicating the uncanny character of human freedom (which, of course, must be thought with nature-philosophy), to which the former group of commentators respond by pointing out that freedom – even by Schelling's own admission – is not adequately addressed in his period of absolute philosophy. Our reading overcomes this objection by arguing that the *System of Transcendental Idealism* is in some sense a subversion of transcendental idealism insofar as it subordinates practical philosophy (and the tenet that freedom is an infinite progress toward an ideal) to an act that is, as we might say, 'more free than freedom itself': a creative or a positive freedom (to use Schelling's later terminology), an early name of which is aesthetic intuition. Aesthetic intuition and its capacity for mythological 'communitarianism,' is, for Schelling, superior to practical philosophy and the emphasis on natural rights and ethical precepts (which, I might add, can – and as I would argue in a work of a different nature, should – be read as a set of rules for governing the ownership of, and transactions of, property). Not that aesthetic intuition – or positive freedom – is immune to ideological exploitation. Whether Schelling recognized it or not, it is difficult to ignore the political motives behind his appointment to the chair in philosophy formerly occupied by Hegel (and before him Fichte) at the University of Berlin in 1841; there were royal expectations that Schelling could root out the 'dragonseed of Hegelian pantheism' and its concomitant political criticism (quoted in Matthews's introduction to Schelling, 2007a: 6). Schelling's insistence that the material crises of the 1840s were more importantly spiritual rather than material, earned him the enmity of his young Hegelian critics (such as Frederick Engels) as a kind of Prussian philosophical revanchism.[20]

Yet it is a long way from the *System of Transcendental Idealism* to Positive Philosophy. Nevertheless, Schelling's insight into the inadequacy of the Kantian-Fichtean concept of freedom is one of his important contributions to early German Idealism, presaging Hegel's criticisms of the 'bad infinity' of practical reason. In the next chapter we will continue the process of showing the continuity of Schelling's philosophy of art. Contrary to the standard interpretation, the *Philosophy of Art*, which was written and delivered as lectures during the period of absolute idealism, maintained all the important features that we introduced as the *Three Conditions* of Schelling's philosophy of art. Each condition is first established in the *System of Transcendental Idealism*:

C1. What philosophy constructs in the ideal, art produces in the real. Thus artistic activity is the highest human vocation because practical philosophy can only approximate its object, which is the moral law.

C2. While both the natural organism and the artwork embody the same identity of real and ideal, of necessity and freedom, the work of art overcomes these oppositions through the identity of conscious and unconscious production, whereas the organism's activity is unconscious.

C3. Artistic production has a socio-political task: it aims to overcome the fragmentary condition of modernity through a new mythology and artistic renewal.

While the first principle of Schelling's system changes, all three of these conditions obtain in the *Philosophy of Art*. While it is true that they are no longer guaranteed by the self's activity, the relationships between nature-, practical-, and art-philosophy are all supported through what Schelling calls a construction of the potencies. However, this is not our only interest in the *Philosophy of Art*. As we will see, these lectures propose a unique perspective on, and a unique solution to, the central problem of absolute idealism.

Chapter 4

Substance and History: Absolute Idealism and Art

4.1. The Light of 1801

After adjudicating the dispute between dogmatism and criticism, delineating a nature-philosophy, and completing, however perfunctorily, a system incorporating these concerns and those of transcendental idealism with a philosophy of art – an impressive achievement for a twenty-six-year-old, let alone for any other recent professor of philosophy at Jena – Schelling did not rest. One year after the *System of Transcendental Idealism* (1800) had been published, he was already announcing *his* system: a philosophy of absolute reason, which later came to be known as absolute idealism or 'identity-philosophy.' This system, which Schelling developed during the period from 1801–1806, holds that the differences between subjectivity and objectivity, self and world, freedom and necessity, ideal and real, and providence and fate, are all grounded on a principle of identity and absolute totality. In other words, these divisions are grounded on an absolute which encompasses all particular manifestations of reason and nature. Thus Schelling abandoned the limits of subjective idealism for the Spinozist monism of absolute idealism, wherein reason and nature are one substance. The *Darstellung meines Systems der Philosophie* of 1801 is the reflection of the fact that, as Schelling will later recall, he had seen the light of the philosophy that led beyond the limits of transcendental idealism (see the letter to Eschenmayer, dated July 30, 1805 in 2003: II, 60–62). Whereas earlier he had held the activity of the absolute self to be the first principle of philosophy, now Schelling posits identity as such. The absolute is the indifference of subject and object: both are contained within the absolute and are only partial expressions of it (which, as we saw in Chapter 3, was suggested by Schelling's parallel systems). From the perspective of reason, all particular things are contained within the absolute; all previous divisions of philosophy comprise partial expressions of the absolute world, whether as nature, history, or art.

This transformation of Schelling's metaphysics presents serious problems for interpreters of his philosophy of art. According to the standard interpretation of Schelling's philosophical development, the philosophy of art serves as an intermediary step toward the discovery of absolute idealism because, the reasoning goes, once he worked out a philosophy of the absolute, beyond the subjective idealism of transcendental philosophy, he no longer needed a philosophy of art. This argument rests on several debatable claims. The first is that Schelling's idea of the absolute stemmed from his work on the *System of Transcendental Idealism* itself, which resulted in his philosophy of art. In Chapter 1, we saw in the *Letters* (1795–1796) that Schelling presents an idea of the absolute that is neither subjective nor objective, but rather the ground of their identity. One could reply, however, that this only serves to support Schelling's claim in the *Darstellung* that he had this idea of the absolute in mind for some time before making it public in 1801 (2001b: 344/IV, 107). Furthermore, even if the claim about the *Letters* is chronologically correct, it does not explain why Schelling hesitates to introduce the absolute in other works, or at least why he subordinates the questions stemming from this principle to those of transcendental inquiry. When, for instance, in the *System of Transcendental Idealism* Schelling introduces the objection that the activity of the self has some other ground outside of consciousness, he states that the ground must be determined by self-consciousness alone, and that some questions can only be determined once the inquiry has been completed: 'Self-consciousness is the lamp of the whole system of knowledge, but it casts its light ahead only, not behind' (1978: 18/III, 357).

We introduced a stronger objection in the previous chapter: that the standard interpretation relies on a confusion between the method of transcendental idealism and what Werner Marx has called the *Bildungsgeschichte* ('history of cultivation') reading of *The System of Transcendental Idealism*, a confusion that has its basis in Schelling's later self-interpretation. The task of transcendental idealism is to demonstrate the conditions necessary for objectivity, to show how the self becomes objective; it is not, as Schelling later claims, a 'Socratic dialogue' where the reader is initiated by the 'philosophical ego' into the Elysian mysteries of philosophy (this account sounds much more like the dialogue *Bruno!*). If these two interpretations are not differentiated, it is possible to hold, ironically, a much more Hegelian interpretation of Schelling's development: that absolute idealism is an overcoming of transcendental idealism, in which the results of the philosophy of art are sublated (*aufgehoben*). Or, as one of the more recent accounts asks, how 'can we understand that art, which in the *System des transzendentalen Idealismus* is still called "the only and eternal revelation"

of the absolute, is no longer needed?' (Braeckman, 2004a: 554).[1] The problem with this interpretation is that, for Schelling, the philosophy of art is
still needed; even if absolute philosophy constructs the world as it is through
reason (and not just through subjective activity) it still requires artistic
production to present this ideal activity in the real world. As I will argue,
both transcendental idealism and absolute idealism rely on the faculty or
power (*Kraft*) of the imagination, which provides the continuity between
theoretical-, practical-, and art-philosophy, and which produces the artwork
as the real presentation of the absolute.

It should be noted, however, that not all accounts of the transition
confuse these arguments. Instead, they often relegate the philosophy of
art to a secondary significance within absolute idealism by neglect. In this
case, art is equated with subjective activity, so once the subject (self-
consciousness) is no longer the first principle, art is no longer central to
the system. Thus in their accounts of the system of identity, many of the
standard commentaries begin with the *Darstellung* and move, for a more
systematic presentation, to the *System der gesamten Philosophie und der Naturphilosophie insbesondere* (1804), better-known as the *Würzburg Lectures*.[2] Xavier
Tilliette dedicates a chapter of his two-volume work to the *Philosophy of
Art*, only to conclude that the system of art is obsolete and that the general
presentation only repeats the central problems of the system of identity
(Tilliette, 1970: I, 439–471). Rather than a justification for neglect, this
repetition should be a reason for investigation.

I argue in this chapter that (1) the philosophy of art is central to absolute
idealism (and therefore cannot be equated with subjective idealism) and
(2) that Schelling's resolution to the central problem of absolute idealism
is not redundant, but that it presents a problematic solution that he tries to
resolve later in the address *Über das Verhältnis der bildenden Künste zu der Natur*
of 1807. Both parts of my argument rest on explicating Schelling's central
difficulty: as he notes, the central task of identity-philosophy, since it does
not begin with the finite, is to demonstrate how the transition from the
infinite to the finite is possible, to show how the finite world arises within
the absolute. What drives our investigation is that the deductions of nature
found in the *Darstellung* cannot overcome the difficulties of this transition
with abstract argumentation. The *Philosophy of Art*, by contrast, provides a
unique attempt at resolving this difficulty by arguing that the determinations of art are the 'highest' presentations of the formation of the absolute
in finite form.

Hence we have Schelling's claim that the philosophy of art 'is the presentation of the absolute world in the form of art' (1989: 7/V, 350). However,

art is not just any presentation: it is the highest presentation of the absolute in the finite world because the production of artwork mediates the separation of necessity and freedom and overcomes this separation in the finished work. Therefore, artistic production is the real presentation of the identity of reason and nature, of the ideal and the real. Of course, these arguments should be familiar from the *System of Transcendental Idealism*. However, now they are extended to identity-philosophy since absolute idealism still recognizes artistic production as the real counterpart to the ideal activity of philosophy. In showing how many of the features of art found in the *System of Transcendental Idealism* are now adapted to identity-philosophy, it is possible to show how the philosophy of art maintains a privileged place in Schelling's thought.

Yet our interest is not limited to how Schelling retains the structural importance of his philosophy of art *vis-à-vis* absolute idealism in general. We are also interested in a solution to the problem of the transition from the infinite to the finite. In the *Philosophy of Art*, he proposes that the imagination acts to 'form-into-unity' or *inform* (*Ineinsbildung*) the infinite into the finite through *both* the content and the particular forms of art. In this chapter we will focus on the historical construction of the content of art in the *Philosophy of Art*, in which Schelling argues that the content of art has its basis in either Greek mythology or what he calls Christian mythology. What makes this account interesting is how the historical construction of the gods (and the Christian God) presents the polytheism of imagination and art as being at odds with the monotheism of reason (to paraphrase the 'System Program'; see Section 2.6). There is a contradiction between substance, eternal and all-encompassing, and history: while the system of identity is grounded on a Spinozistic God, the historical construction of art presents a series of revelations within history.[3] As I will argue, Schelling cannot reconcile these differences in a way that is consistent with his requirement that essence and form be identical. But if essence and form in general are the eternal substance, while the essential content is historically revealed, then history exceeds the formal structure of the philosophy of identity. Schelling will not resolve this problem until 1807, but it is crucial to see why this problem leads to (or at least contributes to) the abandonment of absolute idealism. The crux of the matter is the hypothetical form of the system.

While our approach is limited primarily to the *Darstellung* and the *Philosophy of Art*, it should be noted that Schelling's identity-philosophy is not, despite appearances, a complete relapse into Spinozist dogmatism.[4] Instead, Schelling attempts to maintain a critical approach in the justification of his system, by noting that the principle of absolute identity is a necessary pre-supposition of philosophy.[5] This critical approach is most evident in the *Würzburg Lectures*, where he provides an indirect proof of the principle of identity 'by demonstrating that knowledge remains inconceivable under any other presupposition' (1994a: 141/VI, 138). As Manfred Frank notes, however, Schelling's proofs for absolute identity remain mostly negative and that a positive concept is more elusive (Frank, 1985: 118–132; and also Beiser, 2002a: 577–582, 588–593). Frank writes: 'What, in the beginning of philosophizing, can only be a hypothesis must not in the process remain a hypothesis. In the concept of every beginning lies a lack (VIII, 352). Removing [the lack], by *proving* the hypothesis, is the motive for the development of philosophical reflection. Only at the end can what at the beginning was hypothetically established be grounded' (Frank, 1985: 122–123; the citation is provided by Frank).

Our reading of the *Philosophy of Art* puts Schelling's hypothesis to the test: the justification for the idea of absolute identity relies on the result that will show how the system forms a totality that does not contradict the iden-tity of essence and form. I will argue that Schelling's attempt to construct a philosophy of art overflows the formal structures of absolute idealism. In other words, the plenitude of art pushes Schelling to abandon the stric-tures of identity-philosophy (its 'initial hypotheses') for a more historical approach found in the address *Über das Verhältnis der bildenden Künste zu der Natur* of 1807.

4.2. The Turn to Absolute Reason

We will begin with the *Darstellung* because it outlines Schelling's break with Fichte and transcendental idealism. It is with the *Darstellung* that Schelling announces *his* system of philosophy, one that, in the preface, he says has come too soon and yet has served as the 'guide-star in both transcendental and natural philosophy' (2001b: 344/IV, 107). This philosophy of identity – his philosophy – attempts to elucidate philosophy from the standpoint of absolute reason itself, from a point indifferent to subjectivity and objectiv-ity. In a letter to Fichte dated October 3, 1801, as their debate was escalat-ing, Schelling himself indicates that this standpoint was first mentioned in his *Letters*; and as I discussed in Chapter 3, it seems to be implied in the 'Introduction' to the *System of Transcendental Idealism* (GA, III/5: 85). However, if this is correct, Schelling is left with the unenviable task of explaining why he kept the ground of his system in the shadows. To this question he replies that his previous work served as a propaedeutic, a 'preparation for the integral reception of this philosophy' (2001b: 334/IV, 107).

From the standpoint of the *Darstellung*, it would seem that Schelling's previous goal was to exhaust the possibilities of transcendental idealism – to expose its inner problems – as a path to absolute idealism. As I have argued, the task of the *System of Transcendental Idealism* consists in subordinating Fichte's practical philosophy to a higher principle, which is aesthetic intuition. Yet, despite the assertive tone of the *Darstellung*, Schelling does not yet directly confront Fichte, stating that 'I think it is impossible that we not eventually come to agreement, even if now, at least in my opinion, this point has not been reached' (2001b: 346/IV, 110). It is Hegel's essay *The Difference Between Fichte's and Schelling's System of Philosophy* (1801) that made their break public. Until then Schelling had remained optimistic about reconciling their positions, although he seems to have misjudged Fichte, who seems only to be able to read Schelling as a disciple and not as an equal. Then again, Schelling's confidence is a foregone conclusion of the system itself: regardless of the possessive description of the system, the *Darstellung* argues that reason, and hence a philosophical system, is universally valid beyond the contingencies of the individuals who do philosophy.

However, while Fichte saw that the *Wissenschaftslehre* was troubled by the problem of accounting for the intelligible world, he would not – since he did not develop a system like Schelling's – recognize how Schelling arrived at the system of identity-philosophy.[6] As suggested in the *System of Transcendental Idealism*, neither transcendental philosophy nor nature-philosophy can ground the standpoint from which they can be presented as parallel constructions within a larger system capable of grounding the principles of subject and object (although in that text Schelling states that it should be possible for transcendental idealism to do so. See 1978: 2–3/III, 331). Both transcendental philosophy and nature-philosophy cannot grasp the absolute as identity between subject and object, and, while this identity is represented in art-philosophy, it is difficult to ascertain the discourse from which it becomes possible to articulate this identity of the absolute, unless it is already the discourse of philosophy itself. If one starts from the subject alone – or the object alone – as the standpoint of thinking, one cannot grasp the absolute totality of reason. Schelling states, as a 'possibility,' that Fichte is confined to the standpoint of subjective idealism, which is constrained to an epistemology based on reflection, and thus cannot reach the perilous heights of the absolute. Fichte does begin with the law of identity

(A=A) as the first principle of philosophy, but in the *Wissenschaftslehre*, he holds that this principle is regulative: although identity is the basis of the system, posited as an act of the self, it can only be justified practically (see Section 1.3). The absolute activity of the self is mediated by the not-self. The first section of the *Wissenschaftslehre* presents a contradiction that the remainder of the work attempts to resolve: that the self posits itself as determining the not-self, and that the self posits itself as determined by the not-self. Fichte argues that theoretical philosophy cannot resolve this contradiction between the demand that the self determines the external world and that the finite self necessarily feels itself limited within the world. In the practical part of the *Wissenschaftslehre*, he attempts to resolve the contradiction between self and not-self with a philosophy of striving, with the imperative that the self *ought* to act in such a way that is in conformity with itself.

With the *Darstellung*, Schelling no longer conceives of the absolute as a self, nor does he conceive of it as a regulative ideal. His explicit model becomes Spinoza, who he says 'came nearest my system in terms of content or material and in form' (2001b: 348/IV, 113). Of course, this raises the question: which Spinoza? As we have seen, Schelling's use of Spinoza has never been clear and consistent. In the *Letters*, we were confronted with a dogmatic Spinoza who begins from the first principle of the Object and whose thought both interprets the world through mechanism, and also proposes an ethic of the intellectual love of God. In the *Ideas*, we discovered a Spinoza who first glimpsed a monistic principle grounding the dualism of thought and being, who held to the doctrine of the attributes. And then, in the *First Outline*, a Spinoza whose importance resides in correctly interpreting nature as both producing (*natura naturans*) and product (*natura naturata*).

The shift from subjective idealism to absolute idealism is the shift from the self-producing *Ich* to the Spinozist idea of productive nature (*natura naturans*). This is the point of distinction between Fichte and Schelling that Hegel forced: Fichte exhibits 'nature as an absolute effect and as dead' (1977a: 143) while Schelling grounds his system in living nature. For Schelling, the absolute can be intellectually intuited because it is the identity of reason and nature.

As we have seen, this position is not without precedent, although in partial form: the *First Outline* had suggested that reason could be a 'mere play of higher and necessarily unknown natural forces' (2004a: 194–195/ III, 273–274), while in the *Allgemeine Deduktion des dynamischen Prozesses* (1800) Schelling concludes that 'nature-philosophy gives a physical explanation of idealism' (IV, 76). We should nevertheless be careful with interpreting the natural basis of the system: the distinction between subjective idealism and absolute idealism concerns the relationship between reason and nature. So, if for Fichte (and Kant), reason is something that the subject imposes on nature, or, strictly speaking, something that the subject can only know as an imposition on nature as a regulative ideal, for Schelling, as an absolute idealist, reason operates within nature, or, reason is identified with nature (in the Spinozist sense of *Deus, sive natura*). He attempts to generate both reason and nature from the principle of identity. This task has been the source of much confusion since its inception. As a contemporary of his writes, 'Schelling is reproached with almost always being in suspense between idealism, realism, and even materialism' (quoted in Vater's introduction to Schelling, 1984: 55). The confusion arises from the most difficult part of the system of identity: the transition from the infinite to the finite. This was, for Schelling, the central difficulty of Spinoza's system, and it is no less difficult for absolute idealism. In 1805, he begins his *Aphorismen zur Einleitung in die Naturphilosophie* with the statement that 'There is no higher revelation either in science, in religion or art than that of the divinity of the Whole' (VII, 140). I differ with several recent interpretations of Schelling's absolute idealism (particularly Grant, 2008): while I agree that nature-philosophy is the basis of his absolute idealism, I find it difficult to give a univocal meaning to Schelling's idea of nature. We might say that Schelling leaves reason in suspense: the hypothesis that reason and nature are the same must be explained by unifying all particular forms under this identity; then this identity becomes the ground of the system and not its guiding light. The question is how this unification takes place. Where nature-philosophy as a kind of 'speculative physics' is central to the *Darstellung*, it becomes one part of the larger totality presented in the *Philosophy of Art*. This should not be surprising considering Schelling is attempting to show the unity that grounds the diversity of finite forms.

In the *Darstellung*, the transcendental framework of Schelling's previous work is jettisoned in favor of constructing proofs through axioms, remarks, and corollaries, even if the preface proceeds with some pretense of pursuing a transcendental inquiry into the possibility of subjectivity and objectivity. It should be noted that Schelling's use of the terms 'subject' and 'object' is ambiguous: in the preface, he claims to be grounding the parallel systems of transcendental idealism and nature-philosophy (and their parallel first principles) in a system of identity or absolute reason, but in the deductions and proofs themselves, he is talking about individuals as ideal or real potencies (that is, as emerging from the absolute as particular and finite beings).

Despite the architectonic ambiguity for the system itself, it becomes clear that Schelling draws from Spinoza's doctrine of the attributes: that the absolute is one, although it is expressed in ideal or real terms. Schelling, then, does not proceed from the Object as a first principle, nor does he interpret the world through the concept of mechanism. Instead, the standpoint of absolute reason is indifference [*Indifferenz*].

As stated in the opening paragraph of the *Darstellung*, Schelling defines absolute reason as the 'total indifference of the subjective and objective' (2001b: 349/IV, 114). So 'absolute reason,' which he claims is identical to the totality of the universe, is total indifference, but we are no closer to what indifference is. Our examination of the *Darstellung*, then, must focus on the concept of indifference and then on the relationship between indifference and finitude (as subjectivity or objectivity). This first paragraph provides us with several negative definitions of indifference: it is not subjective, thus neither a psychological state[7] nor limited by finitude of subjectivity; it is not objective, conceived as succession, mechanism, or externality.[8] The problem for Schelling is to define indifference 'positively,' aside from a totality that includes, but is not identical to, subject and object. To state this in another way, even if Schelling can show that indifference, or the absolute, includes subject and object but is not identical to them, he must still show how finitude arises within it. To do this, he will introduce a theory of 'potencies' which express the quantitative difference of finite beings as predominately ideal or real. As I will argue, despite introducing a dynamic physics within his neo-Spinozist system, he cannot demonstrate the transition from the infinite to the finite, which will be addressed in a different manner in Schelling's *Philosophy of Art*.

Let us continue with the *Darstellung*. As totality, Schelling argues, there can be nothing outside the absolute; that is, there can be no qualitative difference between the absolute and the finite. Recall that the categories of quality include reality, negation, and limitation. While the absolute is real, it can neither be negated nor limited in its being if it is to be absolute (2001b: 360/IV, 130).[9] Instead, Schelling argues that the ground of finitude is quantitative difference (unity, plurality, and totality), and he calls this difference an individual's potency (*Potenz*). Like many of the other terms he attempts to define in this premier text of the system of identity, he struggles with a clear definition of potency as well, describing it as an individual's '*amount* of being' or '*magnitude* of being' [*Größe des Seyns*] (2001b: 355/IV, 123). Each individual shows a predominance of either subjectivity or objectivity (or, in other terms, ideality or reality) but never only one (because the central question of the inquiry is explaining the relationship between these terms). Schelling designates, in distinction to the law of identity (which is A=A), potency as A=B, where A is the cognizing principle and B is the real principle. As finite ('A=B is generally the expression of finitude'), a potency contains both a relative unity and quantitative difference. Schelling writes:

> Since A is the cognizing principle, while B, as we shall discover, is what is intrinsically unlimited or infinite extension, we have here quite precisely both the Spinozistic attributes of absolute substance, thought and extension. We do not merely think these attributes are identical ideally (*idealiter*), as people commonly understand Spinoza, we think them completely identical in reality (*realiter*) [. . .] Thought and extension are thus never separated in anything, not even in thought and in extension, but are without exception together and identical. (2001b: 364/IV, 136)

Hence it is clear that Schelling holds that reason and nature are identical, although he does not give this identity a univocal meaning. It is formulations like these that prevent us from deciding whether Schelling, like Spinoza, naturalizes thought or idealizes nature. This problem is especially acute because in his later works the ideal expressions of the absolute, such as artistic production and religion, proliferate. Giving one priority seems to violate his doctrine that substance be thought as both *actually* ideal and real. With this problem of monism, he encounters another problem that he had already found in Spinoza: the transition from the infinite to the finite.

Schelling holds that the absolute admits of no qualitative or quantitative difference whatsoever, but also that individuals differ according to their magnitude of being (their potency). To resolve this contradiction, he argues that subjectivity and objectivity are posited in opposite tendencies, which consequently means that for each predominately subjective potency is counterbalanced by one that is predominantly objective. He states that the absolute's 'form of being can thus be universally conceived through the image of a line':

$$\frac{\overset{+}{A=B} \qquad \overset{+}{A=B}}{A=A}$$

In this line, one tendency (+A = B) proceeds toward the subjective while the other (A = B+) proceeds toward the objective, both being grounded in the indifference of the absolute (2001b: 365/IV, 137). This is the basic model of the potencies and their relationship to the absolute. Additionally, each potency contains both a relative identity and a relative difference, so each potency is, in its existence, isomorphic to the absolute.[10]

This dynamic account of potencies is Schelling's attempt to maintain Spinoza's monism while dispensing with the latter's dependency on mechanism.[11] However, the lack of a concept for the qualitative difference between infinity and finitude forces Schelling to argue that quantitative differences are nothing but appearances (*phenomena*) and not *noumena*; that is, differentiation *appears* to the subject from the standpoint of reflection (2001b: 357/ IV, 126). This stance leads Alan White to note that Schelling's system of identity is 'as homogenous and undifferentiated as the Parmenidean one':

> While opposition is thus beneath the system of identity, differentiation cannot be, or no system would be possible, for there could be no systematic content. Yet if the absolute exists at all, Schelling insists, there must be content: while the essence of the absolute is undifferentiated identity, the form in which the absolute exists is an identity of distinct elements; the absolute exists as identity only if it is the identity *of* something. (White, 1983: 77; and Schelling, 2001b: 353–354/IV, 120–121)[12]

According to White, it appears that all differences are swallowed up by the absolute. And yet, at the same time, others have argued that Schelling's concept of potency provides a conceptual basis for the plenitude within the totality. As Valerio Verra notes,

> Each idea incarnates all the others, not in an indifferent and interchangeable fashion, but following an ascending order of 'potentialization' that culminates in absolute identity, an identity, however, which is not empty, but rich in articulations, tensions and differences. Such a point of view makes it understood that the relationship of the universal and particular becomes more rich, more complex and more concrete than the simple logical or reflected distinction between concept and intuition. (1979: 38)

While the *Darstellung* struggles to account for the finite content, as it were, of the potencies, and the infinity of the absolute, the *Philosophy of Art* will utilize a more developed conceptual vocabulary in the attempt to reconcile the whole and its parts. The promise, at the end of the *Darstellung* to develop truth and beauty as 'highest expressions of indifference' (IV, 212), is fulfilled in the lectures collected as the *Philosophy of Art*.

4.3. The Relationship between Art and the Absolute

The *Philosophy of Art*, which is based on lectures given in Jena in 1802–1803, and then in Würzburg in 1804–1805, is an underappreciated work in Schelling's *oeuvre*. As Jean-François Marquet notes, Schelling stated that the lectures later collected under this title should not be published with the exception of the section on tragedy, advice which was not taken by his son and editor after Schelling's death. This is a fortunate turn of events, because without the *Philosophy of Art* we would lack an important link between the *System of Transcendental Idealism* and his turn away from absolute idealism found in *Über das Verhältnis der bildenden Künste zu der Natur* of 1807 (1979: 75).[13]

When the *Philosophy of Art* has not been overlooked, it is sometimes criticized for its lack of originality. Surprisingly, one of the more disparaging readings comes from Xavier Tilliette, who is usually a more discerning critic. Tilliette finds the text limited in its scope, hastily composed, and reliant on the work of others such as Schiller, Hölderlin, Goethe, and Moritz (1970: I, 444–445). Tilliette's central disappointment seems to come from Schelling's subordination of mythology to the purposes of the philosophy of art (1970: I, 449). Overall, Tilliette finds very little of interest in Schelling's presentation of the absolute in the form of art.[14]

I propose, by contrast, that the *Philosophy of Art* is an important step in Schelling's development. While it is true that his text borrows from his contemporaries, Schelling does so because he is doing much more than constructing a critique of taste, an empirical theory of art, or an aesthetics; Schelling is constructing a philosophy of art by extracting artistic *ideas* from the multiplicity of art.[15] This means that the philosophy of art is not just a philosophical approach to a particular object, like a philosophy of the vehicles or a philosophy of agriculture, but art is worthy of philosophy because it has something to present of the absolute (1989: 14/V, 365).

Schelling begins by asking how a philosophy of art is possible. Ultimately, it is possible because art presents the absolute in sensible form. As Schelling states, the philosophy of art 'is the presentation of the absolute world in the form of art' (1989: 7/V, 350). While these kinds of statements are similar to those found in the *System of Transcendental Idealism*, Schelling no longer has the 'history of self-consciousness' to justify the philosophy of art. Recall that transcendental idealism follows the activity of the self as it strives to produce the absolute, which ultimately results in the production of the work of art through aesthetic intuition. The metaphysics of identity-philosophy dispenses with what Schelling now calls subjective idealism, although he

argues in the 'Further Presentations from the System of Philosophy' that
the *System of Transcendental Idealism* sketches the 'general framework of construction, whose schematism must also be the foundation of the completed
system' (2001a: 396/IV, 410). Schelling's absolute idealism will maintain
the schematism through his use of the potencies without reference to the
activity of the self. The construction of the absolute relies on the power of
the intellectual intuition of reason itself.

In the *Philosophy of Art*, the problem of this relationship can be resolved
in two interrelated steps: the first is to determine the place of art in the
system; the second is to determine why this relationship obtains. As in the
System of Transcendental Idealism, Schelling identifies three domains of
philosophy: nature-philosophy, the philosophy of history, and the philosophy of art (1989: 15/V, 367; 1989: 29/V, 382), which correspond respectively to a predominance of the real (as knowledge), a predominance of
the ideal (as action), and their indifference (as art). These divisions also
obtain as Ideas: Truth,[16] the Good, and Beauty.[17] Thus, for Schelling, to
explain art from the standpoint of understanding (or from the standpoint
of morality) reverses the order of the potencies: a proper appreciation of
art requires explaining beauty by something superior; it requires what we
have already noted as the construction of the philosophy of art. Though art
is the highest potency of the ideal, only philosophy in general can deduce
truth, virtue (*Sittlichkeit*), and beauty from a common source, because philosophy in general explicates the rational structure of the absolute itself.[18]

Now that we have sketched out the systematic relationship between art
and philosophy in general, we come to the much more difficult problem:
why, and how, does this relationship obtain? Schelling's argument is not the
most straightforward, but it hinges on several crucial concepts, drawn from
a vocabulary that he develops after the *Darstellung: Einbildungskraft, Ineinsbildung*, and the opposition between *Urbild* and *Gegenbild.* This vocabulary is
largely developed because Schelling cannot rely on the traditional philosophical vocabulary of representation. The most obvious example of his critique of reflection can be seen in Schelling's use of 'presentation' (*Darstellung*
and its cognates) to describe the embodiment of the absolute in the finite,
in contrast to 'representation' (*Vorstellung*). To take up *ideally* the infinite
from the particular is what Schelling calls construction, which happens not
through the understanding (the faculty of representation), but through
reason itself. Philosophy is interested in art 'only to the extent that it takes
up the entire absolute within itself and presents [*darstellt*] it in itself' (1989:
15tm/V, 367). Philosophy constructs a philosophy of art by intuiting the
universal within the particular, by extracting the ideas of art from the

sensible presentation. Construction is the determination of the '*one* and undivided whole of philosophy in its various *potencies* or from the viewpoint of various ideal determinations' (1989: 14tm/V, 365).[19] Therefore, the choice of 'representation' by the translator of the English edition is misleading. To translate '*Darstellung*' as representation implicitly contravenes Schelling's order of potencies, which progress from knowledge (the standpoint of the understanding), to action (*praxis*), to art (the indifference of the two) (1989: 28/V, 380).

Less problematic is the term *Einbildungskraft*, the imagination, which Schelling defines as the act that realizes, in the concise formulation of Orrin F. Summerell, 'the *unification* of the disparate and the *information* of the formless' (2004: 89). Schelling states that *Einbildungskraft* 'means the power of *mutual informing into unity* (*Ineinsbildung*) upon which all creation is really based' (1989: 31–32/V, 386). The importance of imagination within the system of identity becomes clearer when contrasted with the activity of construction. The latter is the *ideal* intuition of the universal in the particular; in the terms of the *Philosophy of Art*, to intuit the archetype in the particular. Hence construction is the central task of philosophy qua science of reason. Imagination is the *real* counterpart of construction: the informing (*Ineinsbildung*) of the infinite into the finite, whereby the ideal becomes predominantly real. Imagination is the process in which reason is grasped as sensible intellection. Summerell summarizes why art is the highest potency, the highest determination of particular things:

> The imagination is, then, not simply one faculty among others; it is instead for Schelling the capacity which underlies everything in its being, the very dynamic of the absolute itself as the identity conditioning all opposition. Viewed in this sense, imagination is the creative force of identity, the identifying of identity. In the work of art as a product of imagination, then, identification is concretely at work in displaying the original determination of things as what they actually are. (Summerell, 2004: 89)[20]

The role of imagination challenges the common interpretation that Schelling discarded or demoted the role of artistic production in the transition between the *System of Transcendental Idealism* and absolute idealism (see Sections 3.1 and 3.4). Just as the final division of the *System of Transcendental Idealism* revealed the productive imagination (aesthetic intuition) as the basis of the continuity of the 'history of self-consciousness,' the system of absolute idealism holds imagination to be the highest determination (potency) of finite things. The flaw in the earlier system was not aesthetic intuition, but subjective idealism; the role of artistic production/creation is maintained as the real counterpart to philosophy (for Schelling, whether it is 1800 or 1803, art is the *real* counterpart to intellectual intuition). The imagination forms the basis of determination; it renders determination possible as knowledge or action, and it presents the identity of the real and ideal, or the identity of freedom and necessity. The 'organic work of nature' also presents the indifference of the real and ideal, but the organism does not present the relationship as an antithesis.[21] The artwork is superior to the organism because it surpasses (*aufgehoben*) the separation of freedom and nature, informing them into a totality.[22] Far from being a mere artifice, Schelling argues that, as the informing of the infinite into a unity of freedom and necessity, art is the real presentation of 'forms of things as those things are in themselves' (1989: 32/V, 387).

This argument, however, returns us to the division between the infinite and the finite, between reason and imagination, between the absolute and the multiplicity within it. Is it not the case, the objection would proceed, that Schelling is holding that both finitude is *appearance* (just as in the *Darstellung* of 1801) and now, as a product of imagination, a thing as it is *in itself*? Is this not a contradiction? We should concede that this remains a difficulty for Schelling, but note that the temporary solution in the *Philosophy of Art* is that each particular thing is a universe within itself: 'there can be no particular things within the True universe except to the extent that they take up the entire undivided universe into themselves, and are thus themselves universes' (1989: 33tm/V, 388–389).[23] Where the *Darstellung* pursued a Spinozist *more geometrico* in its deductions, the *Philosophy of Art* relies on a combination of Neoplatonism (with the archetypes) and Leibnizian monadology (that each particular thing is a 'universe unto itself'). His Neo-Platonic answer leads us to the conceptual pair of *Urbild-Gegenbild*.

The products, as it were, of construction and imagination correspond to Schelling's opposition of *Urbild* and *Gegenbild*. The archetype (*Urbild*) is constructed by philosophy as enduring form, and it is presented as a particular through artistic production as *Gegenbild*.[24] As Schelling states, philosophy is the immediate presentation of reason as such and art is the immediate presentation of 'indifference as such' (1989: 29/V, 381). *Gegenbild* is a difficult term to translate without relating it to reflection. The translator of the English edition chose 'reflected image,' but, as I mentioned above regarding *Darstellung*, this translation introduces ambiguities into Schelling's critique of reflection as the standpoint of philosophy. While this point has been overlooked in English commentaries, it has been debated by the French commentators.[25] Literally, the term could be translated as 'counter image' or 'reflected image,' but following Marquet's example, I will suggest the term 'perfected image.'[26] This has some basis in one of Schelling's brief arguments for the superiority of art as the highest potency. To paraphrase: the degree of reality or perfection increases to the extent that it approaches its own absolute idea, and art, despite its finitude, has the most immediate relationship to the idea as the information of beauty. Thus art is the perfected image (1989: 29/V, 381–382). This is not, however, merely a translation issue: Schelling's terminological choices reflect his difficulty in unifying his system. No matter the translation, it strikes me that *Gegenbild* is a general placeholder for the two modalities of the presentation of the absolute in the form of art, according to whether the artwork is ancient or modern.

Before proceeding to the relationship between ancient and modern art, we should pause to note that we have completed our reconstruction of Schelling's philosophy of art in general. We have established the basic foundation of the philosophy of art as it is included within identity-philosophy. After the construction of the philosophy of art in general, Schelling offers a historical construction of the content of art and a deduction of the particular forms of art. In the remainder of this chapter, we will focus on the historical content of art, which is derived from Greek mythology and Christian mythology. The deduction of the particular forms will be discussed in Section 5.2.

It is in the historical construction of the mythological content of art that a contradiction between the monotheism of reason and the polytheism of imagination appears. This is not to suggest that Greek mythology is identified with polytheism and Christianity with monotheism and reason, but that Schelling grounds identity-philosophy in a Spinozistic God, while also providing a historical construction of the content of art as a mixture of 'living' gods, as it were, a mixture of Greek deities and Christian revelation. That the lecture *Über das Verhältnis der bildenden Künste zu der Natur* (1807) collapses these distinctions between art and philosophy in general – in content and form – is the clearest proof that Schelling has abandoned the foundations of absolute idealism. Thus, we will focus on the historical construction of the mythological content of art within absolute idealism, and the highest expression of art, which is Greek tragedy. In the next chapter, in order to demonstrate Schelling's abdication of identity-philosophy, we will compare the real series of the *Philosophy of Art* (music-painting-sculpture) with the deduction of the plastic arts found in the *Münchener Rede* of 1807.

4.4. The Gods of Art

To establish the contradiction between identity-philosophy and historical construction we will begin with the monotheism of reason, or, the first principle of absolute idealism. While Schelling has replaced the neutral name of the absolute with 'God,' this God of reason is still Spinozistic. The terminology has changed from the *Darstellung* but the essence/form has remained the same: God is the indifference of the real and ideal, a simultaneous self-affirmation and being affirmed. However, 'affirmation' does not make God a personal God because, as indifference, God is neither conscious nor unconscious, neither free nor necessary (1989: 23–24/V, 373–374). As already mentioned, these divisions and differences require a separation within the totality and only form a relative unity and not an absolute unity. God is absolute unity, and as Schelling states later while discussing Dante, the ultimate revelation of *Paradiso* is 'the vision of the colorless, pure substance of the deity itself' (1989: 246/V, 162). So Schelling has yet to bring forth the personal God in the center of the system: he is right to claim in the *Philosophical Investigations into the Essence of Human Freedom* that freedom, good and evil, and personality had not yet been considered (2006: 4/VII, 334), because identity-philosophy (excepting, he says, *Philosophy and Religion* of 1804) retained a Spinozist God.[27]

This distinction is important because the transition from the infinite to the finite should follow the identity of essence and form. Yet, for Schelling, it does not: the separation of Greek antiquity from Christianity and the closure of antiquity in Christian revelation produces a disjunction that is not overcome within the system. While Schelling holds that the transition from one to the other can be understood as a shift in the predominance from the real to the ideal, this cannot explain the closure of the world of antiquity, which can no longer be actual, and the beginning of historical time in Christianity. Furthermore, these changes cannot be reconciled with the eternity of Spinozist substance. This will lead, as we will see in the next chapter, to the abandonment of the formal structure of identity-philosophy.

Nevertheless, without resolving these tensions, we will attempt to provide the strongest account that the *Philosophy of Art* offers. Schelling elides the problem between substance and history (or, the neutral absolute and an inchoate, positive system [Marquet, 2006: 253]) through his 'monadology,' in which he argues that a particular thing is its own universe within the True universe, and to the extent that things are both particular and a totality to themselves, they can be considered as ideas (1989: 33/V, 388–389). These ideas viewed as real, through being informed by art, are the gods. Recall the distinction between *Urbild/Gegenbild*: 'What ideas are for philosophy, the gods are for art' (1989: 35/V, 390).

Hence the gods are the realization of the ideas of reason, which form a totality of a world. This realization will be unique for both Greek mythology and Christianity. Greek mythology is, for Schelling, a symbol of the absolute, while Christianity presents an allegory of the absolute. That Greek mythology has assumed a great importance in his work can be seen in comparison with his brief remarks found in the conclusion of the *Allgemeine Übersicht* (*Survey*) of 1798, where he states that 'Greek mythology was . . . originally nothing other than a historical schema of nature' (I, 472; see also Section 2.6). Thus the conceptual shift from mythology as schema to mythology as symbol is illuminating. Schema, allegory, and symbol are the three modes of presentation made possible by the imagination: schematism is the intuition of the particular in the universal, allegory is the intuition of the universal in the particular, and the symbolic is the synthesis of particular and universal *in the real* (1989: 46/V, 407). So, in contrast to the *Survey*, Schelling now holds that 'it would be impossible to comprehend mythology . . . simply as a schematism of nature' (1989: 47/V, 408). Literally, mythology is a symbol (*Sinnbild*: 'sense-meaning/image') of the absolute: the gods have meaning in their being, 'by simply *being* as they are without any reference to anything else . . . [they] allow the meaning itself to be dimly visible' (1989: 49/V, 411). The presentation of absolute indifference is only possible symbolically; what is True of the gods is True of the ideas. From there, an entire set of analogies follow: just as the ideas follow from one another, so do the gods arise through a theogony of procreation (§36); just as reason is neither conscious nor unconscious, nor is mythology intentional (§42); just as reason is the indifference of freedom and nature, Greek mythology brings 'nature itself back to us in art' (§42, 1989: 51/V, 415).

Because Greek mythology presents a totality of symbols of the ideas, Schelling holds that the Greeks also possessed the highest manifestations of art: they were exemplary in both sculpture and tragedy, the former presenting the indifference of the real, and the latter the indifference of the ideal. In tragedy, as a presentation of indifference, freedom and necessity are viewed as they are in reason: 'That this guilty person, who after all only succumbed to the superior power of fate, nevertheless is punished, was necessary precisely in order to show the triumph of freedom, and was the recognition of freedom and the honor due to it' (1989: 253/V, 696–697; cf. 1980: 193/I, 336–337). Schelling himself reminds us that this was the account given already in the *Letters*, but this elides a crucial difference.

There, the measure of tragedy is practical philosophy and the demand is that freedom be the highest principle of *praxis*. Because the hero eventually succumbs to fate, tragedy cannot provide a system of ethics for mere mortals, only 'a race of titans, and . . . without this presupposition, it would turn out to be utterly detrimental to humanity' (1980: 194/I, 338). Thus, in conclusion, Schelling states that Greek tragedy could not reconcile freedom and necessity.

In the *Philosophy of Art*, however, tragedy is the highest symbol of the absolute indifference of freedom and necessity. Tragedy, in its performance, literally enacts (produces or presents: *darstellen*) the identity of freedom and necessity. Schelling rejects Aristotle's thesis that misfortune befalls the tragic hero due to some error in his or her actions. Instead, Schelling argues that the highest possible misfortune is 'to become guilty without genuine guilt' through fate (1989: 252/V, 694–695). Yet tragedy would not be adequate to its idea if this were the only necessary condition: fate must also be subordinated to the hero's 'sublime' disposition, which is realized in the voluntary acceptance of being punished for an involuntary transgression (1989: 254/V, 698). It is no coincidence that Oedipus is a central figure in Schelling's account because despite his 'unmerited guilt' he pursues the consequences of fate at the cost of his own dignity and life. Finally, after a predominance of fate, and then free action, tragedy also requires an inner reconciliation to complete it as a work. So, in *Oedipus at Colonus*, Sophocles brings about the 'inner reconciliation' of harmony, an equilibrium between freedom and fate, when Oedipus disappears from the eyes of mortals (1989: 258/V, 703–704). Taken in Schelling's strict sense, the essence of tragedy is the symbol of the restoration of indifference.

Peter Szondi is right to claim that with Schelling there is a shift from a poetics of tragedy, inaugurated by Aristotle, to a philosophy of tragedy. With a poetics, one takes as an object the elements of successful tragedy, while with Schelling, one explicates the idea of tragedy (Szondi, 2002: 1). For Schelling, Aristotle views tragedy from the mimetic play of pity and fear without uncovering the cause, which is the idea. It is not the combination of poetic elements but the realization of the identity of freedom and fate that makes tragedy sublime. If tragedy reaches these sublime heights, it is because it presents the perfected image of the absolute in a public and ritual event, wherein the identity of freedom and necessity is embodied (like sculpture, he says) in the finite.[28]

Yet Schelling does not draw nostalgic consequences from this account of Greek tragedy. Instead, he interprets this totality of Greek mythology and its embodiment in drama as a harbinger of the future. Thus we can see why he finds mythology attractive: the harmony of the Greek world points toward the possibility of the future reconciliation of all the divisions that mark modernity.[29] Like the *System of Transcendental Idealism*, Schelling writes that the poesy of mythology is the 'primal matter from which all else issued, the ocean, to use an image the ancients themselves used, from which all rivers flow out and to which all flow back' (1989: 52/V, 416). This reconciliation he calls providence.[30] The shift from the nature (the real) to the ideal (freedom) presents an 'odyssey of human consciousness that unfolds according to a schema analogous to that of the metamorphoses of art' (Marquet, 2006: 266). This history of human consciousness separates out its freedom from nature in Christianity along with the promise of a return to the harmony of the mythology of the future.[31] Hence antiquity becomes a part of an eschatology, wherein to account for the history of modern art, Schelling historicizes all art, without reconciling this history with the ground of the system, the absolute substance. As we will see, where Greek antiquity possessed a unity of mythology and art, modern art is oriented toward the *demand* to create a new mythology. This new mythology, I will argue, is neither Greek, nor Christian, but a reconciliation of the two.

Christianity arises in the decline of antiquity, what Schelling calls the fall of the natural world, and it is distinguished from Greek mythology by the predominance of the idea and a spirit of universality.[32] The antithesis is clearer when Schelling argues that for the Greeks the universe is intuited as nature, while for Christianity the universe is intuited as a moral world, the Kingdom of God (1989: 61/V, 430). When Greek mythology was grounded in the informing of the infinite into the finite form of the gods, Christianity is grounded on informing the finite into an allegory of the infinite.

As we have seen, the intuition of the universal in the particular is allegorical, whereby the particular signifies the universal. Hence the importance of the figure of Christ in Christianity: through Christ's embodiment of the infinite, his sacrifice and his resurrection, the finite is nullified and overcome. Christ simultaneously closes the world of the ancient gods and marks the transcendence of the ideal world over the real world, thereby reversing the relationship between the natural world and the ideal world. This reversal and revelation opens a universal history by closing the particularity and finitude of antiquity and bringing forth the anticipation of future redemption. No longer is the finite the symbol of the infinite:

In Christ it is rather the finite that is symbolized by the infinite than the latter by the former. Christ returns to the supersensible world and promises not himself but rather the spirit, and not the principle that will

enter into and abide in the finite but the ideal principle that is to lead
all of the finite into and to the infinite. (1989: 64/V, 432)

Thus Christ cannot be interpreted as a symbol in his *being*, he essentially
lacks the finitude of the symbolic, unlike the Greek gods who contained
their meaning in their being. Instead, Christian symbolism is embodied
entirely in action and the church. The liturgy of the church gave body to
Christian doctrine, making its 'cult a living work of art, a kind of spiritual
drama in which each member had a part' (1989: 65/V, 434).

However, Schelling struggles with the relationship between mythology,
the Catholic Church, and the 'historical necessity' of the Protestant Church.
He argues that only Catholicism 'lived in a mythological world' but speaks
of this mythology in the past tense (1989: 72/V, 443). While his discussion
of Protestantism is curt, he does acknowledge that its institution gave new
impetus to free thought and invention. It is notable that Schelling mentions that this new impetus took up the 'spirit of classical antiquity' which
implies an impulse to the natural or real principle, although it did not
develop. What did develop was sectarianism. Whither the destiny of Protestantism, though, Schelling's interpretation still implies, albeit politely,
that its emergence has its ground in the decline of the mythological potential of Catholicism. The division of Christianity through the Reformation
forecloses on mythology, and if this is the case, any use of mythology
degenerates into formality (1989: 73/V, 444).

It appears, then, that modernity leaves Schelling nostalgic, that he finds,
by the measure of the possibilities offered for mythology, the ancient world
to be superior to the modern. This image of Schelling's thought, however,
does not take full account of the philosophy of art as a totality. I cannot
agree with Joseph P. Lawrence's verdict that in the 'Christian era it becomes
progressively clearer that art cannot serve as an adequate medium for the
absolute' (1988: 13). Instead, I think Schelling's entire argument is that, to
paraphrase Lawrence, 'in the modern era it becomes progressively clearer
that Christian art cannot serve as an adequate medium for the absolute'
because the one-sided development of an ideal mythology withdraws from
nature and renders it a mystery. So Schelling interprets the transformations
of modernity as a *spiritual* or *religious* crisis. All the conflicts of the modern
world arise from Christianity.[33] Schelling is advocating a renewal of a sense
of public liturgy beyond either Catholicism, Protestantism, or the Deism of
the Enlightenment (see also Williamson, 2004: 60–71). What is required to
resolve this crisis is the reconciliation of the ideal and real principles, or,
in mythological terms, the re-divinization of nature and the naturalization

of the gods. To this *demand*, Schelling sets out a prescriptive diagnosis for the future of art. First, Schelling argues, it is imperative that the individual artist creates from his or her individuality a partial mythology, a work of art which, second, reconciles all the aspects of the artist's era: its history, science, and poetry.

As Schelling states, the necessary law of modern poesy is 'that the individual form that part of the world revealed to him into a whole, and from the subject matter of his own age, its history, and its science, create his own mythology' (1989: 240tm/V, 154; see also 1989: 73/V, 444). In this regard, the individual artist (or poet) must now create what was once the material of the collectivity. In the face of change and transformation, the task of the poet is to create enduring forms out of the fragmentary nature of modernity, to create totality *ex nihilo*. Thus the law of modern poesy requires originality in the combination of the various elements of poetry, history, and science to craft a singular mythology. In a sense, Christianity already provides the form of this law by showing the finite to be transitory, by creating from the finite an allegory of the totality. The fragments, however, must take on a symbolic quality within the totality.

One embodiment of modern poesy in this regard is the novel, which absorbs the various materials of an age to create a totality. Formally, the novel transforms the fragmentary into a totality through narration; it forms from the indifference of prose its own internal rhythm. All the aspects of the age can be utilized to craft a unified narrative, where out of fragments an organic totality is portrayed. The novel, Schelling claims, 'should be a mirror of the world, or at least of the age, and thus become a partial mythology' (1989: 232/V, 676). With such a standard, Schelling claims that 'there have been only two novels': *Don Quixote* and *Wilhelm Meister's Apprenticeship* (1989: 234/V, 679). As partial mythologies, each is the mirror of its age: *Don Quixote* possesses, Schelling states, a universality that draws on 'all the romantic principles extant in Europe' at the time (1989: 235/V, 680), while *Wilhelm Meister* portrays the effort required to unify the 'fragmented circumstances' of Goethe's (and Schelling's) time.

In many ways *Wilhelm Meister* is amenable to an absolute-idealistic interpretation, with its portrayal of the conflict between the ideal and real that structures the protagonist's apprenticeship. The entire novel, according to Schelling, turns on the ironic interplay of Wilhelm being treated 'continually not as a master, as his name implies, but as a *pupil*' (1989: 235/V, 681). In the process, he is repeatedly frustrated in his striving to be an artist or in his desire to ease the sufferings of those around the theater troupe. Wilhelm presents a 'fortunate center' for the unification of the various elements that persist in the background, which come forth into the foreground at the resolution, in order to display 'an infinite perspective on all the wisdom of life behind a kind of illusory game . . . Only the mystery of the apprenticeship itself articulates this wisdom: namely, only *he* who has recognized his own destiny is a master' (1989: 235–236/V, 681). The limited perspective of the characters presents in an ironic and unconscious manner the objective situation of the novel. The imperfection of the protagonist, far from being a limitation, drives the novel; in *Wilhelm Meister* the protagonist comes to recognize himself in 'the impetuous course of action' in the events that surround him (1989: 232/V, 676).[34]

Second, the mythology to come requires the synthesis of history and nature. While the artist must contribute the elements of a partial mythology, and the philosopher, according to Schelling, must produce a speculative physics. The more modernity has turned to the ideal, the more nature has withdrawn in mystery. While originality and freedom are central to modern poesy, they do not suffice to create a new mythology. Freedom, and its manifestation in history, must be reconciled with the real principle of nature. As Schelling states, 'in the philosophy of nature, as it has developed from the idealistic principle, the first, distant foundation has been laid for that future symbolism and mythology that will be created not by an individual but rather by the entire age' (1989: 76/V, 449). The nature-philosopher awaits the gods of speculative physics.[35] An audacious demand, but recall what Schelling expected: (1) that nature-philosophy, properly developed, would be able to reveal the totality of nature as organic; (2) that humanity would be shown to be the highest expression of reason *within* the natural world (and not *above* it); and (3) that all of nature would be organized according to an ascending order of potencies.

These demands are a great responsibility for the poet, one that seems beyond the possibilities of the modern world. However, Schelling finds that one poet has accomplished this mythology, and that work begins the era of modern poesy (1989: 239/V, 686). This is Dante's *Divine Comedy*, which is so singular, Schelling claims, that it requires its own theory, which places it in a 'genre in and for itself' (1989: 239/V, 687). Even if the *Divine Comedy* is hindered by its Ptolemaic science, Dante still remains the model of modern poesy. He takes up all the elements of his age – science, history, religion – and creates a totality that is both allegorical and symbolic: the characters and their actions can be read allegorically (for instance, Beatrice is an allegory of theology), at the same time that each element forms a symbolic totality, in which the individual parts unveil their own inner meaning.

Dante freely created a mythology, because no *living* mythology could provide the content. Instead, the *Divine Comedy* draws on all aspects of its age. The main structure even reflects the 'three great objects of science and culture': the *Inferno* presents an image of the 'eternal night' of nature, *Purgatorio* follows the historical process of purification and transition toward the infinite, and *Paradiso*, anticipates the absolute as reconciled and 'truly within the center' (1989: 243/V, 157–158). Thus Dante's work shows that mythological creation is still possible in modernity. Schelling claims that 'it is prophetic and prototypical for the entirety of modern poesy' (1989: 247/V, 163). Where Christ signified the closure of the ancient world and the beginning of a universal history, Dante's *Divine Comedy* similarly constituted the poetic rupture between ancient and modern poesy. But that Dante's work is a thing of the past, 'cloaked with the sacredness of antiquity' (1989: 239/V, 152) seems to correspond to Schelling's use of the past tense to describe the mythology of Catholicism. This would only lend further evidence to my claim that modern mythology cannot be specifically Christian, but must reconcile ancient and modern poesy. No doubt Schelling saw Goethe's *Faust* as an exemplar, even if he only had access to the fragment.

Yet, were it to be *Faust*, there is one more element required for the new mythology, namely, that the work of art must have a public or communal character. Drama certainly qualifies, since the works of theater present the embodiment of the idea on stage; drama lives its life as public life (along with music, song, dance, and what Schelling calls the 'caricature' of ancient drama, opera). The reconciliation of ancient and modern poesy aims, for Schelling, precisely to revitalize and renew public life. The religious resources of the modern age are not enough, so it is through renewing the spirit of antiquity that a new public life can be organized. As Schelling concludes:

> Wherever public life disappears, instead of that real, external drama in which, in all its forms, an entire people participates as a political or moral totality, only an *inward*, ideal drama can unite the people. This ideal drama is the worship service, the only kind of *truly* public action that has remained for the contemporary age, and even so only in an extremely diminished and reduced form. (1989: 280/V, 736)

As we will see in Section 5.4, in the *Würzburg Lectures* Schelling takes up the political and public aspect of mythology in a philosophy of the state.

4.5. Substance or History?

I have argued in this chapter, contrary to a common image of Schelling's intellectual development, that his absolute idealism does not relegate the philosophy of art to a secondary status within the system. Instead, the philosophy of art retains almost all of its structural importance found in the *System of Transcendental Idealism*. What has changed is Schelling's metaphysical framework: where the activity of the self once grounded artistic production, now Schelling proposes a theory of potencies that can be derived from absolute identity. Despite this change, he still maintains that the imagination is the 'power' (*Kraft*) that produces art and the unity of the potencies. It was in researching the similarities and continuities within the philosophy of art that I gradually began to recognize another set of similarities and problems shared by identity-philosophy and Schelling's work after 1807. The distinctions and differences constructed in the *Philosophy of Art* are collapsed in *Über das Verhältnis der bildenden Künste zu der Natur* of 1807. I have argued that these distinctions, especially between the first principle of identity-philosophy in general and the historical construction of the gods resulted in a contradiction within the system: if Schelling retained the Spinozist first principle of an impersonal absolute, he would lose the abundance of the historical construction of the gods (they would be merely illusory appearances, which contradicts the infinite side of the gods, and the Christian God), and to maintain the historical construction of the gods as actual, Schelling would need to abandon the eternal immutable substance of the absolute. For the remainder of the period of identity-philosophy, Schelling upheld the Spinozist core of the system, but by 1807, in his address in Munich, he discarded the immutable form of Spinozist substance in order to develop an account of the historical revelation of the absolute in both art and nature. In *Über das Verhältnis der bildenden Künste zu der Natur*, Schelling presents a system that attempts to unify the True, Good, and Beautiful through the historical expression of artistic production.

Chapter 5

From Art and Nature to Freedom
and Revelation

Natur und Kunst sie scheinen sich zu fliehen,
Und haben sich, eh man es denkt, gefunden;
Der Widerwille ist auch mir verschwunden,
Und beide scheinen gleich mich anzuziehen.
Nature and Art, they go their separate ways,
It seems; yet all at once they find each other.
Even I no longer am foe to either;
Both equally attract me nowadays.
—Goethe, 'Natur und Kunst' (2005: 124–125)

5.1. The Moment in Munich

The focus of this chapter is Schelling's *Über das Verhältnis der bildenden Künste zu der Natur*,[1] which was delivered at the *Akademie der Wissenschaften* in Munich on the occasion of the King's Name-day on October 12, 1807 and later included in Schelling's *Philosophische Schriften* with his *Philosophical Investigations into the Essence of Human Freedom.*[2] While today, the *Münchener Rede* receives little attention, it was, according to Xavier Tilliette, an important event (over five hundred people, including Crown Prince Ludwig, were in attendance), earning the praise and scorn of many of Schelling's friends and erstwhile colleagues within the German intelligentsia.[3] As Caroline Schlegel-Schelling describes the event to Luise Gotter, 'Schelling spoke with a dignity, virility and enthusiasm that friend and foe were overcome . . . several weeks later and in the court and city the only talk (*Rede*) is Schelling's talk (*Rede*)' (quoted in Sziborsky, ed., 1983: 69–70).[4] After receiving a copy from Niethammer, Hegel writes that 'Just as the ocean produces grain, the Arabian desert wine, and Gotthard oranges, so Munich flourishes with pentameters and hexameters . . . as also with aesthetic-philosophical addresses' (to Niethammer, dated November 1807, in Hegel, 1984: 149). Jacobi, who presided over the address, was appalled, although he initially saved his scorn for his epistolary exchanges.

Despite the attention the address generated in its time, the *Münchener Rede* is largely neglected today in Schelling scholarship, perhaps because it is his last significant work on the philosophy of art before what we might call his 'theological turn' toward the philosophy of freedom.[5] As I will argue, this neglect is unwarranted. The *Münchener Rede* is an important point of transition between the problems that plagued absolute idealism and those that drove Schelling's philosophy of freedom.

As I argued in Chapter 4, Schelling's development of the philosophy of art, during the period of absolute idealism, results in a contradiction between the deductions of its rational formalism and the historical construction of the mythological content of art. As much as Schelling tried to cover over this contradiction with the formal structures of the system of identity (such as dividing between the real, ideal, and indifference), the more his account dealt with particular details, the more it overstepped these structures. This problem is especially visible in the historicism implied in the transition from Greek antiquity to Christianity.

In the *Münchener Rede*, these formal structures of absolute idealism – that is, the distinctions between philosophy in general, the historical construction of the content of art, and the construction of the particular forms of art – are abandoned. What we find in the *Münchener Rede*, by contrast, is a kind of unified philosophy of nature, history, and *ethos* of art. It is remarkable that the *Münchener Rede* is the only time that Schelling unifies the true (science and nature-philosophy), the good (history and practice), and the beautiful within an *ethos* of artistic production, in which art both reveals nature as it produces itself and demonstrates a moral force in its productions.[6] In its relationship to nature, true art draws on the living power of nature to reveal its divine character, but it also reveals the very history of natural production itself. As Dieter Jähnig states, '*What* art produces is the *producing* itself' (Jähnig, 1969: II, 133). The relationship between nature and art also has consequences for morality, because Schelling presents an ethic of artistic production that shows how the artist presents the world morally through subordinating human passions to the realization of the beautiful or the sublime. In so doing, Schelling argues that art reveals what is divine in humanity and nature.

The first part of this chapter will disentangle this account from Schelling's allusive rhetoric of the address itself. The exegetical difficulties lie in the rhetorical structure, which builds through allusion and repetition, and the anticipation and evocation of ideas – which are then only later developed – in order to produce the emotional rhythm of the speech. In this regard, the *Münchener Rede* is (as *his* contemporaries recognized!) a singular text in Schelling's *oeuvre*, far from the dry axiomatic deductions and aphorisms of the lectures of identity-philosophy.

If we recognize this singularity, however, we are also confronted with the question of why Schelling proceeded to abandon his philosophy of art. Its rapid disappearance is, for the Schelling scholar, puzzling. Various answers have been proposed, and because they draw on different aspects of Schelling's later thought (which continued to develop for over four more decades), they are not even incompatible. Odo Marquard proposes that Schelling's aesthetics give way to an emphasis on medicine as a technique to render the power of nature unthreatening. Marquard marks the shift from aesthetics to medicine from 1800 to 1806, at the same time that Schelling 'distanced himself from the actual project of carrying out his aesthetics, he gave medicine a significant philosophical revaluation' (Marquard, 2004: 21). This is the most speculative and difficult solution to defend, since the *Münchener Rede* post-dates Marquard's chronology of these developments. For Jean-François Marquet, the philosophy of art is replaced by a philosophy that presents Christ as a cosmological *puissance*, this shift begins in 1809 and it is developed in the *Weltalter* and the later *Philosophy of Mythology* (Marquet, 1979: 87). Drawing on the later philosophy, Dieter Jähnig proposes that Schelling abandons the philosophy of art because of the ineffectiveness (*Wirkunglosigkeit*) of artistic production in transforming history (Jähnig, 1969: II, 313–319).[7]

In contrast to these previous answers, I will argue that the creative power of artistic production is transferred by Schelling to a new idea of freedom, which he rethinks outside of the Kantian-Fichtean formalism of the moral law. When this happens, Schelling no longer requires the higher *ethos* of the philosophy of art. Hence, from *Of Human Freedom* (1809) onward, Schelling's ecstatic account of freedom takes the place of artistic production. However, tracing the continuities and differences between these two texts proves both difficult and highly speculative due to the near absence of references to art in *Of Human Freedom* (for an exception see 2006: 75–76/VII, 414).

The *Stuttgart Seminars* from 1810, however, deals with both the theological and philosophical concerns of the *Freiheitsschrift* and the *Münchener Rede*.[8] I will argue that one of the most important shifts in Schelling's philosophical orientation concerns his view of history. While the texts on art are oriented toward the future and a new mythology that could overcome the fragmentary nature of humanity, the *Stuttgart Seminars* is oriented toward the past. In the latter text, Schelling argues that the Fall of humanity is a real historical event with consequences for human freedom. Thus his emphasis shifts from the future 'redemption' of a new mythology to explaining how the Fall precipitates the features of what Schelling considered to be the human condition. This change in orientation transforms his conception of artistic production: where art was once the highest vocation of humanity, it is now limited to expressions of an artist's individuality or of longing for a lost connection to nature. In the place of artistic production, Schelling now prescribes the cultivation of freedom through a universal religious knowledge.

We will conclude by examining the political implications of the idea of a new mythology. Like many of his contemporaries, Schelling eventually turns away from revolutionary enthusiasm to either political quietism, mysticism, or some degree of conservatism.[9] This shift from a revolutionary and utopian vision of the new mythology to a statist apologetics takes place in what I will call the mythologization of politics, until Schelling abandons his philosophy of art altogether. By 'mythologization of politics' I mean the gradual conceptual unification of art, mythology, and the state, in which mythology serves, or is proposed, as an ideological component of legitimating political power. However, let me be clear that the mythologization of politics is not equivalent to what Walter Benjamin calls the 'aestheticization of politics,' by which *aesthetic* judgments become *political* judgments regarding events such as war (Benjamin, 2002: 120–122). In this way, we avoid falling into the generalizations that allow Lukács, in his book *The Destruction of Reason*, to argue that irrationalism leads (as the subtitle indicates) 'from Schelling to Hitler' (Lukács, 1980: 123–192).[10] Not only are the factors that Benjamin takes as the material basis of the mobilization of fascist politics (such as the level of technological development) absent, but the conceptual framework is different. The aestheticization of politics is a reactionary and militaristic politics, while what I have called a mythologization of politics is closer to what Marx would call a mystification: an idealization of social relationships. This idealization does not preclude it from being gradualist, reformist, or quietist, but what is important is that it places *Bildung* or cultivation of peoples or publics over direct or democratic political engagement. This, however, does not excuse pernicious political concepts, such as so-called organic communities or peoples, from criticism; it is meant to show the tensions and ambiguities of Schelling's political or social philosophy.

As we can see *today*, ideologically Schelling was close to a dangerous political stance when he envisioned an organic totality of a people who, as if they embodied a single poet, create a new mythology. Conceived under the form of the state, this idea of a people brings with it unacceptable political consequences: for instance, it can result, through political implementation, in the exclusion from political or public life those groups who are not considered part of the community; those who do not participate in the 'essence' of a people or nation are excluded or marginalized. Viewing this problem through the lens of a theory of hegemony, the stakes become clear: the a priori conception of universality *as organic totality* ignores or disregards the fact that the political space itself is the domain of the struggle over what the definition of universality (and political inclusion) is. That Schelling turns away from the mythologization of politics when he changes his focus to a universal history of religion – just at the time when German politics becomes increasingly nationalistic – appears well advised in retrospect.

It is testimony, for better or worse, to the power of art that both of Schelling's visions of art took on a life of their own after the end of his philosophy of art. On one hand, the mythologization of politics, with art expressing the essence of a nation, had a long history in Germany (see Williamson, 2004), which culminated philosophically in Heidegger's essay 'The Origin of the Work of Art.'[11] On the other hand, the revolutionary and utopian idea of art reemerged in the avant-garde of the 20th century and is still the focus of contemporary debates on the relationship between politics and art.[12]

5.2. From the 'Living Center' of Nature and Art . . .

For purposes of presentation, I left aside from the previous chapter the construction of the particular forms of art in order to present here the contrast between the *Philosophy of Art* and the *Münchener Rede*. In the former, Schelling follows the form of the triad 'real-ideal-indifference' throughout the construction of the arts, which, as I argued, is precisely how the historical construction of the content of art results in an antithesis between the system's formalism and history. But Schelling also presents a deduction of the particular forms of art which reprises the formal sequence of the real-ideal-indifference that is organized as follows in Table 5.1[13]:

Table 5.1 The Particular Arts

Real Series	**Formative Art**	**Verbal Art**	*Ideal Series*
Real	Music	Lyric Poetry	Particular
Ideal	Painting	Epic Poetry	Universal
Indifference	Plastic Arts	Drama	Indifference

To show how he abandons the formal construction of art found in the *Philosophy of Art*, in favor of a historical production of art, we will outline Schelling's construction of the plastic arts, the sequence music-painting-plastic arts, which begins with the construction of music.

Music is the first in the series of the plastic (*bildenden*) arts. Therefore music is the real potency within the series, followed by the ideal, which is painting, and the informing of indifference, which is sculpture. For Schelling, the beginning is always the most difficult, and his construction of music is no exception to the rule. I have attempted to provide the most simplified outline for ease of presentation (see 1989: 107–109/V, 488–491).[14] Music has its ground in the (speculatively) physical dynamic of sound (*Klang*). Sound is the absolute form of time in the world of art, while matter would be that of space. Thus sound and matter relate like concept and being, soul and body; sound requires external bodies to resonate, although, in pure form, absolute sound does not require matter. Resonation requires the externality of other bodies, but also that they cohere to some degree. If matter is being, then sound is activity, and the point of indifference is hearing, which is the organic unity of the medium (matter) and activity (sound).

Sound, constructed as an art form, is music (1989: 109–114/V, 491–499), which is divided between rhythm (real), modulation (ideal), and melody (indifference).[15] Rhythm is the informing of multiplicity from homogeneity, which is why time is the universal form of music. However, it is not that music is given meaning by time, but that the rhythm of music organizes ('self-counts' as Schueller remarks) succession and thus gives meaning to time. Where rhythm informs quantitative difference (recall the resonances, as it were, with Schelling's deduction of individual things as quantitative differences in the *Darstellung*, see Section 4.2), modulation, the movement to higher or lower tones, is qualitative difference (modulation taken as totality, is harmony).[16] When rhythm and modulation are posited as indifference, melody is constructed; melody is the succession of modulation within rhythm. Melody is the point of indifference because tonality is subordinated to rhythm, which is the most universal aspect of music. Unsurprisingly, the Greeks perfected melodic music, and modern music (contemporary with Schelling) subsumes rhythm within harmony (1989: 112–113/V, 496–497).[17]

From music, the entire foundation of the particular arts is built in the *Philosophy of Art*, and an entire set of analogies is drawn: in the real series of art, rhythm is the musical element of music (and thus allegory), modulation that of painting (schematism), and melody the plastic element (symbolism)[18] (1989: 112/V, 496); in nature-philosophy, music is the real expression of '*pure* movement as such'[19] and the form of being of the cosmic bodies. This, of course, suggests a similarity to Pythagoras, who, according to Schelling, did not 'say that these movements *cause* music, but rather that they themselves *are* music'; in other words, the inner, pure movement in the solar system needs no external medium (1989: 116/V, 502).

The *Münchener Rede* abandons these formal structures of absolute idealism. The brief outline of Schelling's metaphysics of music, in all its details and analogies, shows the weight of the architectonic structure of the *Philosophy of Art*. It is easy to see how the *Philosophy of Art* can get caught up in antitheses. We have already identified one important antithesis between substance and history. Clearly the construction of the particular forms of art, such as music, proceeds according to the formal structure of the system (its logical differences), and not historically.

By contrast, the art-philosophy of the *Münchener Rede* unfolds according to a natural-historical series. Missing are all the deductions and divisions between philosophy in general and the philosophy of art, the philosophy of history, and nature-philosophy. Also missing is *music*. Schelling refers only to two of the plastic arts, sculpture and painting. These plastic arts are considered in a historical form: the first principle, the *Wesen* or 'living center,' unfolds in the realization (*Verwirklichung*) of nature and the presentation (*Darstellung*) of art (1968: 342/VII, 310). In accordance with *Münchener Rede*, we will set out the historical account of the production of art and nature, and then outline its metaphysical framework.

The theoretical structure of the *Münchener Rede* draws on Schelling's metaphysics of potencies, in which finite things are expressed according to an ascending series of perfection.[20] Recall that in the *Philosophy of Art*, the same order of potencies could be found in nature, history, and art. For example, Schelling states that works of art present the intellectual world in the finite world:

> music is nothing other than the archetypal rhythm of nature and the universe itself, which by means of this art breaks through into the portrayed (*abgebildliche*) world. The complete forms that the plastic arts produce are the objectively presented archetypes of organic nature itself. The Homeric epic is identity itself as it lies at the basis of history within the absolute. Every painting discloses the intellectual world. (1989: 17tm/V, 369)

The continuities are clear: while Schelling no longer discusses music in the *Münchener Rede*, sculpture still reveals the inner forms of organic nature (that is, where music was once the origin, the point of creation, of the formative arts, sculpture now is), and painting still discloses, despite a change in terminology, something like the entirety of the revealed (formerly called 'intellectual') world. The similarities go beyond the particular arts. The ascending order of potencies or powers reappears in the *Münchener Rede*:

> Nature, in its broader sphere, always presents the higher simultaneously with its lower: *creating* the divine in man, it produces in all other products the mere material and ground thereof, so that essence as such shall appear in contrast to it. Indeed, in the higher world of man the great mass once more becomes the basis to which the divine, that has preserved its purity in the few, is manifested in lawgiving, dominion and the founding of religious faiths. Hence, where art operates with more of the manifoldness of nature it [art] may and must exhibit, alongside the highest measure of beauty, its groundwork and, as it were, the material of the latter in its own forms (*Bildungen*). (1968: 339tm/VII, 308)

While the potencies recur in nature, humanity, and art, to properly understand the difference between the *Münchener Rede* and Schelling's previous philosophy we need to place the emphasis on *creation*: it is not just that these formal structures reoccur, but that the same *Urkraft* (primal power) is expressed in all finite forms in ascending potencies. As Jean-François Marquet points out, the *Münchener Rede* is the first place where 'the origin of the world will be envisaged,' in the work of Schelling, 'as creation' (Marquet, 2006: 343). Each successive revelation *raises* the previous potency to a higher power. The task of the *Münchener Rede* is to show *how* these potencies are produced.

The problem, however, is the origin. We will discuss it in two moments, first as it is produced in nature and art, and then as it pertains to the absolute as first principle of the essay's metaphysics, which sketches a philosophy of freedom *in nuce*. The difficulty of the beginning arises from the modern alienation from nature. Recall the diagnosis found in the *Philosophy of Art* and the second edition of the *Ideas for a Philosophy of Nature*: the more the ideal world is perfected, the more nature withdraws as mystery (see Section 4.4; and 1989: 76/V, 449; 1988: 54–55/II, 72–73). As the cited passages show, Schelling understood nature-philosophy as a contribution to unraveling this mystery, to decode the 'poem lying pent in a mysterious and wonderful script' (1978: 232/III, 628). The *Münchener Rede* is Schelling's first attempt to discover the *Urkraft* at the common point of creation of both nature and art, which is why he begins by rejecting the usual debate of whether art should imitate nature or recreate it as an ideal. All previous answers to this false dilemma have not grasped the living center of nature; they only see nature as either quantity of individual objects, a container, or place for these objects, or as the source of goods to be exploited (1968: 325/VII, 293).[21] In order to reveal nature as living, Schelling argues, all these interpretations must be rejected.[22] The essence of nature must be seen as the common ground of living nature, humanity, and the divine power of art. As different expressions of a common power, or *Urkraft*, we should expect each stage of the realization of this creative source to be repeated in nature, humanity, and art.

So to begin, in nature, as in art, essence strives for realization and pre-sentation, which is brought forth initially as form. Nature comes forth from out of chaos and the formless in order to appear in the individual, the latter of which is only possible through limitation and opposition. As Schelling states, 'without bounds the boundless could not be manifested [and] if there were no harshness, mildness could not exist' (1968: 342/VII, 310). In contrast to the 'labor of the negative' found in that famous book of 1807, written by one of Schelling's erstwhile comrades, limitation is not negation, but an affirmation of a higher potency; the ability to take on self-limitation is how the individual 'appears as truly meaningful force (*Kraft*),' through limitation an individual comes to subsist within the *Urkraft* of nature. If one is tempted to ask 'why the absolute even bothers,' Schelling has an answer: essence takes on limitation in creation because in its origins, its highest and divine power only lies dormant or unfulfilled. Thus the historical series is a necessary self-revelation (what *necessary* means in this context will only be explained later, in the *Stuttgart Seminars*). The struggle of the essence of nature to obtain the fullness of form through limitation is accomplished first in what Schelling calls the severity of form.[23] In its initial formation, the individual is singular, isolated, inaccessible. But where the bringing forth of form is the beginning, Schelling argues that the beginning must be elevated within nature, just as it is in mankind and the divine images of art. Like the first stage of revealed nature, sculpture began with the most severe; the goddess Athena was the 'only muse of plastic art.' Yet nature must be elevated from form toward beauty. Concerning sculpture:

> In depicting the most perfect or divine natures it was not merely neces-sary for the fullness of forms, of which the human nature as a whole is capable, to become united: this union must also be of the kind that we can visualize in the universe itself, namely one in which the lower forms,

or those related to lesser qualities, were subsumed under higher ones and finally under one highest form, in which, to be sure, they were all mutually extinguished as particular forms, but endured in their essence and power (*Kraft*). (1968: 337–338tm/VII, 306–307)

To show how the forms are elevated toward their essence, Schelling moves from this initial revelation of nature to an anthropology of the soul, which stands as the human link between the divine and nature. Then he argues that this sequence of the production of nature reoccurs in art. The conceptual series of this progressive revelation – a kind of anthropology and theology of artistic creation – proceeds from the *Urkraft* of nature to the characteristic of grace (*Anmut*) in the equipoise of body and soul, which itself is based on divine love. This anthropology of the soul anticipates the accounts of human freedom found later in the essay *Of Human Freedom* and the *Stuttgart Seminars*, although in the *Münchener Rede* it is presented as the ethos of art, which has a natural and moral force.

The elevation of nature from the severity of form takes place through the soul, and the activity, as it were, of grace. Through grace form is consummated and overcome – the spirit that laid dormant in nature is revealed through the soul. Natural beings begin to reveal a gentleness and perfection, or the terms of Schelling's earlier nature-philosophy, the organism reaches a point of indifference between its being and activity: the 'spirit of nature (*Naturgeist*) becomes free from its bonds and feels its kinship with the soul' (1968: 342tm/VII, 311). This kinship is possible through grace. Although it is not yet the soul in its divine essence, which can only be actualized in humanity, it is a natural soul (*Naturseele*) or sensuous grace: 'soul and body are in perfect concord; the body is form, grace is the soul.' In art sensuous grace is realized in the image of pure beauty, which is presented by the sculpture of Aphrodite, the goddess of love (1968: 343tm/VII, 311).

That the soul emerges in nature as grace shows that these concepts are not opposed (they only *appear* as opposed), but rather that the ground of nature is elevated to a higher power; nature is the medium of the soul's revelation. At this point, the *Münchener Rede* takes an anthropological turn. The remainder of the essay is dedicated to showing how the powers of nature drive artistic creation through their activity within the soul. Where the soul is active as a potential of nature, it is actual in human being; its revelation is an elevation of human being above the principle of individuality (which is already found in nature itself), grounding human being in a higher principle. Indeed, the principle, which is divine love, is the opposite of individuality:

> in man, the soul is not the principle of individuality, but that whereby he raises himself above all egoism (*Selbstheit*), whereby he becomes capable of self-sacrifice, unselfish love and, the most exalted of all, of the contemplation and cognizance of the essence of things, and, precisely thereby, of art. (1968: 343/VII, 311–312)

However, if the soul is revealed unconsciously in nature, it must be consciously realized by the artist. One would think, from the apparently idyllic portrait of human personality as the equipoise of body and soul through the contemplation of art and the essence of things, that the artist's task is uncomplicated, but the more tragic vision found in *Of Human Freedom* and the *Stuttgart Seminars* looms in the background. The precursor of the 'natural' or 'dark' principle of human being found in the latter essays appears in the *Münchener Rede* as the passions.

Yet we gain no insight into why the passions are introduced in the *Münchener Rede* by pointing out the continuities with later texts. We must also ask whether the passions reveal any continuity between the *Münchener Rede* and Schelling's previous presentations of the philosophy of art. In the previous texts artistic activity was the highest expression of the absolute within the real because art overcame the separation of freedom and necessity, the ideal and the real, through artistic production. The result was the conscious reestablishment of identity in the finite world. Despite the change in terminology, the passions play the role of the disruption of unity (where, previously, this was often cast in terms of consciousness necessarily arising through the separation of freedom and nature). They are, however, not a wholly negative force in themselves, because 'living unity can show itself in action and activity only as the result of the forces composing it being incited to rebellion by some cause or other and departing from their equilibrium' (1968: 341/VII, 309–310). Artistic production brings forth in itself an *ethos* of beauty.

The goal of the artist is to moderate the passions through the realization of beauty, but Schelling points out that this act of moderation is a positive, and not a negative, force.[24] Thus beauty moderates the passions by the higher force of beauty, or, in the case of tragedy, the sublime. In the case of beauty limitation is not negation: 'the true requirement is rather to oppose passion by positive force. For just as virtue does not consist in the

UNIVERSITY OF WINCHESTER
LIBRARY

absence of passions, but in the power of the spirit over them, so beauty is not safeguarded by their removal or reduction but by the power of beauty over them' (1968: 341/VII, 310). The task of the artist is to show in the plastic arts this conflict of the passions and soul without letting their opposition destroy the proportion of beauty. However, this account can only be completed by showing how the soul reestablishes its equilibrium through the power of the sublime. That Schelling cannot manage to avoid a reference to tragedy (or, for that matter, Homer) in a text on the plastic arts is not completely incongruous because this supplemental inclusion of Greek tragedy brings with it explanatory power regarding the unfolding of his artistic sequences. For, Schelling argues, the greatest power that can struggle against the calm of the soul is not the 'inferior natural spirits' but rather the insurrection of the spirit itself. The tragic hero again enters the philosophical stage: this greatest insurrection occurs when the protagonist falls into 'guiltless error':

> when unbearable pain, or even madness ordained by punitive gods takes away consciousness and the power of thought, [grace] still stands beside the suffering figure as a protective daemon and sees to it that he does nothing inept, nothing contrary to humanity, but that when he falls he at least falls as a pure and undefiled victim. (1968: 345/VII, 313)

As we saw in Section 4.4, the truly sublime and ethical protagonist of tragedy endures fate with magnanimity, which Schelling now incorporates into the metaphysics of the *Münchener Rede*: the truly sublime and mortal act of the individual is to face and accept annihilation over breaking the bond of the soul and divine love. In this ethical act he or she chooses the sublime over evil. In a cryptic passage, Schelling writes: no 'external power can do more than take away external goods, it cannot reach the soul; it can tear apart a finite link, but not dissolve the eternal bond of a truly divine love' (1968: 345/VII, 314). Thus while the external power of fate cannot dissolve this bond, the question remains, what can?

I think it is possible to answer this question with reference to the *Stuttgart Seminars*. There, Schelling argues that evil is neither a privation nor a feature of physical finitude, which is a stance that breaks with the modern philosophical tradition.[25] According to Schelling, evil is the inversion of the two principles (light and dark) through spirit itself. This inversion is possible because spirit can revolt against the divine essence of the soul. Evil is the self-willing of a human actor to turn this elevation above nature into a 'positive disharmony': the elevation of the dark ground above the true cause of human freedom, that of eternal love (1994a: 232/VII, 468; see also 2006: 34/VII, 365). Through what is divine, a human agent – like one of any number of Sade's villains – wills evil and unleashes a destructive will against creation itself.

Thus we can complete Schelling's account: no external power can break the bond of love, only an inward power can; it is precisely the grace of the acceptance of fate, rather than acting contrary to virtue (which is evil), that gives tragedy such a sublime power. The revelation of divine love (although still under the form of fate) leads to the final exemplar in the series of sculpture, which is presented in the figure of the goddess Niobe. The Florentine Niobe (which is a replica of an antique work) moderates the horror that has befallen her through beauty; according to Schelling, after all the cruelty endured – as Apollo and Artemis slaughter her fourteen children– 'through grief, fear and indignation there radiates, like a divine light, everlasting love' (1968: 346/VII, 314). Thus in the series 'Athena-Aphrodite-Niobe' sculpture progresses, like nature itself, from severe form through sensuous grace to their unity in the equipoise between the body and soul.[26] Although the final figure in the series, Niobe, reveals everlasting love, Schelling holds that sculpture, since it 'presents its ideas by corporeal things,' is limited to 'the perfect equipoise between soul and matter' (1968: 347–348/VII, 316). Only painting, he says, can bring forth truly divine love.

Unlike sculpture, painting can exhibit both the suffering and divine power of the soul, and can present the whole of the striving of essence beyond the embodied individual.[27] The medium of painting expresses its subject matter in images, and not as individual objects like sculpture: through the techniques of chiaroscuro and the use of color, painting could be considered a more spiritual medium. Painting, in contrast to the equipoise of sculpture, may 'reduce the characteristics of force and activity to the advantage of the soul, whereby it appears that man became more receptive . . . to higher influences' (1968: 349tm/VII, 317). As it leads to the basis, through the portrayal of the soul's suffering as basis of 'higher revelations' (love), this division of sculpture and painting corresponds to the division between the most perfected of ancient and modern art. As noted in Chapter 4, in the *Philosophy of Art* this division between ancient and modern art rests on the revelation of Christianity, which transfigures fate into providence and necessity into freedom, and breaks with nature to introduce the moral and ideal world. It would seem that this account informs that of the *Münchener Rede*, but it is noteworthy that the first principle of this text is not explicitly Christian. Schelling is less specific about *why* the transition from the ancient world to the modern world occurred than the fact *that* it occurred. The only remnant of the *Philosophy of Art*'s Christian mythology found in this address is that the content of painting possesses universality, which is a feature of the Christian religion. In any case, the history of nature and the arts of antiquity – from severity, to grace, to love – recurs in the 'boundless universality of painting' exhibited in the work of the great masters: Michelangelo, Correggio, and Raphael (1968: 349/VII, 318).

The discussion of painting in the *Münchener Rede* is the peak of the text, where Schelling treats his audience to a paean dedicated to the classicism of the Renaissance.[28] First, Schelling states, Michelangelo presents the epoch of nature struggling toward form, including the 'untrammeled energies in monstrous births,' the myths of a primeval world, the 'heaven-storming' Titans, and the predominance of natural energy over charm. The second epoch is exhibited in Correggio, the painter of grace, who demonstrated the sensuous charm closest to antiquity, and whose 'total expression' of chiaroscuro merged the darkness of matter with light, fusing them into one essence. Finally, with Raphael, the soul is turned toward the divine in 'perfect equipoise.' At this peak of human spirit and the divine, Raphael is 'no longer a painter, he is a philosopher, and poet at the same time.' Schelling writes of Raphael:

> After the confines of nature have been overcome and the monstrous, the fruit of the initial liberty, is suppressed, shape and form are beautified by the presentiment of the soul: the heavens brighten, the softened earthly is able to merge with the heavenly and the latter, in turn, with the gently human. (1968: 351tm/VII, 320)

Therefore, for Schelling, painting presents the same sequence that is revealed in nature itself. Interestingly, the trio of the Italian masters, in Schelling's interpretation, reproduce the mythological content of antiquity (the gods of art, discussed in Section 4.4) even when, curiously, the subject matter of the painting is drawn from Christianity, such as *The Last Judgment*. Schelling's accuracy, however, is less important for our inquiry than the fact that he has collapsed all the distinctions found in the *Philosophy of Art* into the search for one common power, or *Urkraft*, that realizes itself in nature, humanity, and the arts, a unification of the true, good, and beautiful in the ethic of artistic production.

Now, at the pinnacle of the *Münchener Rede*, we can take stock of the relationship between the plastic arts and nature. While much of his interpretation of particular artists or artworks remains similar to the *Philosophy of Art*, their relationships have changed between Jena and Munich. The most general shift occurs in the relationship between the plastic arts: the *Münchener Rede* omits the account of music, and Schelling has modified the organization of painting and sculpture. Where in the *Philosophy of Art* sculpture was the indifference point and painting was the predominantly ideal, the *Münchener Rede* drops the formal structures of identity-philosophy to argue that both reveal the same sequence found in nature, although one expression is ancient, while the other is modern.

As Marquet argues, the modified sequence of the Italian masters is telling: Schelling modifies their succession by inserting – 'regardless of all chronology'– Correggio between Michelangelo and Raphael.[29] This minor detail reveals the important shift between the *Philosophy of Art* and the *Münchener Rede*. In the former, Schelling organizes the potencies from the first (the origin) through the third (the perfection or the 'grand style' of the indifference and identity of real and ideal) to the second, which portrays decadence and an excess of soul. We have already seen this above in the philosophy of music, wherein rhythm and melody are respectively origin and perfection, while harmony is a modern excess of ideality. This order and value of potencies is also seen in the account of Italian painting, which progresses

> from the severity of Michelangelo to the softness of Correggio by the unique point of perfection, Raphael . . . the beginning is marked by a kind of excess of formal rigor . . . [the second potency] on the contrary is an excess of soul, intellectuality, of sense: the central perfection is the equilibrium of the two. (Marquet, 1979: 85–86)

In the *Philosophy of Art*, then, Correggio's work is the fall toward decadence or intellectuality, or even softness; in the *Münchener Rede*, the excess of soul comes after the troika Michelangelo-Correggio-Raphael, in the work of Guido Reni (1968: 352–353/VII, 320–321). Nevertheless, the chronological imposture indicates that Schelling had to finesse the history of painting to make it correspond to the revelation of nature and sculpture found in the *Münchener Rede*, that is, to make the history of painting fit into the common schema of the revelation of nature, humanity, and art.

We can summarize by showing that the three necessary conditions of the philosophy of art obtain. For Condition 1, the argumentative structure of the *Münchener Rede* shows that art presents in the real what philosophy only demonstrates ideally: Schelling's claims about the 'evolution' of nature are not supported by complex proofs drawn from contemporary science, but rather are supported by the philosophical interpretation of artistic sequences. It is in this sense that we have said that art is the revelation of revelation itself. For Condition 2, I have argued that the *Münchener Rede* maintains that art is produced through the reestablishment of equilibrium between the parts of soul, which are interrupted by the passions. While the epistemological implications are lacking, this argument corresponds to the previous presentations of the philosophy of art where artistic production is a higher potency than nature because it presents the identity of freedom and necessity, conscious and unconscious, real and ideal, *after* these oppositions are produced, thus producing a reconciliation. Furthermore, while we will address the topic below, we can anticipate Schelling's conclusion by noting that the *Münchener Rede* closes by calling for a renewal of art (Condition 3) – not specifically as a new mythology, but Schelling's presentation as such is itself establishing the frame of reference for a modern mythology should such an artistic renewal arise in Germany.

The possibility of this renewal of mythology rests in the productive capacity of nature itself. Schelling does not discuss the Italian renaissance, for example, as a model for imitation. Instead, he argues that the contemporary artist should bring forth the same inspiration as the Italian masters: a 'different inspiration falls to the lot of different epochs. . . . To be sure, an art the same in all respects as that of past centuries will never come again; for nature never repeats itself' (1968: 356/VII, 327–328). Thus the originality of the art to come is rooted in an implicit historicism and emphasis on finitude, on the particular social context in which art arises. That this context – which is conceived as the place and time of a people or nation – has clear political implications will be discussed below (in Section 5.4). For the moment, we will complete our account of the *Münchener Rede* by turning to the question of *what* god is, or, *who* is this god, revealed through this history?

What, of course, appalled Jacobi about Schelling's address was what appeared to be a kind of vitalistic pantheism.[30] While Jacobi may not have been, in this case, the best listener, Schelling's presentation is unclear. Instead of *Gott* (the name of the absolute in the *Philosophy of Art*), he relies on the more neutral *Wesen* (which, accordingly, I have translated as 'essence,' although it could also be rendered as 'Being'), even if the *Philosophy of Art* possessed a much stronger rationalist-Spinozist core. Dieter Jähnig utilizes Schelling's later distinctions between ground (*Grund*), essence (*Wesen*), and existence (*Existenz*) or appearance (*Erscheinung*), to make sense of the first principle or deity at the center of the *Münchener Rede*: ground and essence are separated by the appearance (Jähnig, 1969: II, 259). Ground and essence are separated by existence of history because essence can only be realized through opposition and self-affirmation. Schelling's idea of God or *Wesen* remains impersonal. Although the *Wesen* opens toward self-revelation, this is not explicitly based on any type of religious series, but rather it follows the outline of a history of art. The emphasis on nature as primal power (*Urkraft*), whose creation is made conscious through the repetition of artistic creation, has the sound of a thoroughgoing pantheism, but the 'historical revelation' is opposed to the eternal and immutable Spinozist substance.

In the texts immediately following the *Münchener Rede*, Schelling turns to revelation to answer '*who* is this god?' In doing so, he introduces, against his previous Spinozism, a personal God, who is revealed within history. In this transformation, the primacy of the philosophy of art and the persistent difficulties with the divisions of art and nature, model and image, real and ideal, are replaced with a 'living idea of freedom' and a theological anthropology based not in artistic production, but in the Fall of humanity.

5.3. . . . to Theological Anthropology

The *Stuttgart Seminars* offers the most immediate contrast to the philosophy of art of the *Münchener Rede* because it discusses the essence of God, his revelation in history, and the relationship between anthropology and art. While the *Münchener Rede* is arguably Schelling's most pantheistic and pagan text, the *Stuttgart Seminars* presents a history grounded in a series of revelations deeply indebted to Christian theology; while the *Münchener Rede* points toward the future through its call for a renewal of a national art, the *Stuttgart Seminars* is oriented toward the past, and more specifically, on the self-revelation of God and an anthropology based on both the Fall of man (as a historical event, not as a mythological symbol) and the redemption of Christ, the latter of which forms the basis of human freedom. This shift in orientation, which seeks to explain human freedom and the origins of good and evil through the Fall, is the most obvious indicator that (to paraphrase Hegel's well-known verdict on art) the philosophy of art, considered as the highest vocation, is for Schelling a thing of the past. If we are searching for an immanent opposition within Schelling's philosophy, it has shifted from the relationship between philosophy and an artistic *ethos* to the relationship between the system and freedom, which is where the *Letters* began, although, of course, this relationship has changed.

In the *Stuttgart Seminars*, Schelling's anthropology is fundamentally bound to the Fall of Man as a historical event. This reconception of history as oriented around the Fall marks a decisive break (already found in

Of Human Freedom) with the orientation of the *Münchener Rede*, which was turned toward the future renewal of art. That the Fall is a necessary event, Schelling argues, can be seen by (1) the present form of nature, which appears in an opaque lawfulness that still appears to lack total necessity, and which remains in a constant state of unrest when it should have attained perfection; this argument is supported by (2) the presence of evil in the moral world and the presence of poison, disease, and death in the natural world (1994a: 225/VII, 459).

This argument is based on Schelling's conception of the relationship between nature and God. In this account, Schelling conceives of God's revelation through the potencies of ground, existence (*Existenz*), and essence (*Wesen*), which form the foundation of God's self-revelation as an event, as the basis of history and human freedom.[31] While the *Münchener Rede* constrained its references to a more neutral *Wesen*, the *Stuttgart Seminars* attempts to show how this tripartite structure reveals the personal God that was only previously hinted at in the last text of the philosophy of art. The first stage is that of the ground, what Schelling calls the 'contraction' (*Contraktion*) of God, in which God raises himself from the formless and affirms his individuality by separating out what is not of his essence: nature as primal matter. As Schelling states, God separates 'Himself *qua being* (*Seyendes*) from His *Being* (*Seyn*)' (1994a: 208/VII, 436). Or, in our terms, God sets his existence (*Seyendes*) in opposition to his ground (*Seyn*). This opposition is the basis of all life and history; 'without opposition [there is] no life' (1994a: 208/VII, 435). This opposition, Schelling argues, is a progressive revelation of the absolute, from ground to essence.[32] In the middle of these two points, in his existence, God reveals himself not just as personality and individuality, but also as divine love, which gives form to primal matter, and in divine love, nature, history, and humanity are grounded.

Humanity stands at the center of existence, between nature and the divine, the consciousness awakened from the unconscious activity of nature (1994a: 208/VII, 435), and therefore human being, or spirit, is divided between temperament (*Gemüth*), spirit (*Geist*), and soul (*Seele*): temperament is the natural or dark principle, soul is the light or divine principle, and spirit their indifference or bond. Human freedom, Schelling writes, 'consists precisely in the spirit being subordinate to the soul on the one hand while standing *above* the temperament on the other' (1994a: 234/VII, 471). The Fall, and evil, happened because humanity elevated the natural principle over the divine, and cut its ties with God. However, Schelling maintains that this bond between the divine and the human was restored through Christ's sacrifice, which was revealed as the model of human freedom and which showed, through his actions, what the original relationship between

Table 5.2 The Divisions of the Spirit

	Temperament	*Spirit*	*Soul: expressed as:*
Temperament	Longing	Egoism	Art and Poetry
Spirit	Desire	Proper Will	Virtue
Soul	Feeling	Understanding	Philosophy

humanity and nature was supposed to be (1994a: 228/VII, 463). To show precisely what is divine in the human, and what is of nature, Schelling turns to a theological anthropology, in which it becomes clear that virtue and religion, and not artistic production, are now the highest potencies of human activity.

As mentioned above, Schelling divides human being into temperament, spirit, and soul. This is similar to the tripartite schema of the *Münchener Rede* (the passions, spirit, and soul), but the *Stuttgart Seminars* create additional complexity by showing how the three potencies relate to one another (See Table 5.2). Temperament has its basis in the dark or natural principle, and its first potency realized in longing (*Sehnsucht*), which is expressed in melancholy. Schelling states that melancholy is manifested by all life, because life is grounded on something separated from it, just as human being is not identical to either nature or God (1994a: 230/VII, 465–466). The second potency of temperament is desire or appetite (*Begierde*), which is an insatiable 'hunger for being (*Seyn*).' Recall that *Seyn* is the dark or natural principle of humanity, and thus the appetite is the basis for the desire to overturn the divine principle and turn one toward evil. The third power is that of feeling (*Gefühl*), which is the ideal expression of temperament.

The second general potency is spirit and personality, which is divided into the individual will (*Eigenwille*), the understanding (*Verstand*), and the proper will (*eigentliche Wille*): the first is the basis of individuality, the second the act of cognition, and the third the point of indifference; the proper will mediates between the temperament and the soul. This stance rests on Schelling's argument that spirit cannot be the highest potency because it is the point, in its relative independence from both nature and God, in which human freedom is enacted for good or evil. As mentioned above, evil is not privation, but a reversal of principles; it is the inversion of the natural principle over the divine, and it 'wages the most vehement war against all *being* (*Seyn*); indeed, it wishes to cancel (*aufheben*) the very ground of all creation' (1994a: 232tm/VII, 468).

However, if the spirit is subordinated to the soul, the highest activity of humanity becomes possible. Unlike the previous two potencies (temperament and spirit), the soul is undivided; however, it may express itself in relation to the lower potencies to produce art, philosophy, and the aforementioned highest activity, virtue. This order of the soul's expressions, or products, shows how Schelling's thought has changed. The first important shift is in his conception of philosophy, which is the result of the soul's activity with the understanding and feeling. The understanding is no longer interpreted as merely an inferior faculty of reflection opposed to intuition (reason), but as a personal aspect of knowledge, as opposed to the impersonality of reason, and there is also a theological aspect to this division: 'the spirit has knowledge because it also contains the possibility of evil' (1994a: 232/ VII, 469).[33] Hence understanding is considered as an activity (it can choose, through its knowledge, to partake in good or evil), while reason is the 'understanding in its submission to the higher [potency] of the soul' (1994a: 234tm/VII, 472).

Schelling draws an analogy between reason in philosophy and pure space in geometry: in geometry, a false concept 'will not be accepted by space but is rejected; e.g., a triangle whose longer side were to face the smaller angle' (1994a: 235/VII, 472). Likewise, reason will reject all that is not submitted to the soul, as that which still bears the subjective traits of personality. The passive role of reason can also be explained by the change in Schelling's view of what a system can do: where in identity-philosophy, it was necessary to construct the system of reason as it was in nature, after the *Münchener Rede*, it is necessary to *discover* in all its obscurity the system of the world itself. Systems *created* by philosophers are more like 'historical novels.' By contrast, Schelling claims that

> long before man decided to create a system, there already existed one: the system of the world (*System der Welt*). Hence our proper task consists in discovering that system. The true system can never be *created* [by the philosopher] but only uncovered as one that is already *inherent* in itself; that is, in the divine understanding. (1994a: 197tm/VII, 421)

This world-system ultimately rests on God's revelation. Reason is the process whereby the personality of the understanding is rejected for the soul and the divine. We can state, then, that reason plays a negative role, or a critical function, but it cannot discover a priori the positive revelation of the system. Instead, God's revelation must be his inner law, not an external law. Schelling calls previous systems, such as Leibnizianism, historical novels since they began with external laws, such as the law of sufficient reason (which was at the center of the Pantheism Controversy), and then applied them to God. For Schelling, if such laws obtain, it is only through God that they do; they are all God's inner laws, and his revelation has mastery over them. To illustrate this point, Schelling cites the last stanza of Goethe's poem 'Natur und Kunst.' The first stanza of this poem, which appears above as an epigraph, could just as well describe the importance of the relationship between nature and art for Schelling through the *Münchener Rede*. But when Schelling cites the final stanza, he interprets it according to the metaphysics of the *Stuttgart Seminars* (1994a: 203/VII, 429). The images of mastery, constraint, and limitation are not primarily the expression of artistic creation, but divine creation itself, God's self-revelation. This beginning of God's self-revelation, which Schelling calls 'contraction,' is the affirmation of mastery over the lower potencies (and thus not negation through limitation):

> *Wer Großes will, muß sich zusammenraffen;*
> *In der Beschränkung zeigt sich erst Meister.*
> To achieve great things, we must be self-confined:
> Mastery is revealed in limitation. (2005: 124–125)

Schelling's citation of the poem stresses the character of creation, but he has omitted the final line, which reads '*Und das Gesetz nur kann uns Freiheit geben,*' which Luke translates as 'And law alone can set us free again' (2005: 124–125). This omission is telling because it draws attention to Schelling's decisive break with the Kantian-Fichtean conception of freedom. With his separation of law from freedom, Schelling no longer thinks freedom as law, as a regulative moral law, or as a negative concept, but as a positive, creative power. The positive character of freedom, its ecstatic character, cannot be determined a priori through practical philosophy. Thus philosophy, which has the task of discovering the 'progressive demonstration of the absolute,' (1994a: 199/VII, 424) is not the highest *activity*. The highest activity is virtue.

Virtue, Schelling argues, arises in the interaction of the soul and will and desire. This interaction is the basis of freedom, and with the proper order of principles (when the spirit stands above desire, but is subordinated to the soul) brings about '*virtus*, purity, propriety [and] fortitude of the will' (1994a: 235/VII, 473). Like the rejection of the priority of law over revelation, Schelling rejects the formalism of previous accounts of practical philosophy. He writes:

> The truth of the different systems of morality . . . converges, I believe, in
> the following, supreme principle: 'Permit the soul to act within you, or

act as a thoroughly holy man.' Kant derives from that principle only the *formal* expression. 'Act according to your soul' means simply to act not as a personal being (*persönliches Wesen*) but in an entirely impersonal manner, without allowing your personality to disrupt its influence on you. (1994a: 235/VII, 473)

While Schelling agrees that impersonality is the highest and most divine potency, he rejects Kant's interpretation of the moral law as a regulative idea. In Schelling's reading, a regulative idea conceives of activity as approximate – that the finite subject can only infinitely approximate the divine (hence 'Act according to your soul'). Schelling's reversal of this maxim rejects the formalism by placing the divine in nature through the mediation of humanity (hence 'Permit the soul to act within you, or act as a thoroughly holy man'). Therefore the products of freedom – virtue, the good, and evil – are realized within the finite world. In virtuous activity, humanity takes God's revelation as a model. Just as God separates 'Himself *qua being* (*Seyendes*) from His *Being* (*Seyn*), [in] the highest moral act' man separates his being (*Seyendes*) from his ground (*Seyn*) (1994a: 208/VII, 436).

When Schelling rethinks freedom as the *realization* of its activity in the finite world, rather than the infinite approximation the moral law, art becomes subordinated to philosophy and virtue. The holistic *ethos* of the *Münchener Rede*, which unified the true, the beautiful, and the good, is once again separated. Art and poetry, according to the *Stuttgart Seminars*, is the expression of the soul in relation to longing (in the temperament) and the individual will (in the spirit). While Schelling holds art to be 'entirely ideal and yet as real as a work of nature – which is innocence restored' (1994a: 234/VII, 471), this stance fulfills none of our conditions for a philosophy of art. Where art was once the expression of the highest potency, it is now the expression of the longing for a lost object, and even a kind of naivety. In E. F Georgii's notes on the *Stuttgart Seminars* – corrected by Schelling himself – Schelling states that 'If the soul relates to longing and ego dynamism (*Selbstkraft*), [and] if it stands in conjunction with longing, then it [the soul] creates art. In art individual will and ego dynamism appear in their naivety' (1973: 189). Where a new mythology once held out the expectation of the reconciliation of humanity and nature, now Schelling holds that only religion can effect this reconciliation. Now that we have seen how art is subordinated, in the *Stuttgart Seminars*, to science (philosophy) and virtue, we will conclude by examining the political destiny of the new mythology.

5.4. The Politics of Mythology and the Mythology of Politics

Artistic production is explicitly linked to politics through the idea of a new mythology. Since art expresses the idea – the absolute – in the finite world, it possesses the ability to render the idea sensible. This is, for Schelling, the unique power of mythology, and it was the concept of a new mythology that opened the possibility of a future reconciliation of the divisions that define modernity. We will conclude, then, by examining the ambiguous politics of mythology, as it shifts from revolutionary enthusiasm to a mythologization of politics.

The conditions of the emergence of the idea of a new mythology should not be ignored. The critique of representation engaged by the early Romantics and German idealists is not just a philosophical issue but a political one. The fundamental political problem is the relationship between the individual, groups (whether conceived as nations, peoples, communities, parties, movements, classes, etc.), and the state: should their relationship be governed by representation, wherein individuals or groups interact within a social framework organized toward maximizing formal rights, or is there another way to conceive of this relationship? Is there not a purpose to which the state should be subordinate? We, of course, cannot resolve this question here, but we can evaluate Schelling's approach to the question through his work on new mythology, society, and the state. As Manfred Frank argues (1982: 153–211), the new mythology emerges as renewal of the public sphere, but it is important to show how Schelling's various conceptions relate to this public sphere, for they are not all alike. While Schelling recognizes the 'legitimation crisis' (Frank) that had emerged in Germany in the transition to industrial capitalism, his various presentations on the new mythology supply different solutions to this crisis. It is here, finally, that we discover why the Greek arts 'count as a norm and as an unattainable model' (K. Marx, 1973: 111): Schelling's idea of the new mythology seeks to reconcile the Greek idea of nature as *physis* with the advances in philosophy in order to overcome the separations that alienate humanity from its community.

Whoever the author, the idea of a new mythology first appears in the 'System Program' as the touchstone of a new, emboldened, post-Kantian philosophy. In this brief text, the new mythology, in mediating 'the monotheism of reason and polytheism of imagination,' shines with revolutionary fervor above, and in contrast to, the lifeless mechanism of the state (see the translation in Krell, 2005: 23–26). As mechanism, the state has no true idea, and hence any idea of freedom must aim for some higher purpose, which ultimately is that of beauty, in which the good and the true are unified. The purpose of the new mythology is to make this unity of the good, true, and beautiful sensuous, to bring forth a sensuous religion and mythology of reason; its task is formative (in the sense of *Bildung*): to educate the people (*Volk*) through poesy. The defining feature of this mythology, insofar as it unites the various revolutionary classes (philosophers and the people as the masses), against sages, priests, and the state, is that the 'eternal unity' it brings about is conceived as egalitarian. The state cannot realize true freedom and egalitarianism through its formal mechanisms; some higher idea must govern the philosopher's inquiry. Against the hierarchies of statism and institutionalized religion, the 'System Program' is clearly animated by the author's enthusiasm for the French Revolution.

By the time of the *System of Transcendental Idealism*, the revolutionary enthusiasm that Schelling once shared with the other possible authors of the 'System Program' (Hegel, Hölderlin) had become tempered, although the idea of a new mythology maintained its socio-political prominence. It was one thing to suggest the unity of the good, true, and beautiful within a new mythology; it was another thing entirely to render this unity systematically, and the resulting difficulties are on display in the *System of Transcendental Idealism*. There, the opposition between practical philosophy and the philosophy of art results in an inconsistent separation of history and mythology. While in Chapter 3, we focused primarily on the difficulties with unifying Schelling's idea of providence with the announcement of a mythology to come, the same problems hold for the relationship between the state (which we discussed with reference to the philosophy of history) and mythology.

In the *System of Transcendental Idealism*, the state is conceived as a mechanism for the realization of individual rights, although it cannot maintain any moral force, because 'all attempts to transform [the state] into a moral order present themselves as detestable through their own perversity, and through that most dreadful kind of despotism which is their immediate consequence' (1978: 196/III, 584). Although the state acts *materially* like providence (that is, toward the collective realization of freedom), it does not do so in form, nor with judgment and forethought. Hence the state, with its foundation in natural law, is subordinated to providence, which is a higher realization of freedom in history. Even in the practical section of the *System of Transcendental Idealism*, the state is subordinate to a higher principle, which is perhaps Schelling's version of the revolutionary thesis calling for the withering away of the state. Yet this does not render the relationship between providence and the new mythology any more con-sistent. It is clear, nevertheless, that the utopian potential of mythology is superior to Schelling's cursory and unenthusiastic deductions of the role of the state in the system.

Nevertheless, the *System of Transcendental Idealism* displays a cosmopolitan-ism (in the Kantian sense) lacking in Schelling's later presentations on the relationship between art, the nation, and the state. In both the *System der gesamten Philosophie und der Naturphilosophie insbesondere* (of 1804, hereafter referred to as the *Würzburg Lectures*) and the *Münchener Rede*, Schelling no longer opposes mythology and the state. Instead, the new mythology, or a renewal of artistic creation, will contribute to the formation of the state as a moral force. The shift toward the mythologization of politics parallels a change in Schelling's conception of the state, for in the latter texts, he argues against Kantian cosmopolitanism in favor of the organic state (VI, 575) and enlightened paternalism (1968: 355/VII, 327). On this basis, the appearance of a new mythology becomes the means of public participation within the paternalist and monarchist state. Or, to make a more critical assessment, mythology becomes the ideological representation of public participation: one can participate through a public set of rituals and beliefs without participating in the structures of political empowerment.

In the *Würzburg Lectures*, Schelling presents the state as the ultimate realization of science, religion, and art. His remarks on art are brief, and are oriented toward his conception of a public sphere. As Schelling states, the modern world lacks a proper *Symbolik* (6: 571), which, in German usage, is 'not only a system of symbolism but also a coherent doctrine of faith' (Williamson, 2004: 336, n. 35). As mentioned in the *Philosophy of Art*, the modern condition has only created partial and fragmentary mythologies, such as in the work of Dante, Shakespeare, Cervantes, and Goethe (VI, 572; see also Section 4.4). The diagnosis, according to Schelling, is that a truly public sphere can bring about a truly organic state:

Lyrical poetry lives and exists truthfully only in a universally public life. Where all public life collapses into the particulars and dullness of private life, poetry more or less sinks into this same sphere. Epic poetry requires chiefly mythology and is nothing without it. But even mythology is not possible in the particular; it can only be born in the totality of a nation that as such acts simultaneously as identity and individuality. In dramatic poetry, tragedy grounds itself in the public law, in virtue, religion, heroism – in a word – in the holiness of the nation. A nation that is not holy, or which was robbed of its holy relics, cannot have true tragedy.

[. . .] The question of the possibility of a universal content of *poesie*, just as the question of the objective existence of science and religion, impels us to something higher. Only in the spiritual unity of a people, in a truly public life, can true and generally valid *poesie* arise – as only in the spiritual and political unity of a people can science and religion find its objectivity. (VI, 572–573)

The political unity of a people arises organically in the nation-state, not in the private pursuit of individual right within a state. Instead, the state develops organically, through the development of religion, science and art, into their highest expression. As Schelling recognizes, this state has never existed, but he is here giving a prescriptive account of a future state. The important shift to recognize is that the state is the apex of the system. Unlike the previous potencies – science, religion, and art – the state is *Potenzlos*, which means that it has no opposition; any opposition is the result of the state oppressing one or more of its living elements (VI, 575). Although he gives very little indication of how this state is to come about, he claims that the relationship of reason to the universe is analogous to that of philosophy to the state: just as reason realizes itself in the universe, philosophy realizes itself through the public life of the state.[34]

Despite the lack of an explicit reference to the idea of a new mythology, the *Münchener Rede* is not just about the common source of nature, history, and art; it also argues for a thoroughgoing renewal of art within the German *Volk*. The entire question of how nature should inspire art is not only of interest to the art historian, but rather points forward toward the realization of art within a unified people or nation. The task, for the artist, is to draw inspiration from nature in order to renew German art. Just as German thought brought forth a revolution in thought, so should it bring forth a revolution in art:

This people (*Volk*), from which the revolution of thought in the new Europe proceeded, to whose intellectual power the greatest inventions bear witness, which has given laws to the heavens and whose investigations have penetrated most deeply into the earth, in whom nature has implanted more deeply than any other a steadfast feeling for the right and an inclination toward the recognition of first causes, this people must reach its conclusion in an original art. (1968: 357tm/VII, 328)

Thus the advances of German thought remain ideal; artistic production, then, still functions in the role of the new mythology, insofar as it should, according to Schelling, realize the revolution of thought for and through the people.[35] This, I think, designates an inchoate project of nationalism that conceives of a people as an organic totality. By contrast, Peter Oesterreich argues that Schelling's call for an original German art is not nationalistic, rather it argues that all original artforms draw on the productive power of nature. That Schelling recognizes the originality and singularity of other national arts (such as the Italian Renaissance) shows for Oesterreich a national pluralism: 'for Schelling, the visible principle of original variations should also rule the world of nations. The equality (*Egalität*) of peoples, therefore, does not consist in sameness (*Gleichheit*), but rather the similar originality of their cultural forms, which present themselves as characteristic art' (Oesterreich, 1996: 107). While I agree that Schelling argues that original art must draw on the productive power of nature, the problem with this argument is that recognizing the diversity of cultural forms is not incompatible with nationalism. Schelling also 'recognizes,' as it were, the singularity of the French, who 'have an exclusively literal understanding of almost all the more exalted subjects,' in a long excursus on the misunderstanding of what it means to imitate or emulate the ancients (1968: 364/ VII, 325). Yet it is not just that Schelling is juxtaposing the virtues and vices of peoples (who are interpreted as nations), but that his conception of a people is that of an organic totality, a concept with dangerous political implications because it masks the internal divisions of society with an ideological homogeneity, excluding in practice those who are not properly members of the community. The issue is not whether Schelling was a nationalist himself, it is whether or not his work resonated with emerging German nationalism. In this regard, Schelling's rhetoric shows some similarity to proto-nationalist sentiment, especially in the way that he proposes a communal role for the new mythology that was once played by religious mythology (see Chapter 4 and Anderson, 2006: 12–19). *This* community imagined through mythology is the problem with what I call Schelling's *mythologization of politics.*

When the *Münchener Rede* praises the 'charitable dominion of a paternal regent' who allows for the proper cultivation for the public reception of art, these compliments are not politically neutral (1968: 355tm/VII, 327). The superiority of the paternal regent arises from preventing the leveling that Schelling associates with democracy in general and the French Revolution in particular, which he claims subordinates the majesty of artistic creation to popular applause. By contrast, according to Schelling, Bavarian paternalism allows for the cultivation of the firmly established taste and public opinion of a whole people (1968: 355–356/VII, 327).[36] The cultivation of the public sphere thus becomes an ideological justification for the Bavarian state-form.

We have focused primarily on the ideological component of the mythologization of politics, and the features which can, beyond the work of Schelling, justify either antidemocratic or oppressive measures when they are taken up within a statist or nationalist project. It would be an incomplete and undialectical (and very Lukacsian) account of Schelling's politics if we did not also discuss the material conditions of this ideological position. Hence, we should turn to Schelling's situation in Munich, where it appears, despite all the grandiose rhetoric of the *Münchener Rede*, that he also had a much more practical and pedagogical goal.

Schelling contributed to the cultivation of the public sphere from 1808–1821 through his appointment as Secretary General of the *Akademie der bildenden Künste* in Munich. Sziborsky shows that Schelling's involvement included writing the constitution of the *Akademie*. She cites a letter to Cotta, dated May 15, 1808, in which Schelling states that most of his ideas have been realized in the constitution, which provided for a society for art open to the larger public for the purposes of appreciation and cultivation (1986: 39–64).[37] In an essay published in 1808, despite its largely descriptive tone, Schelling again reaffirms his views that mythology should be cultivated as the living ideal of art, and that this art is grounded in the essence of a nation (VII, 559–560, 567–568). But if pedagogy is the goal, these stances have much less ideological and political force, and sound, in this context, like a hyperbolic grant application: it is not that the renewal of art justifies the state, but that an art institution musters all the available arguments it can for continued patronage. In retrospect, it seems ill advised, though hardly a trip to Syracuse, as it were. In fact, soon Schelling's enthusiasm for art would wane, due, in all likelihood, to his change in philosophical orientation from his interest in artistic production to the relationship between freedom and system (see also Tilliette, 1978: xxxvii–xlvii).

With this change in orientation, found in the *Stuttgart Seminars*, Schelling includes a critique of the state, and by consequence, a self-critique. There, the inclusion of the Fall into his account of history leads to a reconceptualization of the state as an external or material unity, or even a 'consequence of the curse that has been placed on humanity' (1994a: 227/VII, 461). At its basis, the state cannot escape the central contradiction of moral force: because morality is a higher potency than the institution of the state, any attempt to realize a moral power through the natural means at its disposal (whether in the French Revolution or through Kantian concepts) will result in failure. If the state realizes the conditions of the highest realization of freedom, then it is deprived of coercive force, or, granted coercive force, it turns to despotism (1994a: 227/VII, 461–462). The possibility of the unity of humanity, and its realization through freedom, is only possible through religious knowledge:

> only the supreme and most diverse culture of religious knowledge will enable humanity, if not to abolish the state outright, then at least to ensure that the state will progressively divest itself of the blind force that governs it, and to transfigure this force into intelligence. It is not that the Church ought to dominate the state or vice versa, but that the state ought to cultivate the religious principles within itself and that the community of all peoples ought to be founded on religious convictions that, themselves, ought to become universal. (1994a: 229/VII, 464–465)

If Schelling still has a program, a 'system program,' as it were, for the future, for some way to reconcile the fragmentary condition of humanity, it is through religious study: not through the institution of the church (itself divided internally and externally), but through the study of that peculiar doctrine of knowledge itself, philosophy. For Schelling, this will take place far from the public eye, until his arrival in Berlin in 1841, ten years after the death of Hegel, and seven before the publication of *The Communist Manifesto*. The development of subsequent answers to the problems of modernity and its philosophy, which, in the 19th century, included positive philosophy, the phenomenology of spirit, and historical materialism, is itself another story.

Conclusion

The *Philosophical Investigations into the Essence of Human Freedom* (1809) and the *Stuttgart Seminars* (1810) mark Schelling's return to the question of the relationship between freedom and the system, which is exactly where the *Philosophical Letters on Dogmatism and Criticism* (1795–1796) began. I have argued that the path from freedom to artistic activity and back is everything: Schelling's return to the primacy of freedom should be understood by way of his development of a philosophy of art. This philosophy of art, which holds that artistic activity realizes the ideas of philosophy in the world, anticipates his philosophy of freedom, wherein Schelling develops an *ecstatic* account of freedom as a creative force within finitude, and not as a formal conception according to the imperative of a moral law. To conclude, I will reconstruct Schelling's path toward a philosophy of freedom.

The *Letters* is one of the early stages on Schelling's way. This multifaceted text remained a consistent touchstone as Schelling sought to establish the continuity of the development of his philosophical thought. First, Schelling refers to it in his later epistolary debates with Fichte over the status and legitimacy of nature-philosophy and absolute idealism. Then it 1809 it was included in his *Philosophische Schriften* insofar as it plants the 'seeds of later and more positive views' (2006: 3/AA, I/4: 58). Finally, in his lectures in Berlin in 1841, Schelling refers to the *Letters* as an early anticipation of the division between negative and positive philosophy (2007a: 146/XIII, 82).

Schelling's later interpretations rely on two features found in the *Letters*: first, its distinction between two systems of philosophy, each of which attempt to interpret an absolute that is neither subjective nor objective, and second, its insistence that the only ground of a system's validity is its practical consequences. Schelling holds that neither criticism nor dogmatism can be refuted theoretically, but only refuted practically. This practical contest plays out in how the philosopher lives her system. The dogmatist, in practice, identifies her activity with what Schelling calls the absolute object (the world or God as absolute necessity), which he argues risks the moral ruin of human agency. The risk of moral ruin is derived from *identification*: the dogmatist interprets her activity merely as a modification of the causality of absolute necessity. By contrast, the critical philosopher interprets her activity as an infinite striving toward the absolute. Practically speaking, criticism is a superior system, Schelling argues, because it can account for the infinite activity of the self through freedom. Although Schelling does not force all the consequences of the *Letters* in his early work, the text anticipates his later attempt to reconcile the systematic nature of philosophy with human freedom. Freedom is explicitly thought as an infinite activity of creation: were a system completed, and no longer *lived* by its creator, at that 'very moment [its creator] would cease to be *creator* and would be degraded to an instrument of his system' (1980: 172tm/I, 306). It is this idea of creativity that Schelling later elevates over Fichte's and Kant's formalism.

In the *Letters,* however, Schelling's concerns are constrained to the rivalry of criticism and dogmatism. The rivalry turns on how each philosopher lives her system: this ethical life presents several problems for the dogmatist, who identifies her own actions with absolute necessity, thus misrecognizing the free choice at the basis of the system. The critical philosopher, however, not only holds that 'I act freely,' or that 'I will act freely,' but she also recognizes this free choice retroactively, by looking back at the initial act through the future anterior, that 'I will have acted freely.'[1] The initial act, to draw a comparison with Schelling's later thought (not to mention, perhaps, Sartre or Heidegger), is an ecstatic moment of freedom, and the problem that drives Schelling's thought is how a system can be realized that accounts for this freedom. The primacy of freedom becomes even clearer when compared, in the 'Tenth Letter,' to Greek tragedy. While tragedy presents the ultimate tribute to human freedom, it cannot be the basis of an ethics because the idea of fate diminishes the potential of freedom. So, where the critical philosopher states that 'I act freely,' the model of tragedy falters because it could allow the self to act in bad faith: 'I would act freely but for fate . . .'

After the *Letters,* Schelling turns his attention to researching a 'speculative physics.' The result of this research, which Schelling develops as nature-philosophy, is decisive for his philosophical trajectory. Without due consideration of the impact of nature-philosophy, it is impossible to grasp the role of the philosophy of art, and later, the idea of human freedom that animates the *Freiheitsschrift* and beyond. He argues in this text that the whole of modern philosophy lacks a philosophy of nature (2006: 26/VII, 356). As early as the *Ideas for a Philosophy of Nature* (1797), Schelling criticizes modern philosophy for interpreting nature as a mechanistic universe that has some unexplained relationship to the free activity of the mind because this stance divorces the self's productivity from the world. The critique of modern philosophy, and Fichte's idealism in particular, sharpens as Schelling extends the explanatory power of nature-philosophy within his system. In the *Ideas*, Schelling restrains the task of nature-philosophy to the demand that 'Nature should be Mind made visible, Mind the invisible Nature' (1988: 42/II, 56). He attempts to make good on this demand by drawing on the thought of Spinoza and Leibniz, along with Kant's concept of teleology, to show how self-consciousness emerges within nature. These ideas are further developed in the *Introduction to the First Outline of a System of the Philosophy of Nature* (1799), where Schelling argues, drawing on Spinoza, that nature is both producing (*natura naturans*) and product (*natura naturata*) (see Section 3.3). The common source of subjective and objective productivity, the *natura naturans*, became central to Schelling's absolute idealism (Chapter 4).

This gradual extension of nature-philosophy from one side of the system to the framework of the system itself – that is, the transition of transcendental idealism to absolute idealism – has been a stumbling block for readers of Schelling's work; it has led to his reputation as a protean thinker rather than a systematic one. I have argued that Schelling's emphasis on creation, whether it is manifested as the idea of freedom or as artistic production, demonstrates the continuity of his thought.

The guiding thread of this continuity is *how* this creative activity becomes Schelling's alternative and superior principle compared to the formal accounts of freedom offered by his predecessors. First, in the *System of Transcendental Idealism*, Schelling's philosophy of art takes on a subversive character vis-à-vis Fichte's transcendental idealism. Fichte had sought to ground philosophy in practical reason, in the infinite striving of the subject's activity. In the *System of Transcendental Idealism*, Schelling reinterprets the self's activity as absolute productivity, as the ground of both subjectivity and objectivity. Thus to close the circle of the system, Schelling must search for a principle that can produce this identity objectively.

From this perspective, practical reason and its emphasis on the infinite striving toward objectifying the categorical imperative can no longer suffice to ground the transcendental system. It cannot ground the system because practical reason is itself grounded through the division between subject and object. As Schelling argues, the self is both unconsciously and consciously productive, and this distinction makes the *appearance* of freedom possible. On one hand, the self produces representations of objects, and on the other, the self, as practical, seeks to transform objects according to its activity, but practical reason cannot overcome this distinction between the unconscious and conscious production (see Section 3.2.2). Instead, practical reason becomes the basis of the transcendental distinction between the in itself and appearances. While in itself the self's activity is both free and necessary, in appearance the self acts freely within a world of representations that bring with them a feeling of necessity. Schelling concludes that freedom is a necessary illusion, although only through practice do the representations of reality obtain. Thus practical reason cannot explain the identity of subject and object; rather, practical reason *is explained* by the distinction between subject and object.

By contrast, artistic production meets Schelling's demand for a conscious activity that produces objectively the identity of subject and object, of freedom and nature. Where practical reason can only infinitely approximate its object, which is the moral law, artistic production realizes the identity of freedom and necessity in the work of art. Artistic activity – which he calls aesthetic intuition (the objective equivalent of intellectual intuition) – gives the objective proof of that which philosophy demonstrates ideally. Artistic production does not follow a formal rule, but rather produces the inner harmony of the artwork only through its realization. Not only does aesthetic intuition ground practical reason, it also demonstrates with consciousness the identity of free production and natural compulsion, an identity that we can also see in an unconscious form in nature (see Section 3.3). By grounding the entire system in aesthetic intuition, Schelling deduces a conceptual structure that I have argued forms the *Three Conditions* of his philosophy of art:

C1. What philosophy constructs in the ideal, art produces in the real. Thus artistic activity is the highest human vocation (*Bestimmung*) because practical philosophy can only approximate its object, which is the moral law.
C2. While both the natural organism and the artwork embody the same identity of real and ideal, of necessity and freedom, the work of art overcomes these oppositions through the identity of conscious and unconscious production, whereas the organism's activity is unconscious.
C3. Artistic production has a socio-political task: it aims to overcome the fragmentary condition of modernity through a new mythology and artistic renewal.

The third condition proves decisive in the fate of Schelling's philosophy of art, for, once stripped of its socio-political consequences, the philosophy of art and the central role it gives to artistic production is subsumed under higher forms. In the *System of Transcendental Idealism*, Schelling's discussion of a new mythology remains brief but full of promise. He argues that, since art makes objective what philosophy has proved in ideal form, and since it perfects the development of the sciences that were first 'nourished' by poetry, that the complete philosophy and its various sciences would 'flow back like so many individual streams into the universal ocean of poetry.' The medium for this return will be a new mythology that will be the creation of a new 'race' personifying 'a single poet' (1978: 232–233/III, 629). While the *System of Transcendental Idealism* claims that the problem of how this mythology is to arise must be resolved in the 'course of history to come' (1978: 233/III, 629), Schelling nevertheless develops a possible answer in the lectures collected in *The Philosophy of Art*.

While the metaphysics of absolute idealism reject the commitments of transcendental idealism – for absolute idealism claims to begin from the standpoint of reason itself, instead of from the transcendental self's activity – during this period Schelling still argues that art presents or realizes what philosophy intuits ideally. Art plays this role because of the priority Schelling gives to the power of imagination (*Einbildungskraft*) within the absolute system: art is the *informing* (*Ineinsbildung*) of the infinite into the finite; imagination is the complementary power to philosophical construction, which intuits the universal in the particular. Thus the *Philosophy of Art* provides a unique answer to the central problem of the system of identity, the problem of finding the transition from the infinite to the finite.

The *Philosophy of Art* attempts to explain this transition in a unique way, through the historical construction of the mythological content of art (Chapter 4). Mythology presents the sensuous informing of the ideas of reason. In this account, however, Schelling encounters a contradiction between the formal deduction of substance and the historical construction of mythology. The substance of the system, its first and all-encompassing principle, is an eternal and impersonal God, while the construction of Greek mythology and Christian mythology presents the Greek gods and Christian God as revealed in the finite world. I have argued that Schelling is faced with a contradiction between the first principle, which is absolute and eternal, and historical revelation through mythology. If Schelling maintains the first principle (the absolute, eternal substance), this renders mythology as mere appearance or illusion, and yet, if he maintains the actuality – or informing – of the revelation of the gods, this contravenes the form of the immutable, eternal substance. Schelling does not resolve this contradiction because of the socio-political importance of the new mythology, because his analyses of art and mythology are driven by his search for a social form that can overcome the fragmentary structure of society and unify it in an organic totality. The modern artist, he argues, must create a unified whole in the work of art out of the fragmentary relationships that govern the individual's role in society. This is the role of novelists and dramatists such as Goethe. Just as the philosopher can think the totality of the world, the artist produces it in objective form.

These problems are taken up yet again in the address *Über das Verhältnis der bildenden Künste zu der Natur* (hereafter the *Münchener Rede*), in which Schelling turns to a historical or revealed account of the development of nature, history, and art (Chapter 5). In the *Münchener Rede*, Schelling argues that nature's productive power (*Urkraft*) is repeated in human history and artistic production. So while nature is the ground of art, it is only through art that nature's productivity is revealed. The difference between the *Philosophy of Art* and the *Münchener Rede* is that in the latter text substance is revealed in history. Schelling's previous Spinozism gives way to a historical revelation of divine essence through art. At the same time, Schelling presents a self-creating artistic *ethos* of the *Münchener Rede*, which is a positive, creative power that can overcome the various passions in the formation of beauty or the sublime in the work of art. This singular ethics unifies the true (of nature and science) and the good (in overcoming the passions) through the beautiful, which at the same time reveals the history of nature's production.

Through its emphasis on history and revelation, the *Münchener Rede*, then, prefigures the concerns of the *Philosophical Investigations into the Essence of Human Freedom* (1809) and the *Stuttgart Seminars* (1810). However, in the latter texts, Schelling undergoes a theological turn: his construction of history is no longer oriented toward the production of various, monumental series of artworks, such as those of Michelangelo-Correggio-Raphael from the Renaissance, nor does he call for a renewal of art through the proper approach to nature; now, in the *Stuttgart Seminars*, history is constructed with the inclusion of both the Fall of humanity and Christ's redemption as real events. The focus is no longer on artistic activity, which is relegated in this text to a kind of longing for a lost bond with nature, but rather on the human capacity for good and evil. This capacity is possible because human being *exists* at the point of indifference, or mediation, between nature and God. The relative independence or distance from both nature and God becomes the basis of human freedom. Thus in Schelling's philosophy, freedom emerges where artistic activity once was.

In the trajectory from freedom to artistic activity and back to freedom, the path is everything: freedom did not just emerge *ex nihilo* in Schelling's thought in 1809 or 1810, it had been slowly developed at first through a philosophy of art as a kind of artistic *ethos*. Hence this return to freedom is grounded on an entirely different conception than Schelling's early work. Whereas in his more Fichtean phase, Schelling held that freedom was conceived according to the imperative of the moral law, he now holds that freedom demonstrates its own creative power in the finite world through virtue. Freedom is not thought in conformity to the a priori moral law, but is now conceived as an ecstatic act: freedom is possible because humanity *stands out* from nature and the divine, something that, in different terms, was once reserved for artistic activity.

Schelling's turn from the *ethos* of art in favor of a renewal of a universal religion, was to have decisive effects on the reception of his thought, for in post-Enlightenment Germany – through Hegel, Feuerbach, Marx, and before them, the young Schelling himself – religion itself was in question.[2] Religion became, in the work of Marx, a mystified expression of both real suffering and the objective conditions of human activity. Religion in the realm of politics became ever more criticized as oppressive and religious criticism became ever more criticized as obscurantist. We will not render a judgment on the later Schelling, who entered Berlin in 1841 with his system of positive philosophy to root out the dragon seed of Hegelianism. However, we can say that in his turn *toward* a universal philosophical religion, Schelling turns *away* from the *demand*, of the *Philosophy of Art*, that modern art collect the fragments of subjective life and unify them within a totality that could express the objective conditions of human existence.

To close, we will return to the epigraph of the present study, which reproduces Marx's comments on Greek art. How, he asks, does Greek art still 'count,' under the material conditions of capitalism, 'as a norm and as an unattainable model?' Marx concludes with the verdict that Greek art (and mythology) exercises a continued charm that is the result of the fact 'that the unripe social conditions under which it arose, and could alone arise, can never return' (1973: 111). Without disputing Marx's verdict, his emphasis on Greek art obscures the general problem of art in the age of mechanical reproduction: why does art seem to offer a utopian sociopolitical promise? If Greek art and mythology remain the norm and unattainable model of Schelling's philosophy of art, it is not because he thought Greek society could be reborn in Germany; rather, it is because it offered a model for a new mythico-political space that could resolve the contradictions of the rapid transformation of German social life in the 19th century. That this particular political vision is untenable nevertheless does not mean art is for us a thing of the past.

Schelling is one of the first modern philosophers to grasp artistic production as a form of socio-political criticism, which makes him an important predecessor to those who, a century later, returned art to the forefront of philosophical thought, such as Walter Benjamin, Martin Heidegger, and Alain Badiou. What they share is a critical and philosophical interest in artistic production – in its truth, or in its activity – despite their differences over what the conditions of human activity *are*. I hope to have shown that Schelling's philosophy of art merits the same careful attention that has been given to his better-known successors.

Notes

Introduction

[1] The idea of freedom has been cast as Schelling's fundamental thought by Heidegger (1985) and, despite his many criticisms, White (1983); on nature-philosophy see Merleau-Ponty (2003); Grant (2008); and Esposito (1977). On the relationship between Schelling and Hegel see Frank (1975); Bowie (1993); and Žižek (1996).

[2] Although their reasoning varies, this includes, among others, Braeckman, 2004: 551–569; Lawrence, 1988: 5–19; Bowie, 1990: 84–88; and Beiser, 2002a: 584–585.

[3] Schelling never loses his interest in mythology, but reconstructing the relationship between mythology, religion, and positive philosophy in his work after 1809 requires a separate study.

[4] By 'mythologization of politics' I mean the gradual conceptual unification of art, mythology, and the state, in which mythology serves, or is proposed, as an ideological component of legitimating political power (see Section 5.4).

Chapter 1

[1] I will use the term *Wissenschaftslehre* to refer to Fichte's system, apart from any particular attempt at articulating this system. I will refer to *Über den Begriff der Wissenschaftslehre* as *Concerning the Concept of the Wissenschaftslehre*, which is translated in Fichte's *Early Philosophical Writings* (1988: 94–135/I, 29–81) and I will refer to the *Grundlage der gesamten Wissenschaftslehre* by the title provided by the translators of the English edition, *Science of Knowledge* (1982).

[2] These, however, are not Schelling's first texts. By the time he had become interested in critical idealism Schelling had already published works on the origin of evil, and mythology, respectively: *De prima malorum humanorum origine philosophematis Gen. III explicandi tentamen criticum et philosophicum*, and *Über Mythen, historische Sagen und Philosopheme der ältesten Welt*.

[3] For the historical details see Beiser, 1987: 44–126; di Giovanni, 1994: 3–116; and Altmann, 1973, 553–744. Snow directly relates the work of Jacobi to the early Schelling (1996: 1–32).

[4] For their polemics after 1811 see Snow, 1996: 205–215; and Ford, 1965: 75–89.

[5] It seems that for a time Jacobi also appreciated their work. In a letter to Jens Baggesen from 1797, Jacobi writes that 'Fichte and Schelling are now referring ever more frequently, extensively and emphatically to my writings, and in all the works of the latter one can see how he has given them [e.g. Jacobi's writings] flesh and blood. . . . For my part I must try and see if perhaps these men have succeeded in understanding me better than I do myself, and if I might not – through them – learn something better from myself than I knew I was teaching, which would in no way be impossible' (quoted in Snow, 1996: 207–208).

[6] In the following, we will only be interested in Jacobi's reading of Spinoza and other modern philosophers, and not the accuracy, or lack thereof, of his readings.

[7] I have omitted the second point of Jacobi's argument because it is less relevant to our discussion. It says that the '*philosophy* of the cabbala, or so much of it as is available to research, and *in accordance with its best commentators, von Helmont the younger and Wachter is, as philosophy*, nothing but undeveloped or newly confused Spinozism' (1994: 233–234).

8 Although, as Manfred Frank argues, Jacobi's concept of a 'feeling' of faith has some foundation in the work of Kant (2004: 56–75 and 83–84).

9 It should be noted that Jacobi rehabilitates Leibniz when he finds it necessary to confront the emerging Kantian philosophy in *David Hume on Faith, or Idealism and Realism* (1994: 253–338).

10 Di Giovanni goes to great lengths to both deny charges of irrationalism against Jacobi, and to show how Jacobi made great strides toward an 'unfinished philosophy' of 'historical reason' (1994: 82–86). Beiser argues that Jacobi endorses relativism by rejecting the Enlightenment belief in objective inquiry; though others, such as Hume and Helvetius, held that interests and desires governed practical action, Jacobi extends the priority of the will over reason 'in a new and dangerous direction,' to the domain of theory. As Beiser writes, 'Jacobi's chief contention [is] that we cannot separate the realms of theory and practice, because knowledge is the consequence of right action, truth the result of the proper interests' (Beiser, 1987: 85–89). Although Beiser shows that Jacobi later develops his relativistic position, I argue that the 1785 edition of the *Doctrine of Spinoza* holds both that human action is conditioned by its historical situations and that Christianity is a universal (and ahistorical) standard of practical instruction.

11 Recall Schelling's admiration for Jacobi's ability to differentiate between 'absolute, immutable being and every kind of conditional, changeable existence' (1980: 109/I, 216).

12 Beiser argues that despite these arguments against Spinoza and the Enlightenment, Jacobi was also (in his other works) an 'advocate of the fundamental ideals of the *Aufklärung* – liberty of conscience, religious toleration [and] equality before the law' (Beiser, 1992: 138–153).

13 In the *Critique of Practical Reason*, Kant mentions that a comparison of the two *Critiques* would raise the 'expectation of bringing some day into one view the unity of the entire pure rational faculty (both theoretical and practical) and of being able to derive everything from one principle. The latter is an unavoidable need of human reason, as it finds complete satisfaction only in a perfectly systematic unity of its cognitions' (1956: 94/V, 91).

14 Neuhouser discusses these developments within the framework of Fichte's early unpublished writings on Kant (1990, 11–31); Beiser underlines the importance of these skeptical objections to Fichte's development (2002a: 240–259); concerning the 'Review of Aenesidemus,' see Breazeale (1981: 545–568).

15 We focus on the first part because in a letter to Niethammer, dated January 22, 1796, Schelling states that he had not yet read the third part on practical philosophy (AA, III/1: 40).

16 For a discussion of Fichte's dialectical method and its use of formal logic, see Seebohm, 1994: 17–42.

17 I will translate '*Ich*' as either 'I' or 'self' and '*Nicht-Ich*' as 'not-I' or 'not-self.' It should be understood that this 'self' is not the empirical self but conceived as a pure self.

18 Fichte states that the '*form* of ~A is determined absolutely by the act; it is an opposite, because it is the product of an opposition. Its *matter* is governed by A; it is not what A is, and its whole essence consists in that fact' (1982: 104/I, 104).

19 As mentioned above, the status of the absolute subject in the *Science of Knowledge* has been the subject of much debate. Insofar as these demonstrations have methodological, ontological, epistemological, and ethical consequences, I think that interpreting the absolute subject as *either* a theoretical *or* a practical principle rests on a false dilemma. As I have shown, Fichte argues that it is both. Thus there is no reason to attribute a 'fundamental inconsistency' to the foundations of the *Science of Knowledge* as Neuhouser does (1990: 41–53, especially 52). My argument owes much to Beiser, 2002a: 273–288.

20 This requires Fichte to downplay Kant's use of the thing in itself. See Beiser, 2002a: 260–272.

21 Incidentally, Kant also says as much about his dogmatic rivals in the *Critique of Pure Reason*: 'The first step in matters of pure reason, which characterizes its childhood, is dogmatic. The [. . .] second step is skeptical, and gives evidence of the caution of the power of judgment sharpened by experience. Now, however, a third step is still necessary, which pertains only to the mature and adult power of judgment, [. . . which is] the critique of pure reason' (1998: 654/A761/B789).

22 See also Baumgartner, 1999: 241–250.

[23] I have borrowed the term 'extensive' from Grant, (2008: 20), who writes that 'extensity' refers to the range and capacity of a philosophical system. Schelling's system will be more extensive than Fichte's, at this point, because it intends to mediate between Spinoza and Fichte, while later, it is more extensive insofar as it develops a nature-philosophy.

[24] If we oppose Schelling to Jacobi, his Spinozism becomes clearer. The letter of February 4, 1795 continues with Schelling's proof against the idea of a personal God: 'For us there is no supersensuous world other than the absolute I. [. . .] Personality emerges through the unity of consciousness. But consciousness is not possible without an object. But for God, that is, for the absolute I, there is no object *at all*, for it would thereby cease to be absolute – therefore there is no personal God' (AA, III/1: 23). Schelling will hold to an impersonal God until at least 1807 (as I will argue in Chapter 5, the essay *Über das Verhältnis der bildenden Künste zu der Natur* is not clear on this point), and more than likely until around 1809.

[25] See also Frank 1985: 61–70; Marquet, by contrast, suggests that Schelling might have influenced Hölderlin (2006: 73).

[26] Dieter Henrich argues that Hölderlin's argumentation is Spinozist (1997: 71–89).

[27] Due to an editorial interference, the first installment of the *Letters* has the term *Dogmaticismus* (dogmaticism) in the place of *Dogmatismus* (dogmatism). In the Fifth Letter, Schelling distinguishes between the two by stating that Kant had refuted dogmaticism, that is, the metaphysics of the 18th century, such as Wolff and Leibniz (1980: 169/I, 302; and Düsing, 1999: 206–207).

[28] For an illuminating essay on Storr and Flatt, see Henrich, 1997: 31–54.

[29] As Kant states in the *Critique of Practical Reason*, 'most actions conforming to the law would be done from fear, few would be done from hope, none from duty. The moral worth of actions, on which alone the worth of the person and even of the world depends in the eyes of supreme wisdom, would not exist at all. The conduct of man, so long as his nature remained as it now is, would be changed into mere mechanism, where, as in a puppet show, everything would gesticulate well but no life would be found in the figures' (1956: 152–153/V, 147).

[30] If the thing in itself and the transcendental object are different, Kant seems to use them as synonyms in this passage. Later Kant attributes the givenness of space to the transcendental object (1998: 545/A557/B585).

[31] For an account of the importance of this text in Fichte's development, see Breazeale, 1981: 545–568.

[32] Although Fichte does not mention it, in the 'Transcendental Aesthetic,' Kant argues that the transcendental ideality of space and time also implies their empirical reality.

[33] In this regard Schelling cites two passages from Spinoza's *Ethics*: first, 'That thing is said to be free (liber) which exists solely from the necessity of its own nature, and is determined to action by itself alone' (definition 7, Part I; 1992: 31), and second, 'God acts solely from the laws of his own nature, constrained by none' (prop. 17, Part I; 1992: 44).

[34] George ignores the fact that the *Letters* follows Fichte in demarcating the boundaries of theoretical reason in order to demonstrate the practical superiority of criticism, and that Schelling excludes the tragic as a system of practical action. George claims that the Schelling of the *Letters* argues for the following anachronistic, proto-Heideggerian positions: (1) the fractured character of reason, (2) the theme of the end of philosophy, and (3) the attribution of arrogance to systematic philosophy, whether critical or dogmatic. None of these positions are Schelling's. Instead, Schelling argues for (1) the limitation of theoretical reason in favor of practical reason and the power of freedom, (2) the defense of the term 'philosophy' against Fichte's introduction of *Wissenschaftslehre* in its place (1980: 172/I, 307, footnote). Finally, (3) it would be odd to call either dogmatism or criticism arrogant, considering Schelling's sympathy for both Spinoza and Fichte; the problem is neither arrogance nor the 'failure' of criticism, but the claim that one system could assert that it is the *complete* system of philosophy. There are, as I have pointed out, differences between Fichte and Schelling, but certainly not because Schelling is a proto-Heideggerian.

[35] In this regard, my interpretation agrees with that of Szondi (2002) and also White (1983: 24–37).

[36] Where for Kant (1988: 159/IV, 260) this 'dogmatic slumber' is theoretical, for Schelling it is practical.

Chapter 2

[1] Despite its many critics, nature-philosophy has influenced the phenomenology of Martin Heidegger (1985: 137–139) and Maurice Merleau-Ponty (2003: 36–51). Iain Hamilton Grant has argued that nature-philosophy is the core of 'Schellingianism' (see Grant, 2004 and 2008).

[2] This is true whether or not it is Schelling's system that is parodied by the remark that pitting the 'single insight that in the Absolute everything is the same . . . is to palm off its Absolute as the night in which, as the saying goes, all cows are black' (1977b: 9). For the debate over the target of this comment, see Harris (1987: 627–643); Vater (1987: 645–652); and di Giovanni (1987: 653–663).

[3] Grant argues that nature-philosophy is the core and guiding thread to properly understanding Schelling's philosophy, although the strength of his argument is bought at the price of Schelling's interest in freedom and its relationship to the philosophy of art that is the basis of the present book.

[4] The renamed second edition of the Survey (*Allgemeine Übersicht*) is translated as *Treatise Explicatory of the Idealism in the Science of Knowledge* (1797) in *Idealism and the Endgame of Theory* (1994a), 61–138. The English translation of the *Ideas* (1988) relies on that text's second edition.

[5] The original reads: '*eine Naturlehre unsers Geistes.*' I've modified the possessive form in subsequent references.

[6] In the *Second Introduction*, Fichte argues that idealists and dogmatists 'find themselves in two worlds, that are entirely sundered from each other' (1982: 78n/I, 509n), which is a striking contrast with Schelling's opposition of the critical idealist to the dogmatist, who have incompatible philosophies, but of the *same* absolute.

[7] For Kant, this unity of thinking and matter is only hypothetical, because it could not be discovered by theoretical philosophy. See, for instance, this passage from the *Critique of Pure Reason*: 'The problem of explaining the community of the soul with the body' consists 'in the presumed difference in kind between the object of inner sense (the soul) and the object of outer sense, since to the former only time pertains as the formal condition of its intuition, while to the latter space pertains also. But if one considers that the two kinds of objects are different not inwardly but only insofar as one of them appears outwardly to the other, hence that what grounds the appearance of matter as thing in itself *might perhaps not be so different in kind* [my emphasis], then this difficulty vanishes, and the only difficulty remaining is that concerning how a community of substances is possible at all, the resolution of which lies . . . outside the field of all human cognition' (1998: 455–456/B427–428).

[8] As Spinoza states in the *Ethics*, 'whatever can be perceived by infinite intellect as constituting the essence of substance pertains entirely the one sole substance. Consequently, thinking substance and extended substance are one and the same substance, comprehended now under this attribute, now under that' (Scholium, Proposition 7, Part II; 1992: 67).

[9] The translators of the *Ideas* render *Vorstellung* as 'idea' which obscures Schelling's technical distinction between *Vorstellung* and *Idee*.

[10] Recall, as discussed in Chapter 1, that Schelling holds the absolute subject (the I) and absolute object (Spinoza's God) to be conceptually symmetrical. Thus the absolute I, unlike the finite I, acts 'acts solely from the laws of his own nature, constrained by none' just as Spinoza's God does (prop. 17, Part I; 1992: 44).

[11] There is precedent in Fichte's 'Review of Aenesidemus' (1988: 73/I, 19–20). In the *Second Introduction to the Science of Knowledge* Fichte approvingly references Schelling's account of Leibniz (1982: 82–83/I, 514–515).

[12] The reference is to §7 of the 'Monadology': 'Monads have no windows, through which anything could come in or go out' (Leibniz, 1998: 268).

[13] Kant states 'since in any doctrine of nature there is only as much proper science as there is a priori knowledge therein, a doctrine of nature will contain only as much proper science as there is mathematics capable of application there' (2004: 6/IV, 470).

[14] I have made use of several secondary sources for this discussion, including McFarland (1970); Makkreel (1991); and especially Allison (1991).

[15] Schelling's technical use of the terms such as concept and matter have their roots in Kant's definitions of purpose and purposiveness found in the introduction to the third *Critique*: 'the concept of an object insofar as it is at the same time contains the ground of the reality of this object is called an end [or purpose: *Zweck*], and the correspondence of a thing with that constitution of things that is possible only in accordance with ends is called the purposiveness of its form' (2000: 68/5: 180).

[16] Distaso misreads this passage in the *Ideas* and reaches the conclusion that for Schelling 'God creates the ontological horizon of every teleological possibility that unfolds in ourselves and in our intellect' (2004: 140) This conclusion clearly contradicts Schelling's idea of inner purposiveness.

[17] Schelling's 'Cartesian demonstration,' as it were, runs the risk of reducing his position to (1), the problematic idealism criticized by Kant, and/or (2), a theoretical principle instead of a practical principle. Tilliette argues that at the time Schelling was attempting to define a broader sense of the term 'experience' (1999a: 257).

[18] This position is also developed by Fichte in his writings on natural right and ethics. It first appears in the theoretical section of the *Science of Knowledge*. There he states 'No Thou, no I: no I, no Thou' (1982: 172–173/I, 188–189).

[19] Remember that this passage follows Schelling's discussion of moral existence. So does his avoidance of the question mean that, for him, there is no moral obligation toward other species?

[20] From an 'analytic' perspective, Friedman shows how collapsing the distinction between regulative and constitutive principles, in the *Ideas*, directly confronts skeptical problems concerning the status of the knowledge of life (biology) arising in Kant's work (Friedman, 2006: 33–36; and also Huneman, 2006: 9–13).

[21] For a critical edition I have used the version found in Christoph Jamme and Helmut Schneider, eds. *Mythologie der Vernuft* (1984), 11–17; for an English translation I have relied on Krell (2005, 22–26).

[22] For a succinct account of the early debates see Krell (2005: 18–22).

[23] Later, in the *Philosophy of Art*, Schelling states that 'In the novels *Pamela* and *Grandison*, Richardson is little more than a moralistic writer. In *Clarissa* he displays a truly objective gift for portrayal, though entangled in pedantry and diffuseness' (1989: 237/V, 683).

[24] However, see Marquet, who discusses the relationships between Schiller, Schelling, and the 'System Program,' along with the suggestion that Schelling might have influenced Hölderlin (Marquet, 2006: 73, 77–80).

[25] Condition 3: Artistic production has a socio-political task: it aims to overcome the fragmentary condition of modernity through a new mythology and artistic renewal. It seems that the 'System Program' also anticipates Condition 1: What philosophy constructs in the ideal, art produces in the real. Thus artistic activity is the highest human vocation because practical philosophy can only approximate its object, which is the moral law.

Chapter 3

[1] However, this producing is not transparent to the self because it is the product of both conscious and unconscious activity. This is why Schelling says it is the activity that produces out of the identity of freedom and necessity *with consciousness* and not a *self-conscious production*.

[2] Schelling's later interpretation overlooks the subversive sting of the *ST* insofar as it forgets that it is precisely through the limitation of freedom, as an infinite task of approximation, that it opens the way to demonstrating that aesthetic intuition produces the absolute as art, in the finite or real world – that artistic activity *presents* what freedom can only approximate. Schelling does a disservice to his early work when he remembers the apex of the *ST* as 'pure freedom' with no reference to artistic production (1994b: 112/X, 97).

[3] Like many of the terms Schelling chooses, production has both an ideal and a real definition: the ideal production of objectivity finds its limit in the self's productive capacities in the objective (real) world.

⁴ For the relationship between Kant and Schelling and their use of the concept of imagination, see Orrin F. Summerell, 2004: 85–98; and John Llewelyn, 2000: 50–68.

⁵ Compare to Grant (2008: 158–186) despite our differences: he reads the *ST* as a document of nature-philosophy without mention of the philosophy of art. See also Richards, 2002: 289–306.

⁶ We will not discuss reflection because Schelling argues that reflection is the result of an abstraction from the productive activity of the self, hence it is analytic rather than part of the series of synthetic deductions that lead from intellectual intuition to aesthetic intuition (1978: 134/III, 505).

⁷ Unlike the limitations found in the theoretical section of the *ST*, the limitations of practical reason are recognized by self-consciousness. The task of transcendental idealism is to show the conditions of these limitations.

⁸ But Schelling makes sure to distance his philosophically overdetermined use of 'pre-established harmony' from Leibniz: 'the explanation should not venture to extend further, to some absolute principle, which, by operating as the communal focus of intelligences, or their creator and agent of uniformity (concepts wholly unintelligible to us), should contain the common basis of their agreement in regard to objective presentations' (1978: 164/III, 544).

⁹ Schelling's argument is heavily influenced by Kant's 'Idea for a Universal History from a Cosmopolitan Point of View' (in Kant, 1988: 415–425/VIII, 17–31). See also W. Marx, 1984: 1–32; and Habermas, 2004: 43–47.

¹⁰ This conclusion supports my argument, following Werner Marx, that the transcendental method of the *ST* is incompatible with Schelling's later claim that it supplies a *Bildungsgeschichte*. See Section 3.1.

¹¹ I will refer to both as the *First Outline*.

¹² Note also Wilhelm Meister's desire to 'plunge into the flood of destinies that hangs over the world and someday, if fortune favors me, to cull several drafts from the great ocean of living nature and distribute these from the stage to the thirsting public of [his] native land' (Goethe, 1989: 113/Book Three, Chapter Eleven).

¹³ Fichte explains that 'from the transcendental point of view, the world is something that is made; from the ordinary point of view, it is something that is given; from the aesthetic point of view, the world is given, but only under the aspect of how it was made' (2005: 334/IV, 353–354).

¹⁴ An important exception to the general trends of the Enlightenment in this regard is Hamann, who, in his Christian mysticism and/or metaphysics, held that 'Poetry is the mother-tongue of the human race' (from *Aesthetica in nuce* in 2007: 63). For an overview of Enlightenment philosophy and aesthetics, see Ernst Cassirer (1951: 275–360); and for a Marxist interpretation see Terry Eagleton (1990: 13–152).

¹⁵ This does not mean that artistic production can be accomplished without discipline or training. Schelling stresses that art requires conscious thought and reflection along with the *poesie* granted by nature (1978: 223–224/III, 618–619).

¹⁶ My difference with Beiser rests on the priority I think should be given to Schelling's systematic use of the concept of imagination. We will return to this point in Section 4.3.

¹⁷ Recall that, according to Jacobi, 'Lessing could not accept the idea of a personal, absolutely infinite Being, unfailingly enjoying his supreme perfection. He associated an image of such infinite *boredom* with it, that he was troubled and pained by it' (Jacobi, 1994: 197).

¹⁸ As Werner Marx convincingly argues (1984: 1–32), the relationship between history, revelation, and practical philosophy is internally inconsistent. Schelling himself indicates dissatisfaction with the equation of universal rule of law and providence (1978: 196/III, 584). We have multiplied the problems by trying to assess the relationship between mythology and revelation, and practical philosophy and the philosophy of art.

¹⁹ It is interesting to note that both practical philosophy and even the philosophy of art have, if we take this passage on Greek mythology seriously, an intersubjective basis.

²⁰ See, for Frederick Engels, Marx and Engels, 1975: II, 181–264, and for Karl Marx, ibid.: I, 103, and III, 349–351 (which translates Marx's letter of October 3, 1843 to Feuerbach). For a recent account in English see Bruce Matthews' introduction to Schelling, 2007a. For the politics of Schelling's new mythology see Section 5.4.

Chapter 4

1. Braekman's argument attempts to show how the philosophy of art is gradually assimilated by Schelling's metaphysics in general. By contrast, I argue that the philosophy of art maintains a central position during the period of absolute idealism.

2. See Frank, 1975: 103–119; and 1985: 118–132; Bowie, 1993: 55–90; and White, 1983: 81–92. The notable exception is Marquet (2006), who will be discussed below. Frank does discuss the section on art and mythology in 1982: 198–200.

3. Marquet discusses these developments but does not treat them thematically as a central contradiction within the system of identity-philosophy (2006: 238–277).

4. Nor should this reading be taken as *exhaustive* of identity-philosophy. As Marquet notes, the various presentations over the years 1801–1806 are too similar to make it necessary to study each separately and too different to extract a single system-formula supporting each (2006: 208; see also Beiser, 2002a: 560–564).

5. See *Vorlesungen über die Methode des akademischen Studiems* (translated as *On University Studies*) which is concurrent with the lectures given as the *Philosophy of Art* (1966: 9/V, 215).

6. Fichte to Schelling, December 27, 1800 (GA, III/4: 406–407). Fichte finally accuses Schelling of dogmatism in his response to Schelling's letter of October 3, 1801 (GA, III/5: 90–93). Excerpts are translated in Schulte-Sasse, et al. (1997: 73–90).

7. Michael Vater, the translator, points out that '*Indifferenz* is borrowed from English; [Schelling] means "indifference" to be a logical operator; not a psychological descriptor like Gleichgültigkeit' (2001b: 343).

8. In the *First Outline*, Schelling contrasts absolute identity and relative identity (indifference), when he establishes as an axiom that 'No identity in Nature is absolute, but all is only indifference' (2004a: 220/III, 309). In this context, indifference is defined as equilibrium between opposing forces.

9. This is an important difference with both Fichte, who, while deducing the activity of the absolute subject, also deduces the categories of quality (see Section 1.3), and, of course, Hegel, for whom negation is the activity of thought itself.

10. Schelling's proof: 'every point [on the line] can also serve as indifference-point relative to some other, or become now one, now the other of the two opposed end poles' because the line is infinitely divisible, as it is grounded in the absolute (2001b: 365–366/IV, 137–138).

11. After the construction of the potencies, Schelling goes on to deduce the central concepts of nature-philosophy. Marquet notes how some of Schelling's deductions formally anticipate those of Schelling's later work (2006: 215–223).

12. Not even Beiser, who is much more sympathetic to Schelling's work, can resist the Parmenidean image in his interpretation (2002a: 565).

13. Fischbach argues that Schelling's disdain for these lectures arose from their retrospective proximity to Hegel's *Aesthetics*, but while Fischbach notes the similarities, there are numerous differences as well that undercut his hypothesis (Fischbach, 2000: 185–195).

14. This negative judgment is moderated somewhat in Tilliette's *La mythologie comprise* (1984: 31–45).

15. For more on the comparison between an aesthetic and a philosophy of art, see Pascal David, 2002: 179–191.

16. We will distinguish between 'truth' as the correctness of propositions about the natural world from 'Truth' which is absolute, the archetype of truth in its identity with beauty: 'truth that is not beauty is also not absolute Truth, and vice versa' (1989: 31tm/V, 385).

17. Note that Schelling also mentions the organism as an example of beauty. We will return to the relationship between natural organisms and artworks below (1989: 27/V, 379).

18. Schelling again complicates this presentation by stating that 'reason and philosophy can relate to one another as real and ideal. *Since, however, each in itself is absolute identity, this relationship does not constitute any real difference* [my emphasis]. Philosophy is merely reason that has become or is becoming aware of itself; reason is merely the matter or objective model of all philosophy' (1989: 28–29/V, 381).

19. For more on construction, especially in relation to Kant, see Verra, 1979: 27–47.

[20] My only problem with this account is the use of the term 'faculty' (instead of 'power'), which implies that imagination is a faculty of a subject.

[21] The triplicity real-ideal-indifference recurs in nature as matter (being) – light (activity) – and the organism, which 'constitutes such a condition of indifference, since its essence as an organism is inseparable from the subsistence of its form, and since being also immediately constitutes activity within it' (1989: 27/V, 379).

[22] Recall that, in the *System of Transcendental Idealism*, theoretical philosophy was grounded in an unconscious producing of subject and object, practical philosophy demonstrated freedom and necessity as an antithesis, and art-philosophy overcame this antithesis through the production of the work of art.

[23] Schelling's answer in the *Würzburg Lectures* introduces the concept of an 'absolute life' (Schelling, 1994: 174–175/VI, 187; and Frank, 1985: 118–132).

[24] Compare to the Schelling's distinction between philosophy as esoteric and art as exoteric in the dialogue *Bruno, or, On the Natural and the Divine Principle of Things* (1984: 131–133/IV, 230–232).

[25] Jean-Marie Vaysse utilizes '*effigie parfaite*' (2004: 41) and Fischbach chooses '*reflet imagé*' instead of Jean-François Courtine's choice of '*contre-image*' (Fischbach, 2000: 188 and 194, n. 21).

[26] Marquet leaves the term untranslated in the chapter 'Le modèle et l'image' with one exception where it appears as '*image parfaite*' (2006: 238–277; in particular 274).

[27] It is interesting, though, that Schelling's discussion of language in the *Philosophy of Art* touches on the idea, developed later, of God's word as the living word of creation. However, where the *Freiheitsschrift* argues that God's revelation brings to form the chaos of nature, here Schelling writes that 'Language as the infinite affirmation that expresses itself in a *living* fashion is the ultimate symbol of chaos eternally residing in absolute knowledge' (1989: 101/V, 484).

[28] Schelling is not alone in grasping the public character of theater, which has also drawn the attention of Nietzsche, Sartre, and more recently, Alain Badiou, who discusses the *mise en scene* of theatrical-ideas in his *Handbook of Inaesthetics* (2005: 72–77).

[29] Or, more specifically, Schelling *ascribes* this harmony to the Greek world because he overlooks many of its social divisions and conflicts.

[30] Schelling states that fate and providence are also identical within the absolute: fate is a form of providence intuited within the real while providence is also fate, but intuited within the ideal. Fate is natural, providence historical (1989: 61/V, 428). See also the Eighth Chapter of *On University Studies* (1966: 82–91/V, 286–295).

[31] The 'odyssey of human consciousness' should not be mistaken for Schelling's 'history of self-consciousness': the former refers to the historical series of human events (in the Western world) while the 'history of self-consciousness' in his earlier work is limited to describing the necessary conditions of consciousness.

[32] It should be noted that Schelling recognizes other mythological systems from the 'Orient' only to dismiss them or to show how it is 'necessary that the Oriental ideas [are] planted in Occidental soil' (1989: 59/V, 426–427). For a concise account of Schelling's attitudes toward Indian literature and religion, see Sedlar, 1982: 41–46.

[33] This is precisely what Marx would call a religious mystification of material production. The idea of *spiritual* crisis has a long history because it is one answer to the tendency inherent to capitalism to produce material crises through the constant revolutionizing of the means of production (see also Section 5.4).

[34] Schelling repeats Goethe's ironic commentary (which presents itself as the conclusions drawn from a discussion between Serlo and Wilhelm) in Book Five, Chapter 7 (1989: 185): 'In the novel it is predominantly sentiments and events that are to be presented; in drama, characters and deeds' (compare to Schelling, 1989: 232/V, 676). Goethe continues 'The novel must move slowly and the sentiments of the main personage must, in some way or another, hold up the progression of the whole toward its resolution' (1989: 185).

[35] Compare to Schelling's programmatic statement at the end of the 1803 edition of the *Ideas for a Philosophy of Nature*: 'The ideal world presses mightily toward the light, but it is still held back by the fact that nature has withdrawn as a mystery. The very secrets which the

ideal harbors cannot truly become objective save in proclaiming the mystery of nature. The still-unknown deities, which the ideal world is preparing, cannot emerge as such until they can seize possession of nature. After all *finite* forms have been struck down, there is nothing more in the wide world to unite mankind but collective intuition, it can only be the contemplation of absolute identity in the fullest objective totality that afresh, and in the final development to religion, unites them forever' (1988: 54–55/II, 72–73).

Chapter 5

[1] Abbreviated in the following as the *Münchener Rede*.
[2] The *Philosophische Schriften* also included *Vom Ich*, the *Letters* and the *Allgemeine Übersicht der neuesten philosophischen Literatur*, the latter of which was revised (revisions included cutting the final section from 1798, which is discussed here in Section 2.6) and renamed the *Abhandlungen zur Erläuterung des Idealismus der Wissenschaftslehre*.
[3] Those in the know included Goethe, the brothers Schlegel, Niethammer, Johann Wilhelm Ritter, Henrik Steffens, and Friedrich Tieck (Tilliette, 1978: xxxi–xxxiii; and Sziborsky, ed., 1983: 69–79).
[4] The letter is dated October 12, 1807, although this seems to be in error.
[5] Recent texts that develop the concerns of the *Münchener Rede* include Marquet, 2006: 354–363; and 1979: 75–88; Jähnig, 1969: II, 66–70, 130–137, 259; Oesterreich, 1996: 95–109; and Lawrence, 1988: 15–19.
[6] Here Nietzsche could object that existence is only bearable as an aesthetic phenomenon and not as a moral phenomenon (*The Gay Science*, Section 107; 1974: 163–164). One might answer that the worldview of the *Münchener Rede* is more melancholy than what is traditionally thought as moral, and that in subsequent texts Schelling's worldview becomes ever more tragic. In the essay *Of Human Freedom*, Schelling calls finitude the source of a 'deep indestructible melancholy of all life' that affects even God himself (2006: 62–63/VII, 399). My criticism of Schelling's *mythologization* of politics is developed below.
[7] As Schelling says in the lectures published as *The Grounding of Positive Philosophy: The Berlin Lectures*, 'history shows us no example of an age that deeply divided, confused, and doubtful of itself has reconciled and healed itself through poetry' (2007a: 96/XIII, 12).
[8] Braeckman also draws connections between Schelling's philosophy of art and the *Stuttgart Seminars*, but his omission of the *Münchener Rede* leaves his account incomplete (2004b: 67–83).
[9] For a constellation-view of these changes, see Sturma (who focuses on Schelling), 2000b: 219–238; Peter, 2004: 191–208; and for an account of conservatism in Germany in the 1790s, see Beiser, 1992: 281–334.
[10] See Adorno's critique in 'Reconciliation Under Duress,' in which he writes that in a 'highly undialectical manner, the officially licensed dialectician sweeps all the irrationalist strands of modern philosophy into the camp of reaction and Fascism. He blithely ignores the fact that, unlike academic idealism, these schools were struggling against the very same reification in both thought and life of which Lukács too was a dedicated opponent' (Adorno, 1977: 152).
[11] According to Heidegger, great art instigates history, which is 'the transporting of a people into its appointed task as entry to that people's endowment' (1993: 202). This should be read in the context of Heidegger's politics in the 1930s. His later work on poetry and technology turns away, through a possible self-critique, from political engagement.
[12] See, for example, Alain Badiou, *The Century* (2007); the 'Third Sketch of a Manifesto of Affirmationist Art' (2006: 133–148); and Jacques Rancière's *Malaise dans l'esthétique* (2004).
[13] This is a simplified schema of Schelling's categorizations. See also Douglas W. Stott's introduction to the *Philosophy of Art* (1989: l); for comparison see also Tilliette's schemes of other presentations of absolute idealism (1970: I, 417–421).
[14] This is also complicated by the fact that Schelling's determinations of music are sometimes incorrect; for instance, Schelling's ideal deduction of sound discusses absolute sound, and with more difficultly, its relation to magnetism, which I have not been able to square with

the basic definition of sound as a vibration or wave, which is formed by the oscillation (periodic displacement) of a medium such as air. To get Schelling's account in order, I have consulted Marquet, 2006: 262–263; Schueller, 1957: 461–476; and Stott (1989). Let me remark that, as a musician, I thought it would be easier.

[15] In correspondence to the potencies, rhythm 'qualifies music for reflection and self-consciousness, [modulation] for feeling and judgment, and [melody] for intuition and the power of imagination' (1989: 112/V, 496).

[16] Harmony is referred to as the vertical relationship between tones, what Schelling refers to as their coexistence, and melody is then the horizontal relationship between tones. Schelling is correct to state that the use of cadence – 'the movement toward the release of tension, toward absolute repose' (to quote Rosen, 1975: 26) – and counterpoint (the use of dissonance to create tension), structures the modern music of his time; most melody in modern Western music up to the end of the 19th century also followed harmonic resolution (see Schelling, 1989: 114–115/5: 498–501; and Rosen 1975: 23–62).

[17] Schueller notes that the stance that 'melody is "superior" to harmony is an assumption of the 18th century' just as 'melodic exploitation is a characteristic of "classical" music up to Beethoven' and 'harmonic experimentation is characteristic of 19th century musical composition' (1957: 472, n. 44; 473, n. 46).

[18] So, for example, architecture is 'solidified or frozen (*erstarrte*) music' (1989: 165/V, 576).

[19] This also implies, as Schueller points out, the *real* expression of mathematical relationships (1957: 470).

[20] Note, however, that where the *Philosophy of Art* uses *Potenz* the *Münchener Rede* uses *Kraft*.

[21] This passage indicates the influence of Schelling on Heidegger's development of his critique of technology (Heidegger, 1985: 137–139).

[22] See Lucia Sziborsky, 1986: 41. Sziborsky phrases it in Spinozist terms: for Schelling the artist should imitate nature as production (*natura naturans*) and not nature as object (*natura naturata*).

[23] Compare to this passage in the *Aphorismen zur Einleitung in die Naturphilosophie* from 1805: 'just as, in Winckelmann's terms, the still harsh and severe style of the most ancient sculpture must have preceded the products embellished through grace in later art, and as only those states which begin from stricter legislation have the ability to become great, so must have serious and severe scientific education (*Bildung*) restrained the ignorance of the heart (*Gemüthen*) before the more delightful fruits of philosophy are able to ripen. The Platonic [injunction] "let no-one uninitiated in geometry enter here" held a much more general significance' (VII, 143).

[24] Schelling does not discuss if the work of art should arouse the passions of the spectator.

[25] A reader would not gather this by reading Susan Neiman's *Evil in Modern Thought* (2002). Although she makes three references to Schelling (pages 62, 96, 260), she never mentions that he wrote about the problem of evil.

[26] Compare to 1989: 187–192/V, 609–617.

[27] Compare to 1989: 126–160/V, 517–568.

[28] The following paragraph is a summary of 1968: 350–351/VII, 318–320.

[29] This paragraph follows Marquet, 1979: 85–86. Here are the chronological dates: Michelangelo (1475–1564); Correggio (1489[?] –1534); Raphael (1483–1520); and Guido Reni (1575–1642); for an explanation of Reni's inclusion in this list, see below.

[30] Jacobi writes: 'Schelling's creation of the world (*Weltschöpfer*) produces, from a world without end, nothing other than time. . . . The one nontemporal Life . . . is transformed into an infinitely multiple transience so that Life is lived. There is only one quality, Life as such. All other qualities or properties are only different quantities or restrictions of this one quality, which is at the same time substance and all reality (*Wesen*). Mankind has thereby more [reality] than the dung beetle, but in itself nothing better or higher. All that lives only lives the one and the same Life' (Jacobi to Fries, November 26, 1807, in Sziborsky, ed., 1983: 74).

[31] Schelling has returned to the usage of *Potenz* for potency.

[32] Thus the *Stuttgart Seminars* closes with an account of the final judgment, when God is revealed as 'divine matter,' visible and corporeal, the basis of all that is: 'Then God is in all actuality everything, and pantheism will have become true' (1994: 243/VII, 484).

UNIVERSITY OF WINCHESTER LIBRARY

[33] Marquet shows how this shift is anticipated in several of Schelling's works from 1806–1808, although understanding does not yet have a theological aspect (2006: 355–356; 441).

[34] A similar schema organization of these relationships appears in a footnote (VII, 184) in the *Aphorismen zur Einleitung in die Naturphilosophie* (1805):

	God The All	
All: relative-real		All: relative-ideal
gravity (A^1), matter		truth, science
light (A^2), motion		the good, religion
life (A^3), organism		beauty, art
the world-system	reason	history
man	philosophy	the state

[35] Recall Marx's sarcastic remarks, made decades later, that 'we Germans have experienced our future history in thought, in philosophy. We are philosophical contemporaries without being *historical* ones. German philosophy is the ideal prolongation of German history' (K. Marx, 1977: 67).

[36] Concerning the French Revolution, see also *On University Studies* (1966: 52–55/VII, 258–261).

[37] Sziborsky also mentions that the constitution of the *Akademie*, in comparison to the constitutions of other academies at the time, is fairly progressive in its mandate.

Conclusion

[1] This should make the *Letters* of some interest to Žižek, who stresses the retroactive character of subjectivity.

[2] Marx, in the appendix to his dissertation, turns the *Letters* against the later Schelling. He quotes the final sentence from the Second Letter ('*The time has come* to proclaim to the *better part* of humanity the *freedom of minds*, and *not to tolerate any longer that they deplore the loss of their fetters*'), and then adds, 'When the time already had come in 1795, how about the year 1841?' (in Marx and Engels, 1975: 103; the emphases are Marx's; see also Schelling, 1980: 162–163/I, 292).

Bibliography

German Editions of Schelling Consulted

1. Complete Editions

(1927–1959), *Schellings Werke. Nach der Original Ausgabe in neuer Anordnung.* 12 vols. Ed. Manfred Schröter (Munich: Beck). This edition reproduces the pagination of K. F. A Schelling's edition of *Schellings sämmtliche Werke* (Stuttgart, Cotta: 1856–1861). My citations of German sources reproduce the volume and pagination of this latter volume, by volume (in Roman numerals) and page.

(1976–), *Historisch-kritische Ausgabe.* (Abbreviated as AA) Ed. H. M. Baumgartner, W. G. Jacobs, H. Krings (Stuttgart: Frommann-Holzboog, 1976–). It contains three divisions: I: Works, II: the Nachlass, III: Letters (Cited as AA, Division (in Roman numerals)/Volume/Page).

2. Other Works Consulted

(1973), *Stuttgarter Privatvorlesungen.* Ed. Miklós Vetö (Turin: Bottega D'Erasmo).

(1983), *Über das Verhältnis der bildenden Künste zu der Natur.* Ed. Lucia Sziborsky (Hamburg: Felix Meiner Verlag).

(1985), *Ausgewählte Schriften.* 6 vols. Ed. Manfred Frank (Frankfurt am Main: Suhrkamp).

(1992), *System des transzendentalen Idealismus.* Ed. Horst D. Brandt and Peter Müller (Hamburg: Felix Meiner Verlag).

(2003), *Aus Schellings Leben In Briefen.* Ed. G. L. Plitt. 3 Volumes (Hildesheim: Georg Olms Verlag).

(2004b), *Texte zur Philosophie der Kunst.* Ed. Werner Beierwaltes (Stuttgart: Reclam).

Schelling in English

(1966), *On University Studies.* Trans. E. S. Morgan (Athens, Ohio: Ohio University Press).

(1968), *Concerning the Relation of the Plastic Arts to Nature* (1807), trans. Michael Bullock, in Herbert Read, *The True Voice of Feeling* (London: Faber and Faber), 323–364.

(1974), *Schelling's Treatise on 'The Deities of Samotrace.'* Ed. Robert F. Brown (Missoula, Montana: Scholar's Press).

(1978), *System of Transcendental Idealism.* Trans. Peter Heath (Charlottesville: University Press of Virginia).

(1980), *The Unconditional in Human Knowledge*. Ed. Fritz Marti (Lewisburg: Bucknell University Press). Includes *Of the I as Principle of Philosophy, or On the Unconditional in Human Knowledge* (1795) and *Philosophical Letters on Dogmatism and Criticism* (1795–1796).

(1984), *Bruno, or, On the Natural and the Divine Principle of Things*. Ed. Michael G. Vater (Albany: SUNY Press).

(1988), *Ideas for a Philosophy of Nature*. Trans. Errol E. Harris and Peter Heath (Cambridge: Cambridge University Press).

(1989), *The Philosophy of Art*. Trans. Douglas W. Stott (Minneapolis: University of Minnesota Press).

(1994a), *Idealism and the Endgame of Theory*. Ed. Thomas Pfau (Albany: SUNY Press). Includes the *Stuttgart Seminars* (1810), the *System of Philosophy in General and of the Philosophy of Nature in Particular* (1804), and the *Treatise Explicatory of the Idealism in the Science of Knowledge* (1797).

(1994b), *On the History of Modern Philosophy*. Trans. Andrew Bowie (Cambridge: Cambridge University Press).

(2001a), 'Further Presentations from the System of Philosophy,' trans. Michael Vater, in *The Philosophical Forum*, Vol. 32, no. 4, 373–397.

(2001b), 'Presentation of My System of Philosophy,' trans. Michael Vater, in *The Philosophical Forum*, Vol. 32, no. 4, 339–371.

(2004a), *First Outline of a System of the Philosophy of Nature*. Trans. Keith R. Peterson (Albany: SUNY Press).

(2006), *Philosophical Investigations into the Essence of Human Freedom*. Trans. Jeff Love and Johannes Schmidt (Albany: SUNY Press).

(2007a), *The Grounding of Positive Philosophy: The Berlin Lectures*. Trans. Bruce Matthews (Albany: SUNY Press).

(2007b), *Historical-Critical Introduction to the Philosophy of Mythology*. Trans. Mason Richey and Markus Zisselsberger (Albany: SUNY Press).

Additional Sources

Adorno, Theodor (1977), 'Reconciliation Under Duress,' in Adorno et al. *Aesthetics and Politics* (London: Verso), 151–176.

Allison, Henry E. (1991), 'Kant's Antinomy of Teleological Judgment,' in *System and Teleology in Kant's* Critique of Judgment. Ed. Hoke Robinson. *Southern Journal of Philosophy*, Vol. 30: Supplement, 25–42.

Altmann, Alexander (1973), *Moses Mendelssohn: A Biographical Study* (Alabama: The University of Alabama Press).

Anderson, Benedict (2006), *Imagined Communities*. New Edition (London: Verso).

Badiou, Alain (2005), *Handbook of Inaesthetics*. Trans. Alberto Toscano (Stanford: Stanford University Press).

— (2006), *Polemics*. Trans. Steve Corcoran (London: Verso).

— (2007), *The Century*. Trans. Alberto Toscano (Cambridge: Polity Press).

Baum, Manfred (2000), 'The Beginnings of Schelling's Philosophy of Nature,' in *The Reception of Kant's Critical Philosophy*. Ed. Sally Sedgwick (Cambridge: Cambridge University Press), 199–215.

Baumgartner, Hans Michael (1999), 'The Unconditioned in Knowing: I–Identity–Freedom,' in *The Emergence of German Idealism*. Ed. Michael Baur and Daniel O. Dahlstrom (Washington, D.C.: The Catholic University of America Press), 241–250.

Beiser, Frederick C. (1987), *The Fate of Reason: German Philosophy from Kant to Fichte* (Cambridge, Mass., Harvard University Press).

— (1992), *Enlightenment, Revolution, and Romanticism* (Cambridge, Mass., Harvard University Press).

— (2002a), *German Idealism: The Struggle Against Subjectivism 1781–1801* (Cambridge, Mass., Harvard University Press).

— (2002b), *The Romantic Imperative: The Concept of Early German Romanticism* (Cambridge, Mass., Harvard University Press).

Benjamin, Walter (2002), 'The Work of Art in the Age of Its Technological Reproducibility,' in *Selected Writings: Volume 3, 1935–1938*. Ed. Howard Eiland and Michael W. Jennings (Cambridge, Mass., Belknap/Harvard University Press), 101–133.

Bowie, Andrew (1990), *Aesthetics and Subjectivity: From Kant to Nietzsche* (Manchester: Manchester University Press).

— (1993), *Schelling and Modern European Philosophy* (London: Routledge).

— (2000), 'German Idealism and the Arts,' in *The Cambridge Companion to German Idealism*. Ed. Karl Ameriks (Cambridge: Cambridge University Press), 239–257.

Braeckman, Antoon (2004a), 'From the Work of Art to Absolute Reason: Schelling's Journey Toward Absolute Idealism,' in *The Review of Metaphysics*, Vol. 57, 551–569.

— (2004b), 'The "Individual Universal": The Socio-political Meaning of the Work of Art in Schelling,' in *Idealistic Studies*, Vol. 34, no. 1, 67–83.

Breazeale, Daniel (1981), 'Fichte's *Aenesidemus* Review and the Transformation of German Idealism,' in *The Review of Metaphysics*, Vol. 34, 545–568.

— (1995), 'Check or Checkmate? On the Finitude of the Fichtean Self,' in *The Modern Subject*. Ed. Karl Ameriks and Dieter Sturma (Albany: SUNY Press), 87–114.

— (1996), 'The Theory of Practice and the Practice of Theory: Fichte and the "Primacy of Practical Reason,"' in *International Philosophical Quarterly*, Vol. 36, no. 1, 47–64.

Cassirer, Ernst (1951), *The Philosophy of the Enlightenment*. Trans. Fritz C. A. Koelln and James P. Pettegrove (Princeton: Princeton University Press).

David, Pascal (2002), 'Schelling: construction de l'art et récusation de l'esthétique,' in *Revue de Métaphysique et de Morale*, Vol. 2, 179–191.

Di Giovanni, George (1987), 'Grazing in the Sunlight: On H.S. Harris's "The Cows in the Dark Night,"' in *Dialogue*, Vol. 26, no. 4, 653–663.

— (1994), 'The Unfinished Philosophy of Friedrich Heinrich Jacobi,' in *The Main Philosophical Writings and the Novel Allwill*. Ed. George di Giovanni (Montreal: McGill-Queen's University Press), 3–116.

Di Giovanni, George and H. S. Harris, eds. (1985), *Between Kant and Hegel: Texts in the Development of Post-Kantian Idealism* (Albany: SUNY Press).

Distaso, Leonardo V. (2004), *The Paradox of Existence: Philosophy and Aesthetics in the Young Schelling* (Dordrecht: Kluwer).

Dodd, James (1998), 'Philosophy and Art in Schelling's *System des transzendentalen Idealismus*,' in *The Review of Metaphysics*, Vol. 52, 51–85.

Düsing, Klaus (1999), 'The Reception of Kant's Doctrine of the Postulates in Schelling's and Hegel's Early Philosophical Projects,' in *The Emergence of German Idealism*. Ed. Michael Baur and Daniel O. Dahlstrom (Washington, D.C.: The Catholic University of America Press), 201–237.

Eagleton, Terry (1990), *The Ideology of the Aesthetic* (Oxford: Blackwell Publishers).

Escoubas, Eliane (2001), 'Philosophie de l'art *versus* esthétique,' in *Critique*, no. 665, 972–983.

Esposito, Joseph L. (1977), *Schelling's Idealism and Philosophy of Nature* (Lewisburg: Bucknell University Press).

Fackenheim, Emil L. (1996), *The God Within: Kant, Schelling, and Historicity*. Ed. John Burbidge (Toronto: University of Toronto Press).

Fichte, J. G. (1964–), *J.G. Fichte: Gesamtausgabe der Bayerischen Akademie der Wissenschaften*. (Abbreviated as GA) Ed. Reinhard Lauth, Hans Jacobs, and Hans Gliwitsky (Stuttgard-Bad Cannstatt: Fromann-Holzboog).

— (1982), *The Science of Knowledge*. Ed. Peter Heath and John Lachs (Cambridge: Cambridge University Press).

— (1988), *Early Philosophical Writings*. Ed. Daniel Breazeale (Ithaca: Cornell University Press).

— (2005), *The System of Ethics*. Ed. Daniel Breazeale and Günter Zöller (Cambridge: Cambridge University Press).

Fischbach, Franck (2000), 'Différence et correspondence entre les arts chez Hegel et Schelling,' in *Hegel Jahrbuch 1999: Hegels Ästhetik*, Vol. 1. Ed Andreas Arndt, Karol Bal, and Henning Ottmann (Berlin: Akademie Verlag), 185–195.

Ford, Lewis S. (1965), 'The Controversy Between Schelling and Jacobi,' in *The Journal of the History of Philosophy*, Vol. 3, 75–89.

Frank, Manfred (1975), *Der Unendliche Mangel an Sein* (Frankfurt: Suhrkamp).

— (1982), *Der kommende Gott: Vorlesungen über die Neue Mythologie*, Vol. 1 (Frankfurt: Suhrkamp).

— (1985), *Eine Einführung in Schellings Philosophie* (Frankfurt: Suhrkamp).

— (2004), *The Philosophical Foundations of Early German Romanticism*. Trans. Elizabeth Millán-Zaibert (Albany: SUNY Press).

Frank, Manfred and Gerhard Kurz, eds. (1975), *Materialien zu Schellings philosophischen Anfängen* (Frankfurt: Suhrkamp).

Friedman, Michael (2006), 'Kant, Skepticism, and Idealism,' in *Inquiry*, Vol. 49, no. 1, 26–43.

George, Theodore D. (2005), 'A Monstrous Absolute: Schelling, Kant, and the Poetic Turn in Philosophy,' in *Schelling Now: Contemporary Readings*. Ed. Jason M. Wirth (Bloomington: Indiana University Press), 135–146.

Goethe, Johann Wolfgang von (1989), *Wilhelm Meister's Apprenticeship*. Ed. Eric A Blackall with Victor Lange (Boston: Suhrkamp).

— (2004), *The Sorrows of Young Werther*. Trans. Burton Pike (New York: The Modern Library).

— (2005), *Selected Poetry*. Ed. David Luke (New York: Penguin).

Grant, Iain Hamilton (2004), ' "Philosophy Become Genetic": The Physics of the World Soul,' in *The New Schelling*. Ed. Judith Norman and Alistair Welchman (New York: Continuum), 128–150.

— (2008), *Philosophies of Nature After Schelling* (New York: Continuum).

Habermas, Jürgen (2004), 'Dialectical Idealism in the Transition to Materialism: Schelling's Idea of a Contraction of God and its Consequences for the Philosophy of History,' in *The New Schelling*. Ed. Judith Norman and Alistair Welchman (New York: Continuum), 43–89.

Hamann, Johann Georg (2007), *Writings on Philosophy and Language*. Ed. Kenneth Haynes (Cambridge: Cambridge University Press).

Harris, H. S. (1972), *Hegel's Development: Toward the Sunlight 1770–1801* (Oxford: Clarendon Press).

— (1987), 'Cows in the Dark Night,' in *Dialogue*, Vol. 26, no. 4, 627–643.

Hegel, G. W. F. (1968–), *Gesammelte Werke*. Ed. Rheinisch-Westfälischen Akademie der Wissenschaften (Hamburg: Felix Meiner Verlag).

— (1970), *Philosophy of Nature*. Trans. A. V. Miller (Oxford: Oxford University Press).

— (1975), *Hegel's Aesthetics: Lectures on Fine Art*. Trans. T. M. Knox (Oxford: Oxford University Press).

— (1977a), *The Difference Between Fichte's and Schelling's System of Philosophy*. Ed. H. S. Harris and Walter Cerf (Albany: SUNY Press).

— (1977b), *The Phenomenology of Spirit*. Trans. A. V. Miller (Oxford: Oxford University Press).

— (1984), *The Letters*. Trans. Clark Butler and Christiane Seiler (Bloomington: Indiana University Press).

Heidegger, Martin (1985), *Schelling's Treatise on the Essence of Human Freedom*. Trans. Joan Stambaugh (Athens, Ohio: Ohio University Press).

— (1993), *Basic Writings*. Ed. David Farrell Krell (San Francisco: HarperCollins Publishing).

Henrich, Dieter (2003), *Between Kant and Hegel*. Ed. David S. Pacini (Cambridge, Mass.: Harvard University Press).

— (1997), *The Course of Remembrance and Other Essays on Hölderlin*. Ed. Eckart Förster (Stanford: Stanford University Press).

Hölderlin, Friedrich (1943–1985), *Sämtliche Werke*. (Abbreviated as HSA) Ed. Friedrich Beissner (Stuttgart: Verlag W. Kohlhammer).

— (1988), *Essays and Letters on Theory*. Ed. Thomas Pfau (Albany: SUNY Press).

Huneman, Philippe (2006), 'From the *Critique of Judgment* to the Hermeneutics of Nature: Sketching the Fate of Philosophy of Nature after Kant,' in *Continental Philosophy Review*, Vol. 39, 1–34.

Jacobi, Friedrich Heinrich (1994), *The Main Philosophical Writings and the Novel Allwill*. Ed. George di Giovanni (Montreal: McGill-Queen's University Press).

Jähnig, Dieter (1969), *Schelling: Die Kunst in der Philosophie*, 2 vols. (Pfüllingen: Neske).

Jamme, Christoph, and Helmut Schneider, eds. (1984), *Mythologie der Vernunft* (Frankfurt am Main: Suhrkamp).

Kant, Immanuel (1900–), *Gesammelte Werke* (Berlin: de Gruyter).

— (1956), *Critique of Practical Reason*. Trans. Lewis White Beck (Indianapolis: Bobbs-Merrill Co.).

— (1988), *Kant: Selections*. Ed. Lewis White Beck (New York: Macmillian).

— (1998), *Critique of Pure Reason*. Ed. Paul Guyer and Allen M. Wood (Cambridge: Cambridge University Press).

— (2000), *Critique of the Power of Judgment*. Ed. Paul Guyer (Cambridge: Cambridge University Press).

— (2004), *Metaphysical Foundations of Natural Science*. Ed. Michael Friedman (Cambridge: Cambridge University Press).

Krell, David Farrell (1998), *Contagion: Sexuality, Disease, and Death in German Idealism and Romanticism* (Bloomington: Indiana University Press).

— (2005), *The Tragic Absolute: German Idealism and the Languishing God* (Bloomington: Indiana University Press).

Lachs, John (1972), 'Fichte's Idealism,' in *The American Philosophical Quarterly*, Vol. 9, no. 4, 311–318.

Lawrence, Joseph P. (1988), 'Art and Philosophy in Schelling,' in *The Owl of Minerva*, Vol. 20, no. 1, 5–19.

Leibniz, G. W. (1998), *Philosophical Texts*. Ed. R. S. Woolhouse and Richard Francks (Oxford: Oxford University Press).

Llewelyn, John (2000), *The HypoCritical Imagination: Between Kant and Levinas* (London: Routledge).

Lukács, Georg (1980), *The Destruction of Reason*. Trans. Peter Palmer (London: Merlin Press).

Makkreel, Rudolf A. (1991), 'Regulative and Reflective Uses of Purposiveness in Kant,' in *System and Teleology in Kant's* Critique of Judgment. Ed. Hoke Robinson. *Southern Journal of Philosophy*, Vol. 30: Supplement, 49–63.

Mandt, A. J. (1984), 'Fichte's Idealism in Theory and Practice,' in *Idealistic Studies*, Vol. 14, no. 2, 127–147.

Marquard, Odo (2004), 'Several Connections between Aesthetics and Therapeutics in Nineteenth-Century Philosophy,' in *The New Schelling*. Ed. Judith Norman and Alistair Welchman (New York: Continuum), 13–29.

Marquet, Jean-François (1979), 'Schelling et le destin de l'art,' in *Actualité de Schelling*. Ed. G. Planty-Bonjour (Paris: Vrin), 75–88.

— (2006), *Liberté et existence*. 2ⁿᵈ Edition (Paris: Les Éditions du Cerf).

Marx, Karl (1973), *Grundrisse*. Trans. Martin Nicolaus (New York: Penguin Books).

— (1977), *Selected Writings*. Ed. David McLellan (Oxford: Oxford University Press).

Marx, Karl and Frederick Engels (1975–2005), *Collected Works* (New York: International Publishers).

Marx, Werner (1984), *The Philosophy of F.W.J. Schelling*. Trans. Thomas Nenom (Bloomington: Indiana University Press).

McFarland, J. D. (1970), *Kant's Concept of Teleology* (Edinburgh: University of Edinburgh Press).

Merleau-Ponty, Maurice (2003), *Nature: Course Notes from the Collège de France*. Ed. Dominique Séglard. Trans. Robert Vallier (Evanston: Northwestern University Press).

Morgan, S. R. (1990), 'Schelling and the Origins of His *Naturphilosophie*,' in *Romanticism and the Sciences*. Ed. Andrew Cunningham and Nicholas Jardine (Cambridge: Cambridge University Press), 25–37.

Neiman, Susan (2002), *Evil in Modern Thought* (Princeton: Princeton University Press).

Neuhouser, Frederick (1990), *Fichte's Theory of Subjectivity* (Cambridge: Cambridge University Press).

Nietzsche, Friedrich (1954), *The Portable Nietzsche*. Ed. Walter Kaufmann (New York: Penguin Books).
— (1974), *The Gay Science*. Trans. Walter Kaufmann (New York: Vintage Books).
Oesterreich, Peter L. (1996), 'Die Gewalt der Schönheit,' in *Schellings Weg zur Freiheitsschrift: Legende und Wirklichkeit*. Ed. Hans M. Baumgartner, Wilhelm G. Jacobs (Stuttgart-Bad Cannstatt: Frommann Holzboog), 95–109.
Peter, Klaus (2004), 'History and Moral Imperatives: The Contradictions of Political Romanticism,' in *The Literature of German Romanticism*. Ed. Dennis F. Mahoney (Rochester, NY: Camden House), 191–208.
Piché, Claude (2004), 'Fichte et la première philosophie de la nature de Schelling,' in *Dialogue*, Vol. 43, no. 2, 211–237.
Pippin, Robert B. (1989), *Hegel's Idealism: The Satisfactions of Self-Consciousness* (Cambridge: Cambridge University Press).
Rancière, Jacques (2004), *Malaise dans l'esthétique* (Paris: Galilée).
Reidhold, K. L. (1985), 'The Foundation of Philosophical Knowledge (Excerpt),' in *Between Kant and Hegel: Texts in the Development of Post-Kantian Idealism*. Ed. George di Giovanni and H. S. Harris (Albany: SUNY Press), 52–103.
Richards, Robert J. (2002), *The Romantic Conception of Life* (Chicago: University of Chicago Press).
Rosen, Charles (1975), *Arnold Schoenberg* (Princeton: Princeton University Press).
Schiller, Friedrich (1982), *On the Aesthetic Education of Man*. Trans. Elizabeth M. Wilkinson and L. A. Willoughby (Oxford: Oxford University Press).
Schmied-Kowarzik, Wolfdietrich (2000), 'Kunst zwischen Natur, Geschichte und Absolutem bei Schelling und Hegel,' in *Hegel Jahrbuch 1999: Hegels Ästhetik*. Vol. 1. Ed. Andreas Arndt, Karol Bal, and Henning Ottmann (Berlin: Akademie Verlag), 178–184.
Schueller, Herbert M. (1957), 'Schelling's Theory of the Metaphysics of Music,' in *The Journal of Aesthetics and Art Criticism*, Vol. 15, no. 3, 461–476.
Schulte-Sasse, Jochen, et al., eds. (1997), *Theory as Practice* (Minneapolis: University of Minnesota Press).
Schulz, Walter (1992), 'Einleitung,' in *System des transzendentalen Idealismus*. Ed. Horst D. Brandt and Peter Müller (Hamburg: Felix Meiner Verlag), ix–xliv.
Schulze, G. E. (1985), 'Aenesidemus (excerpt),' in *Between Kant and Hegel: Texts in the Development of Post-Kantian Idealism*. Ed. George di Giovanni and H. S. Harris (Albany: SUNY Press), 104–135.
Sedlar, Jean W. (1982), *India in the Mind of Germany* (Washington, D.C.: University Press of America).
Seebohm, Thomas M. (1994), 'Fichte's Discovery of the Dialectical Method,' in *Fichte: Historical Contexts, Contemporary Controversies*. Ed. Daniel Breazeale and Tom Rockmore (New Jersey: Humanities Press), 17–42.
Seidel, George J. (1974), 'Creativity in the Aesthetics of Schelling,' in *Idealistic Studies*, Vol. 4, no. 2, 170–180.
Snow, Dale E. (1996), *Schelling and the End of Idealism* (Albany: SUNY Press).
Spinoza, Baruch (1992), *Ethics, Treatise on the Emendation of the Intellect, and Selected Letters*. Trans. Samuel Shirley (Indianapolis: Hackett).
Sturma, Dieter (2000a), 'The Nature of Subjectivity: The Critical and Systematic Function of Schelling's Philosophy of Nature,' in *The Reception of Kant's Critical*

Philosophy. Ed. Sally Sedgwick (Cambridge: Cambridge University Press), 216–231.

— (2000b), 'Politics and the New Mythology: The Turn to Late Romanticism,' in *The Cambridge Companion to German Idealism*. Ed. Karl Ameriks (Cambridge: Cambridge University Press), 219–238.

Summerell, Orrin F. (2004), 'The Theory of the Imagination in Schelling's Philosophy of Identity,' in *Idealistic Studies*, Vol. 34, no. 2, 85–98.

Sziborsky, Lucia, ed. (1983), 'Aus zeitgenössischen Briefen,' in *Über das Verhältnis der bildenden Künste zu der Natur*. Ed. Lucia Sziborsky (Hamburg: Felix Meiner Verlag).

— (1986), 'Schelling und die Münchener Akademie der bildenden Künste,' in *Welt und Wirkung von Hegels Ästhetik*. Ed. Annemarie Gethmann-Siefert and Otto Pöggeler (Bonn: Bouvier Verlag Herbert Grundmann), 39–64.

Szondi, Peter (2002), *An Essay on the Tragic*. Trans. Paul Fleming (Stanford: Stanford University Press).

Tilliette, Xavier (1970), *Schelling. Une philosophie en devenir*. 2 vols. (Paris: Vrin, 1970).

— (1973), 'Schelling als Verfasser des Systemprogramms?' in *Das älteste Systemprogramm*. Ed. Rüdiger Bubner (Bonn: Bouvier Verlag Herbert Grundmann), 35–52.

— (1978), 'Schelling, l'art et les artistes,' in *Schelling, Textes esthétiques*. Trans. Alain Pernet (Paris: Editions Klincksieck), xi–xlvii.

— (1984), *La mythologie comprise* (Naples: Bibliopolis).

— (1999a), 'The Problem of Metaphysics,' in *The Emergence of German Idealism*. Ed. Michael Baur and Daniel O. Dahlstrom (Washington, D.C.: The Catholic University of America Press), 251–266.

— (1999b), *Schelling: Biographie* (Paris: Calmann-Lévy).

Toscano, Alberto (2004), 'Philosophy and the Experience of Construction,' in *The New Schelling*. Ed. Judith Norman and Alistair Welchman (New York: Continuum, 2004), 106–127.

Vater, Michael (1987), 'Hymns to the Night: On H.S. Harris's "The Cows in the Dark Night,"' in *Dialogue*, Vol. 26, no. 4, 645–652.

Vaysse, Jean-Marie (2004), *Schelling: Art et mythologie* (Paris: Ellipses).

Velkley, Richard L. (1997), 'Realizing Nature in Self: Schelling on Art and Intellectual Intuition in the *System of Transcendental Idealism*,' in *Figuring the Self*. Ed. David E. Klemm and Günter Zöller (Albany: SUNY Press), 149–168.

Verra, Valerio (1979), 'La "construction" dans la philosophie de Schelling,' in *Actualité de Schelling*. Ed. G. Planty-Bonjour (Paris: Vrin), 27–47.

White, Alan (1983), *Schelling: An Introduction to the System of Freedom* (New Haven: Yale University Press).

Williamson, George S. (2004), *The Longing for Myth in Germany* (Chicago: University of Chicago Press).

Wirth, Jason M. (2003), *The Conspiracy of Life: Meditations on Schelling and His Time* (Albany: SUNY Press).

Žižek, Slavoj (1996), *The Indivisible Remainder: An Essay on Schelling and Related Matters* (London: Verso).

Index

Page numbers in **bold** denote tables.

absolute idealism (identity-philosophy)
2–3, 5–6, 11, 24, 39, 51, 64–5,
67, 78, 82, 87–90, 92–5, 100–1,
103–4, 114, 119, 142, 144, 146,
156n.1, 158n.13
Adorno, Theodor 158n.10
'Reconciliation Under Duress' 158n.10
aesthetic intuition 65–6, 72, 76, 80, 82,
86, 99
aesthetic sense 58–60
in Hölderlin 58
in Schelling 58
Akademie der Wissenschaft 6, 113
allegory 105
Christian allegory 105, 107, 105–11
Allison, Henry E. 153n.14
*Älteste Systemprogramm des deutschen
Idealismus* 5, 41, 56, 60, 62, 67,
79, 83, 154n.24, 154n.25
Altmann, Alexander 150n.3
anthropology 122
Schelling's 129
theological 129–31
archetype (*Urbild*) 50, 100–2, 105, 119,
156n.16
Aristotle 34, 106
artist 53, 69, 79–81, 109–10, 114, 116,
122–4, 128, 138, 147, 159n.22
artistic production 1–3, 5, 37, 62–87
creative freedom of 4
Aufklärung philosophy 10

Badiou, Alain 149, 157n.28, 158n.12
The Century 158n.12
Baggesen, Jens 150n.5

Baumgartner, Hans Michael 151n.22
beauty 3–6, 41, 58, 60–1, 80–3, 98, 100,
103, 120–5, 136, 147, 156n.16
and the philosophy of art 100
Beiser, Frederick C. 16, 150n.2, 150n.3,
151n.10, 151n.12, 151n.14,
155n.16, 156n.12, 158n.9
Benjamin, Walter 116, 149
Berkeley, George 26
idealism of 28
Bowie, Andrew 64–5, 81, 150n.1, 156n.2
Braeckman, Antoon 65, 150n.2, 156n.1
Breazeale, Daniel 151n.14, 152n.31

capitalism 85, 135, 148, 157n.33
Cassirer, Ernst 155n.14
Cervantes, Miguel de 137
Don Quixote 109
Christianity 103–9, 114, 125, 126,
151n.10
and Catholicism 108
and Protestantism 108
and Reformation 108
symbolism in 108
The Communist Manifesto (by Karl Marx
and Friedrich Engels) 141
consciousness 16–20, 27–8, 32, 44,
48–50, 65, 68–71, 74, 80, 82,
84, 89, 107, 123–4, 130, 145,
152n.24, 154n.1, 157n.31
self-consciousness 4–5, 18–21, 23–4,
27, 40–1, 44, 47–50, 53–4, 64,
66, 68–72, 75–6, 79, 89, 90,
99, 101, 144, 155n.7, 157n.31,
159n.15

UNIVERSITY OF LIBRARY